ORAN
GUTAN

GUTAN

A MEMOIR

BRODERICK

THREE RIVERS PRESS • NEW YORK

Copyright © 2009 by Colin Broderick

Published in the United States by Three Rivers Press, an imprint of
the Crown Publishing Group, a division of
Random House, Inc., New York.

www.crownpublishing.com

Three Rivers Press and the Tugboat design are
registered trademarks of Random House, Inc.

Cataloging-in-Publication Data is available on request
from the Library of Congress

ISBN 978-0-307-45340-2

Printed in the United States of America

Design by Maria Elias

1 3 5 7 9 10 8 6 4 2

First Edition

This book is dedicated to the angels in my life,
Renata and Erica

WARNING

I have to warn you: This is not a pleasant story. In
fact, it's downright ugly in places. But it's my story
and I'm not going to apologize for it. It's the truth:
my truth. This is a document of my first eighteen
years living in America as an Irish immigrant, as
a construction worker, as a drinker, and at times
as a writer. So if you still want to read it, go ahead.
From here on in you have nobody to blame but
yourself. And if you don't like it, I don't care.
Stop whining and go write your own damned book.

In the midst of winter, I finally learned that there is within me an invincible summer.

Albert Camus

FNG

"**WANKER**. Hey, wankhead."

Someone was standing over me, yelling. I felt the toe of a boot prodding harshly into my rib cage. I clenched my fists and snapped bolt upright, ready for a fight as I forced my leaden eyelids open.

"That's it. On yer feet and let's go," the voice continued. "You're in New York now, ya little bollox. This is not your mother's house back in Tyrone."

It took me a moment to wrestle the face above me into focus. It was my cousin Sean towering above me.

"Come on. Get up. Move it. Let's go."

I grabbed him by the leg of his pants, determined to halt his onslaught, but released my grip again just as quickly, clamping both hands on my head to quiet the searing pain that was rising behind my eyeballs.

"Oh fuck," I said. "What happened?"

"You drank about a bottle of vodka and ten peppermint schnapps is what happened. Come on, up."

Hearing him say the word "peppermint" triggered a series of vaguely familiar mechanisms that stirred my internal organs into something that felt like a wet dog circling for position on a green shag carpet. I was going to be sick.

I pried myself off the living room floor where I'd been

sleeping and shoved my way past Sean with one hand clamped over my mouth.

"If your mother could see you now, huh," I heard him shout after me as I lurched toward the toilet bowl on my knees. "You'd better be ready to go in two minutes. It's nearly seven thirty; we should've been on the road a half hour ago. This is no good, lads. This is no fucking good at all."

As I hunkered on the floor, hugging the bowl, it was coming back to me. I'd staggered off the plane at JFK the previous evening. My cousin Paul had been there to meet me. We'd driven in over the Triborough Bridge. I remembered seeing it now, Manhattan, a silhouette of skyscrapers, like black headstones against a hazy orange sky. We'd gone straight to an Irish bar in the Bronx to meet the rest of my cousins. I remembered the air-conditioning and the first frosty beer stein. The rest was a blur.

I pried myself off the toilet bowl and splashed some cold water on my face at the sink. The wet dog had found its spot on the rug and was resting peacefully. I took a look at myself in the mirror. There I was: Colin Broderick, twenty years old, an Irishman in New York; I'd made it.

"When you're done admiring yourself there, George Michael, it's time to go," my cousin Paul said, standing in the open door of the bathroom. Sean appeared behind him.

"What do you make of this little bollox, huh? Sick, after a few civil drinks like that."

"It's a sad state of affairs, alright, when a man can't hold hees drink," said Paul.

"It sure is. It just won't do. I'm calling your mother this evening," Sean continued over Paul's shoulder, "and telling her what a show you made of yourself last night, disgracing the Broderick name on your first night in America."

"Sean," I said.

"What?"

"Shut the fuck up, please."

"Oh, I'm calling her." He grinned before breaking into that laugh of his that sounded like a donkey having its balls squeezed. "Mark my words: Claire Broderick's goin' to be hearing from me, I can tell you."

"Great. Say hello for me when you're at it."

"Oh, I will. Don't you worry about that. Right, lads, seriously, let's get the fuck out of here. Paul, you're supposed to be in the city at eight o'clock. Take Des and this useless cocksucker with you and I'll take Ian and the rest of the gang to Brooklyn. Right, lads, come on, let's get this show on the road." I glanced down at the clothes I'd woken up in, a wrinkled and stained white shirt and blue jeans. I'd been wearing them since I'd left my house in County Tyrone early the previous morning.

"Maybe I should put on some work clothes."

"I thought they were your work clothes." Sean laughed again. "Come on, they'll do for the day. Let's fuckin' go." He turned back into the living room and yelled, "The vans are leaving, lads. Anybody who's not outside in two seconds will be looking for a new job and a new place to live this evening."

I moved to the door of the bathroom and took a look around the apartment to see who he was yelling at. There were lads rising, bleary-eyed, off the couch, off the floor, out of the armchairs, from doors that opened off the small living room.

"Jesus," I said to Paul, who was still standing next to me. "How many of us live here?"

"I'm not sure," he said pensively. "I think it was thirteen at last count . . . maybe it's fourteen now that you're here. We'll have to take a head count on rent day."

"So where should I leave my suitcase and stuff?"

"Whatever patch of floor you dropped them on when you came in last night, I suppose. Right, come on, we've got to roll.

We can sort that out later." He turned to the door to follow
Sean out into the hallway, yelling over his shoulder, "OK, Des,
let's hit it, you're with me, time to roll."

I followed him on down the stairs and out into the morning
heat. It was a hot, clammy May morning in New York in 1988
and I was on my way into Manhattan for my first day's work.

I was ushered into the van to sit on a five-gallon drum of
polyurethane that sat on the floor between Paul and Des.

"How come I get to sit on the drum?" I asked. "Shouldn't we
toss for it?"

"That's the way the thing works here in New York, Colly,"
Des said, getting in behind me. "The FNG always sits on the
drum."

"What the fuck's an FNG?" I asked.

"That's you," Paul said, handing us each a smoke. "You're
the Fuckin' New Guy."

Paul and Des were brothers. We'd grown up together.
They'd left Tyrone ahead of me for similar reasons. There was
the issue of the dismal economy, of course, and the miserable
climate as well, but most importantly there was the desire to escape the caged feeling of living as a Catholic in the British-
occupied North of Ireland. It had gotten so bad back home that
a lad couldn't leave the house for a quiet drive anymore without
the prospect of being stopped and harassed at gunpoint by a
pimply-faced British soldier no older than himself. Lads that
we knew had been shot and killed by the British already. Occasionally we could hear bombs as the police stations and army
barracks were attacked by the IRA in the neighboring towns of
Ballygawley, Carrickmore, Omagh, and Beragh. We would go
silent and count off the explosions on our fingers: one . . . two . . .
three . . . four . . . five . . . "They've killed a few with that one, alright," someone would say. "The more the merrier," would come
the reply.

I'd tried London for two years already, but that was worse than living at home. Having to take the worst job on the building site from an English foreman who referred to all Irishmen as Paddy was not part of the life I'd had in mind. And then of course there was the drinking. It seemed no matter where I lived, my drinking was becoming an issue. But it would be different now that I was in America. I was sure of it.

As we roared down the Major Deegan, Paul was pointing out some landmarks. The area to our left was known as the South Bronx, or Fort Apache, as it was more commonly called back then. Red brick buildings tattooed with graffiti towered over the highway, surrounded by garbage-strewn lots and the occasional old couch or busted dresser that seemed to have been tossed out of the dark windows high above. I made a mental note never to go there. And on we thundered past Yankee Stadium, with Des tuning the radio to 92.3 to introduce me to some popular new DJ called Stern, who apparently did nothing but talk for four hours straight every morning. On through the throng of early morning traffic over the Macombs Dam Bridge and onto the island of Manhattan for my very first time, through the streets of East Harlem and onto Lexington Avenue, where Paul got into a yelling match with some black guy with a filthy rag and a squeegee who'd jumped onto our front bumper and refused to budge until Paul tossed him a few coins out of his pocket.

"Asshole," Paul yelled at him as we tore through the green light, almost colliding with a silver hearse that'd apparently jumped the red to our left. Paul jammed on the brakes, slamming Des and me up against the dash and spilling our coffee all over the front of the van. "What the fuck . . ."

The driver of the hearse, a stocky-looking gray-haired woman with a cigarette dangling out of the corner of her mouth, paused in front of us just long enough to flash Paul the middle finger and yell out her open window, "Go suck off ya mudda's ass, ya bastard," before screeching off again, her middle finger held high out the driver's-side window.

"Did you fucking see that?" Paul stammered in disbelief.

"That old granny almost totaled us," Des said, peeling himself off the front window. "Get her."

Paul floored the old blue Chevy van, sending me flying backwards off my bucket as we lurched down Lexington Avenue after her, swerving in and out of the scattered traffic.

"Is that a coffin in the back of that hearse?" I said as I gathered myself for the chase.

"Looks like it," Paul said, almost ripping the front off a yellow taxicab as we flipped furiously from lane to lane.

"Should we be chasing an old lady in a hearse with a coffin on board?" I asked.

"Welcome to New York, pal," Paul said, laughing, and Des joined him, grinning gleefully as we whipped in and out of traffic for about thirty blocks, hot on the trail of the speeding hearse before she pulled a sudden right onto a side street, leaving us with the sight of her middle finger again raised defiantly as we slowed into the steady roll of the traffic. Before me suddenly lay the great canyon of Lexington Avenue as far as the eye could see. Skyscrapers stood on either side of us for miles in a perfectly straight line. I was breathless. There was no way I could ever get to know all of this. It was just too big, too overwhelming. It would take a lifetime to get to the bottom of it all. I thought that the two years I'd spent living in London had prepared me for city living. I was wrong. London couldn't shine New York's shoes. There was just no comparison.

That day Paul and Des introduced me to the floor-sanding business. I was assigned the job of cleaning the corners of the floor where the machines couldn't reach. For about six hours I shuffled around on my sweaty knee pads with a backhand scraper and a file, trying to stay ahead of the roar of the sanding machines. By three thirty we were covered in a fine layer of dust from head to toe as we lashed down a potent coat of shellac on the clean floor and began lugging all the equipment down the service elevator and into the back of the van again.

"There's only one cure I can think of for a dusty throat," Paul said as we bailed into the van again for the ride back to the Bronx and I took my seat on the bucket.

"A man's not a camel," Des said.

"What's that supposed to mean?" I said.

"Can't live on water alone." He grinned.

"I like the sound of that," I said as we roared off up Park Avenue, Bronx-bound. Floor sanding sure was thirsty work.

By the time we pulled up at McKeown's bar on McLean Avenue there was already a line of Irish construction workers' trucks parked outside. The vans were adorned with shamrocks and tricolors, and names like Celtic Construction and Emerald Flooring Service. There would be no hiding our heritage here. I was astounded. I had never lived in a place where I was free to be Irish.

"Looks like Sean and the lads beat us home again," Paul said as he wheeled the Chevy into a parking space and we all jumped out.

The inside of the bar was cool and dark after the bright, sweaty ride home.

"Look, everybody, it's the FNG," I heard a familiar voice shout from up the bar, followed by the unmistakable roar of a donkey's laugh. It was my cousin Sean.

"Watch out," someone else yelled. "More Tyrone men."

"Get these lads a beer," Sean yelled to the bartender as we approached.

"No, no, I got it," another man next to him leaning against the bar insisted.

"It's about time you bought one, ya tight bastard," Sean began. "I was beginning to think somebody'd swiped yer wallet again." He tipped back his head and brayed like an ass and the whole bar joined in the fun.

The atmosphere in the bar was joyous. The beer was served in frosted steins. You couldn't finish one without someone buying you another. There was so much money being flung onto the bar it was impossible to tell after a while who owned what. It didn't really seem to matter. The surface of the bar was littered with cash. It was like Monopoly money; it wasn't real. Big juicy steaks were carried through the throng all night, sizzling on steel plates. All you could eat, mashed turnips and carrots, baked potatoes as big as footballs, smothered in butter. And the girls, oh my God, the girls. I fell in love that first night with at least seven or eight different girls, their perfect smiles, tanned skin, bright, eager eyes. What had I been doing my whole life? Why hadn't I come sooner?

At midnight we left the bar to go on to the real party. Once again I was floored by the heat as I stepped outside. It was midnight and here it was, perfect warmth. I'd spent my whole life warming one piece of my body at a time, against a fire or a radiator, but never this, this allover body heat, like being safely wrapped inside of the womb. About ten of us piled into a little Colt RS and raced off to Bainbridge Avenue.

Bainbridge was the heart of the Irish bar scene in 1988. There were something like thirty Irish bars on a strip of about six blocks, and every one of them was packed. The Roaring Twenties was the most popular of the lot at that time. Once inside we had to wrestle our way to the bar. There were six or seven bartenders, tending to a crowd that stood at the bar like an audience pushed up against the stage at a rock concert. A sea of outstretched arms waving twenty- and fifty-dollar bills, trying to snag the bartenders' attention. Luckily for us, my cousin

Ian knew all of the bartenders and we never had to wait very long for service. He also knew a lot of girls, and I was introduced around as the FNG, a title I was beginning to embrace. I was the Fuckin' New Guy.

The following morning my cousin Sean had me up at seven o'clock again. I was barely asleep when I heard the shout.

"Come on, ye lazy bastard, are ye goin' to lie around sleeping all day?"

"What? It's Saturday. I just got here."

"You're not in London now. Up. You're coming with me."

And off we went again, an army of floor sanders, groaning and rubbing our heads. This was my cousins' flooring company, Hudson Valley Flooring Company. Paul, Ian, and Sean had just started the company weeks before I had arrived, and already they were swamped with more work than they could get to. After a quick stop for coffees and breakfast sandwiches the convoy of vans hit the Major Deegan, dodging and weaving, racing each other through the early morning traffic. Two of the vans branched off for Manhattan, and Sean and I went on toward Brooklyn.

"The sooner we get this job done, the sooner we'll be back on McLean Avenue having a cold one," Sean said as we pulled up outside a miserable-looking brown brick building somewhere in Brooklyn. That was all the incentive I needed.

We grabbed the machines out of the back of the van and blasted through the job in a flash. We slapped down a coat of sealer, gave the floor a quick screening, and lashed on a coat of polyurethane. By one o'clock we were done. Sean collected the check for $450 and we were on our way back to McLean Avenue for brunch. Sean handed me two hundred dollars for my first two days' work. Four crisp fifty-dollar bills. It would have taken me a month to earn that much money before I left Ireland. And here I was barely awake and already I'd earned enough to pay my rent for a month. Everything else was gravy. They were right about America. The streets really were paved with gold.

By two thirty we were sitting in Fibber Magee's bar on McLean Avenue having brunch and a beer. The bars up and down McLean Avenue were already buzzing with activity. The vans were parked up for the day. The bar windows were thrown wide open and the girls strolled by in a constant procession in miniskirts and halter tops. There was an intoxicating air of optimism about the whole thing, like anything was possible. We clinked our frosty steins and toasted America. I'd never felt so free.

Within two months I had rented a two-bedroom apartment on 237th Street just off Katonah Avenue and bought the Colt RS from Paul. My cousin Ian decided to take the other bedroom in the apartment I had rented and we split the rent down the middle. Two hundred and fifty bucks each. No more sleeping on the floor.

We spent two weeks before we moved into the new apartment painting the place and redoing the floors. We stained the living room floor the exact colors and design of a pack of Parliament cigarettes, right down to the silver-and-white borders. The rest of the floors we pickled white. We bought expensive new furniture and a sound system powerful enough to blow the ceiling off. We bought new beds, a dining table and chairs, new blinds for all the windows. We even remodeled the bathroom and retiled the kitchen floor.

Ian was the son of my uncle Brendan, who had died of alcoholism just a few years earlier at the age of forty-two. Ian was a good guy to have as a roommate because he knew firsthand the pain that too much partying could bring. Not that the knowledge stopped him from being a party animal; it just made him more aware. Ian was like my party barometer. He could tell when we were pushing the needle into the red. He'd make sure we cooled off and spent a few nights at home to let the liver take a breather. On our nights off we'd rent a movie, cook a big dinner, and drink a case of beer. We hadn't known each other very well growing up in Ireland, but in the first few weeks we spent with each other in New York we realized we shared a few very important interests: movies, music, girls, and beer.

I had soon decided that floor sanding wasn't for me. I didn't like the dust and the heavy machinery. I'd had my own painting business before I left Ireland. I decided I'd give that a shot instead. My cousin Paul made a phone call for me on a Saturday evening and I was all hooked up to start a new job on Monday morning.

That Monday, Paul dropped me off outside a house on a street just off Broadway in the Bronx. It was seven thirty in the morning.

"Con's apartment's down the driveway in the back. Tell him I said hello."

As I walked down the steep driveway between the two houses, I could hear some kind of a commotion going on in the backyard. I rounded the corner to see a group of about ten guys standing around watching as two guys tore into each other. They pounded each other with a few punches, then the big guy had the skinny guy down on the ground and they both had each other by the throat. There was blood on the big guy's face and he was shouting, "Give it up, for fucksake."

"Fuck you," the skinny guy screamed back. He landed another punch to the side of the big guy's eye and they rolled around some more.

I considered turning and slipping back up the driveway. I was barely awake. I had a hangover. I didn't know these people and this seemed way too violent for a Monday morning. Then one of the guys closest to me, standing casually with his arms folded, turned and noticed me.

"Oh, how are ye?" he said.

"Good, and yourself?"

"Oh, not so bad," he said casually, watching the mayhem as if he were pondering what he was going to have for breakfast. The big guy had the upper hand again, but he was losing blood from his left eye.

"Has this been going on long?" I ventured.

"A little while, yeah, it should be over soon, though. My name's Derrick, by the way," he said, extending his hand.

"Colin. I'm supposed to start a job here this morning."

"Oh, yeah, that'll be with Con, I presume."

"That's right."

"Mmmm. That's Con on the bottom there, the skinny guy. And that's Dessie there on top of him. The two fellas live together here." He motioned to the door of the basement apartment. "They're actually pretty good friends when they're not killing each other."

"That's good to know."

Another lad walked around the corner of the driveway and stood next to me, his eyes wide with surprise at the scene before him. Nobody seemed to notice him either.

"What the hell is going on here?" he whispered to me.

"I'm not entirely sure," I said. "I just showed up here a little while ago to start a job and this is the way I found them."

"I'm supposed to start here myself with some guy called Con."

"That's Con there," I said, pointing to the screaming lunatic on the bottom. "And that's his buddy Dessie there on top, pounding the head off him."

"Nice, nice setup. Lovely stuff. So what do we do now?"

"Wait, I suppose."

The two boys wrestled for a while longer, then Dessie jumped up and backed off out of swinging distance.

"It's over, stop it!" he roared.

Con jumped to his feet but kept his distance, screaming back.

"It's not nearly over. I want you to get your shit moved out of this apartment before I come back here this evening."

"But it's my apartment."

"Get your shit out, Dessie, or I'll throw it out."

"I'll throw you out, you skinny bastard."

"Ah, Con . . . excuse me, Con," Derrick began. "Con, there's a couple of lads here to see you."

Con turned to us, the two FNGs.

"What do you want?" He was flushed red, his shirt was ripped at the neck, and he was bleeding from his lower lip.

"We're here for the job. I'm Colin, this is . . ."

"Right, get in the van," he said, turning and pacing to the van. "And the rest of you fuckers, if you want a job, get in the fuckin' van now."

"Ah, Con . . . ," the other new guy began.

"Get in the fuckin' van now or you'll be left behind."

We all piled into the van. There were six or seven of us in by the time he had the van started and into reverse gear.

"Ah, excuse me, Con," the new guy began again. Con ignored him as he floored the van, the tires squealing as we hurtled backwards up the steep driveway.

"Con!" the guy shouted as the van crashed into something behind us.

"Jesus fucking Christ!" Con screamed. "Who the fuck left a car parked across our driveway?"

"I was trying to tell you, Con," the new guy said, rubbing his forehead. "I didn't get a chance to move it."

"Well, get out and move it now, you bollox." The door was opened and the new guy stepped outside to survey the damage. The front wing was destroyed and the bumper was lying in the street. "Get that piece of shit moved out of my driveway!" Con screamed.

Without responding, the new guy got in the car and backed it up slowly, dragging pieces of the front end with him. Con lunged the van into the street and floored it, leaving the new guy and his wrecked car sitting there in a cloud of smoke.

"Jaysus, Con," Derrick said. "I think you destroyed that poor fella's car."

"He'll be careful where he parks it the next time." Con laughed and everyone sort of laughed along with him. "Put on some Wolf Tones there, Derrick. I'll give the lad a call later and sort him out for the damage."

"Good man, Con. That's the stuff."

And we roared on down the Deegan toward the city, everyone singing along to the Wolf Tones as if nothing had ever happened.

As it turned out, Con and I became very good friends almost immediately. I was good at my job. I was the fastest and tidiest painter on his crew. Within one week he handed me the keys to a van of my own. I was painting apartments in a building just across the Hudson River in New Jersey. I had a studio apartment a day to paint. He allowed me two days to complete a one-bedroom.

I'd start at nine in the morning, horsing the paint on with an eighteen-inch roller, and be on my way home at about two thirty. I did this six days a week for the first two months. On Friday evenings Con would have all the boys into Characters, a bar down on Broadway at 242nd. He'd order beers for everybody and pitchers of kamikazes and we'd all spend a few hours getting hammered together before we'd go our separate ways for the weekend. I'd never seen so much alcohol consumed in all of my life. Not at home. Not in London. Nobody could afford to drink like this anywhere else.

The first time I did cocaine, I was with a friend of mine from Dublin. He was one of the painters I'd met working with Con. He played bass guitar in a band on Saturday nights down at Characters. I had always had this romantic idea about doing cocaine. How could I not? Every time I'd heard about cocaine use while I was growing up it was always some cool rock star with a bevy of beautiful women around him. What could possibly be wrong with cocaine? Let's face it, in the time I'd been drinking— since I was fifteen—I'd known only one person who died from doing cocaine. I'd known tons of people who'd died or gone mad from alcohol. I'd just take it easy on the stuff and everything would be OK. God knows I had plenty of money to buy it.

The first night I did it, I got a taste of how dangerous cocaine could be. I was in Characters. Ronny, the bass player, had the night off, and we were getting pretty hammered when he suggested we take a little trip and pick up some of the devil's dandruff. We left the bar and got into a gypsy cab outside. Gypsy cab drivers in the Bronx, I was to find out, always knew how to get their hands on drugs.

The driver was a Middle Eastern guy. He knew Ronny. He knew where we were going. He took us somewhere in Yonkers, not far from Getty Square. Not too far from my old apartment. It was after midnight and we pulled up near where a few black guys sat on a stoop outside of a run-down shack of a house. All the streetlights were busted and a few old cars sat around on blocks. Two of the guys got up and approached the car.

"What you want? Want some blow, some rock, weed. What you want?"

Our driver did the talking for us.

"They just want a little blow."

"How much, a gram, you want an eight-ball, I'll give you an eight-ball for two-fitty."

"No, just a gram. That's plenty."

"You guys cops. He looks like a cop," he said, pulling a gun out of his belt.

"No, man, we're Irish," Ronny said through the open rear window.

"What about you? You a cop?" he said, tapping the barrel of his gun on the door, pointing it at me.

"I'm Irish, man. Do I look like a cop?"

"Yeah you do. You look like a cop."

"Well, I'm not. When was the last time you heard a cop with an accent like this?"

He pulled the gun back and shoved it into his belt again. "OK, you cool."

Ronny handed him the money and he passed Ronny a small foil wrapper and sauntered off back to the stoop. Our driver pulled away slowly and I slipped down in my seat a little, half expecting a bullet in the back of my head as we drove away.

"Jesus, is it always like that?"

"I told you it was dodgy." Ronny laughed. "Hey, buddy, when you get a chance pull over somewhere so I don't spill this shit."

The driver pulled over and Ronny chopped out a couple of fat white rails on the back of a cigarette box and handed me a rolled-up bill.

"Here, get this into you. And don't fuckin' sneeze."

I leaned over as he held the box up close to my face and I gave it a good snort. I could taste the powder down in the back of my throat. I sniffed a few times to make sure it was all the way up there. Then I held the box for Ronny.

"I don't feel anything, Ronny."

"Oh, don't worry, you will. Just relax."

When we returned to 240th Street we went into the Terminal Bar, and that's when it hit me. My heart was racing. The rush went through my whole body. I was sober—I was super sober. I was talking fifty miles an hour. The rush was so powerful it scared me.

"Just slow down," Ronny said. "Just relax. We'll have a drink. Stop talking so fast or everybody will know you're high."

I wish I'd had a bad experience. I wish I hadn't loved every second of it. It does happen that people do coke once and never want to do it again. No such luck for me. I'd always smoked pot. I'd been smoking pot since I was fifteen, but this, this was what I was looking for. After a few drinks I was off by myself; I'd lost Ronny somewhere in the crowd. I didn't care. I went back to

Characters. The band was in full swing. I was euphoric, unstoppable. More drink. I talked to one beautiful girl after another. I was dancing. I never dance. I am the world's worst dancer.

And then I woke up. I was in bed in my apartment. The sun was shining brightly through the open slats of the blinds and next to me was a beautiful blond-haired girl, naked and sleeping peacefully. I stared at her in disbelief, trying to figure out how this could have happened. I tried to remember leaving the bar. I had no recollection whatsoever. I remembered the cocaine, losing Ronny, dancing, feeling great. I propped myself on my elbow and watched her sleep for a few minutes. She opened her eyes and started to smile and without speaking she began to kiss me, rolling over on top of me. I wish I'd had a horrible experience the first time I did cocaine, but this was the beginning of trouble.

A while later she said she had to go and catch the bus and make her way back to Queens. I offered to walk her to the bus stop, but she told me to stay where I was and maybe we'd bump into each other in Characters again sometime. She kissed me good-bye and she left. I hadn't even asked her name. I was in trouble alright. Trouble with a capital C.

If it's true what they say about addicts always chasing that first high, I had presented myself with an impossible situation. Doing cocaine would never be the same again. Although I was sure going to give it a good try.

When I showed up for work Monday morning I found out Con had been arrested over the weekend for drunk driving. He'd smashed the van down in Bainbridge after watching a World Cup soccer match. He'd spent the weekend in the slammer and they'd taken his license. I was his new driver. It didn't seem to matter that I didn't have a license either. Somehow it made sense.

We were heading down Seventh Avenue that morning at about ten thirty. I remember it was almost a hundred degrees already and we didn't have an air conditioner. We were late for an appointment downtown and stuck in some kind of traffic backup. Con perched up on the edge of his seat, chewing his fingernails and barking directions at me, when suddenly he spotted some guy on the sidewalk.

"Pull over!" he shouted. "Pull over."

"Right here?"

It wasn't easy in all that traffic.

"Yeah, right here." Con laughed. "You have to meet this lunatic."

"Who is it?"

"This guy's crazy." Con calling somebody crazy. This I had to see. I managed to wrestle the van into a bus stop next to the guy Con was pointing to. Con leaned over and shouted to him.

"Hey Caffrey. Caffrey. Come here."

The guy sauntered over and stood next to the truck.

"Ah, Jaysus, Con, how's it goin'?"

"Whassup, Caffrey?"

"Oh, the same old shit." The guy was balding a bit on top; he had a round beer face and the wildest sparkle I'd ever seen in his eyes. The kind of look you might imagine peering at you from behind a row of steel bars.

"I don't suppose you have anything to do with this backup here, do you?" Con said.

"Mmmm. That might be my car there in the middle of it." He smiled, rubbing his forehead with the palm of his hand.

"Where?" Con laughed, looking around, as did I. Sure

enough, there in the middle of the traffic jam, just a few feet ahead, was a brown station wagon stalled right in the middle of Sixth Avenue. "That's your car? The brown one?"

"Mmmm."

"You break down?"

"Mmmm."

"You look like you're not quite over the weekend, Tony."

"Mmmm. I just got out of jail this morning in Boston."

"In Boston?" Con laughed. "How long did they have you?"

"Oh, since Saturday night." He smiled. His eyes glistened in the sun. "But the bastards didn't know about the uppers I was taking. I had a pocket full of those to keep me going." He seemed proud of this little detail.

"They got me too at the weekend."

"Mmmm. Where'd they get you?" He didn't seem at all surprised.

"Bainbridge."

"Mmmm."

"This is my new driver, Colin."

"How's it goin', Tony."

"Oh, great. Just great."

"What are you going to do about that car in the middle of the avenue there, Tony?"

"I think I'm going to go for a drink and have a think about it."

"Sounds like a good idea," I said.

"You sure you don't want us to push it for you?" Con offered.

"No, I think I'm just going to leave it there. There's no plates on it. It's not registered and there's not much in it of value."

"Are you sure?"

"Mmmm. I'm thirsty. I think I'll have to go wet my throat."

"Well, I wish we could join you, but we're late for an appointment."

"I'll see you around, Con," he said. "Nice to meet you, Colin."

"You too, Tony." And off he walked up the block, looking for the nearest bar. I wished I could have gone with him. Tony looked like he had a story or two to tell. God knew where his day was going to take him. I pulled out into the traffic and slipped past his beat-up old brown station wagon and we went on about our business.

"That guy's as crazy as it gets, right there."

"Crazier than you?"

"I'm a choirboy compared to that lunatic, Colin."

After I started doing cocaine, I found it impossible to have a few drinks without the urge to get high. At first I limited use to only Saturday nights, when we would go out and really rip it up. I had found out where all the after-hours bars were in the area, so there was never a closing time; the party could go all night. I could go out for a drink on a Friday evening after work and be home in bed by about ten or eleven on a Sunday night. In those days I could survive on one night's sleep out of three.

On a Saturday night if you hadn't picked up a girl on Bainbridge Avenue by two a.m. it was time to hit the Archway down on Jerome under the elevated train tracks. That way you could scout the bar for any stragglers and if all else failed you were just a few blocks from the Shamrock for after hours, the most popular late-night spot.

The Shamrock was without a doubt the saddest place I ever drank. After four in the morning the place was dark as a coffin. The whole bar smelled like piss. The filthy bathrooms were crammed with cokeheads with empty, murderous eyes sniffing their way to oblivion. Someone was always sprawled on a bench unconscious, or dead for all anybody cared. At least two or three would be slumped facedown on the bar at any given time. There was always a girl or two, differentiated in the smoky haze only by the streamers of dark makeup plastered down their cheeks. Nightmarish stories were mumbled and lost in the din. Someone was always wailing away about the old country. The pool table in the corner at this time of night was about as inviting as a cockfight at a nuclear plant. Tempers would flare. Glass would be broken. Blood was nearly always shed by sunrise. Maybe that's why I loved it so much. The kind of bar crowd that even the devil himself would shake his ornery head at in disgust.

One night after running short on coke, I left the Shamrock and flagged a gypsy cab on Kingsbridge. The driver, a hyper, skeletal black guy, said he knew of only one place but it could be a bit dangerous at this time of night. It was almost five in the morning.

"Sounds good," I said. "Take me there."

I always loved this part of the high. The search. The anticipation. The danger of getting caught or killed. He drove me through the twisted wreckage of the South Bronx to a street like all the others. Brown brick buildings down one side, brown brick buildings down the other. He paused at the end of the block. And turned to me.

"Whatever happens, just go with it. Don't panic."

"Cool. Just don't leave me down here."

"I won't."

He slowly made his way down the block and stopped about halfway down, outside an apartment building with a huge center courtyard. A group of about ten black guys were standing on the pavement outside of the tall steel gates. Three or four guys came to the car immediately, pushing and shoving each other. They were all carrying semiautomatic machine guns.

"What you want. Rock, rock, rock."

"I just wanted a little blow. A gram."

One guy just opened the back door of the car and grabbed me by the shoulder.

"Out. Out!" he shouted, dragging me onto the pavement. "Look at me. Look at me." I looked at him square in the eyes.

"Keep your mouth shut and stay tight to me. Got it?"

"Got it," I said.

He turned, keeping a tight grip on my arm, and held his gun up in front of him.

"Back off," he said to the others. And shoved his way past them toward the gates. "Open them," he shouted, and the gates were opened enough for us to walk through into the courtyard. They clanged closed behind us. Inside the courtyard there must have been fifty guys with semiautomatics and bags of drugs. They waved as they swarmed us like a school of piranha.

"You want rock?"

"Coke?"

"What you want, muthafucka?"

My guide never let go of me. He never stopped moving. He just held out his weapon and kept moving through the courtyard toward the front doors of the building. It was one of those moments in my life where I thought to myself, "This is it, numb-nuts. You pushed it too far this time." I didn't expect to get out of this one alive. I could picture my cabdriver disappearing down the block. No one knew I was here. The pieces of my body would never be found. Maybe I'd been set up. Maybe the cabdriver was in on it. I stayed calm and tried to stay as close to my guide as possible. There was death in the air. Here were a lot of very high guys with enough artillery to start a war. Not even the police cruised these streets at night. This could get ugly in a heartbeat. As we reached the doors to the building, the crowd of guys backed off and went back to adjusting their weapons; the click and clack of magazine clips and gunmetal rattled around the courtyard. I didn't need the coke anymore. I was high enough already. There was enough adrenaline racing through my body to keep me up for the next two days.

The inside of the building was worse. This was a drug fort. No one actually lived here. The hallways were dimly lit. All the apartment doors were wide open; some had been ripped off their hinges and fell against the graffiti-raped walls. We made our way up the dark stairwell. Barking echoed down the hallways. There was the rattle of machine-gun fire and loud angry shouts too muffled for me to decipher. On the fourth floor my guide dragged me into an open doorway. Two rottweilers chained to a radiator lunged at us, their chains snapping them short by just inches. Their teeth bared, drool dripping off their jaws. Another gunman appeared in the lighted doorway of the kitchen. He nodded to my guide and I was led into the kitchen.

There was a guy at a table in the middle of the floor. He was sitting behind a mound of cocaine about the size of a football. He had three guns laid out next to the coke. A semiautomatic, a large handgun, and a small palm-sized gun with a gold handle. There were two other gunmen in the room, one leaning against the wall by the window and another in a chair in the far corner. The guy behind the counter kept staring at me.

"What do you want?" he eventually asked.

"Actually, I just wanted a little bit of blow," I said. "If I'd known we were going off to war I could have brought my rocket launcher."

The guy behind the table let out a huge laugh and looked around at his buddies, who smiled a little. Nobody else laughed.

"You Irish?"

"Yeah, I'm Irish."

"Fuckin' Irish in the house."

"Yup."

"You fuckin' guys are crazy, right?"

"Maybe."

"You got that war goin' on with the English, man, right?"

"You got that right."

"You from Belfast?"

"I'm from the North. Fifty miles from Belfast."

"So you know what I'm talking about."

"I sure do."

"You guys got guns in the IRA, right?"

"I've heard that."

"I know your story. You Irish guys are fuckin' crazy. What do you think of these guns?"

"They look dangerous."

"They look dangerous." He laughed. "Here . . . ," he said, tossing me the big handgun. I managed to catch it without shooting anybody in the process. "What do you think of that?" I held it up and sighted down the barrel, being careful not to point it in anybody's general direction.

"This is a sweet gun. I could use a gun like this back home." It was the first time I'd ever held a gun in my life.

"Go ahead, shoot it."

"In here?"

"Shoot the damn ting."

"Cover your ears, boys. This thing's gonna make some noise." I raised it and blasted a hole in the wall. The dogs in the next room howled ferociously. "Jesus," I said. "This thing's like a fuckin' cannon." My new buddy behind the table laughed again.

"You don't have no guns like that in Ireland?"

"Not that I've seen."

"You're one crazy mutherfucker, Irish. Here, take a seat." He shoved a chair out from the other side of the table and I sat down across from him. He lifted a knife and shoved some coke off to the side and chopped out two big rails and handed me a straw.

"Have one on the house. Slicer, get our buddy here a drink. You like to drink, Irish?"

"That's my specialty."

Slicer poured two dirty glasses of Jack Daniel's and handed them to us at the table.

"Sláinte," I said, raising my glass.

"Sláinte," he said and clinked my glass. "To freedom."

"To freedom."

We finished our drinks in a swallow.

"Thank you," I said. "You're a gentleman."

"I'm no gentleman, Irish," he said, shaking his head.

"You've been very hospitable. You take me in here and you don't even know me, you give me a drink, some free coke. You even let me shoot your gun. I have close friends who don't treat me so well. Unfortunately, I have to go. I have a cab waiting for me and a girl sitting in a bar who thinks I went to use the men's room."

"You have a twenty-dollar bill, Irish?"

"I sure do," I said, taking a bill out of my pocket and handing it to him.

He took the bill and placed it on the table and shoveled a nice heap of coke onto it and refolded it carefully.

"This is for making me laugh," he said, handing me the package. I took it and offered him my hand and we shook.

"Thank you."

"You're welcome, Irish, enjoy it. Mamasboy, make sure this guy gets out of the building safely. No one touches him."

I got up and gave him a quick salute.

"We're alike, you and I, Irish."

"I know it," I said. He saluted back and I slipped out the

door with Mamasboy. Down the stairs and out through the courtyard. This time nobody bothered us. There was my cabdriver, waiting nervously by the gate. I slipped Mamasboy a twenty. He nodded and turned away without speaking.

"Where the hell did they take you?" my cabdriver blurted as we pulled away. "I thought you were a dead man."

"I guess it was my lucky night," I said. "Thanks for waiting. We're going back to the Shamrock on Kingsbridge. I think I need a drink."

"I think I need one myself."

Around this time I got a phone call from my mother saying that my good friend Brian Mullin had been shot by the SAS, the elite hit squad of the British army. He was in a car with his two bothers-in-law. They were ambushed near our home. All three bodies were riddled with bullets; Brian was shot twenty-eight times.

As usual, any truth around the details of the shooting was shrouded in shreds of the real facts woven with conspiracy stories. As usual, no explanation seemed to justify the fact that another three men had been ruthlessly slaughtered when they could have just as easily been captured and imprisoned. I was floored by the news. I never thought they'd get Brian. I was angry with myself for not being there. I felt like a coward. Here I was, three thousand miles away, while my friends were being murdered for standing up for their freedom. For my freedom, and my family's freedom.

I went out and got drunk. I didn't talk about it. Too many guys who knew nothing about it were doing enough talking around the bars. In the bars around Woodlawn, the IRA card was played extensively for the sole purpose of liberating American girls from their underwear. It was a romantic time for the IRA; it's always been a romantic time for the IRA. Actors like Mickey Rourke, Daniel Day-Lewis, Stephen Rea, and Brad Pitt have all portrayed heroic Northern Irish characters, the rogue with a heart of gold. The truth is, if we'd had half these guys who were claiming themselves nationalists actually do something at home, the war could have been over years ago.

What we had in America when I first arrived was real freedom. Freedom to get any job regardless of religious beliefs. Freedom to go out for a drive with your friends without the worry of being harassed or shot for being Irish. Freedom to stroll down the street in broad daylight wearing a T-shirt with an Irish flag on it. Having an Irish accent in New York at that time was like possessing a deck of "Get Out of Jail Free" cards. Every week in the bar you heard another story about one of the guys getting pulled over for drunk driving, or speeding, or running a red light, and getting away with it. The moment the cop realized they were Irish, it was all over.

"Where are you from?"

"Tyrone."

"Ah, my mother's from Cork and my father's from Kerry."

"No shit."

"Go on now. Get out of here. Just slow it down a little bit and keep that bottle down when you're driving, for Chrissakes."

"No problem, officer."

Within one year here I was doing cocaine two or three nights a week. Sometimes more. I started driving out to Queens to party at the weekends. Fewer people knew me there and it was easier to buy cocaine on the street. A lot of the Irish, including most of my own cousins who lived here, did not look kindly on anyone doing cocaine, so I began to alienate myself from the herd. I've always been a bit of a loner, but the cocaine began to make that a necessity.

One night in Queens I couldn't find a dealer anywhere in or around Woodside, the Irish section of Queens. I was drunk. I'd been drinking with some airline pilot all afternoon. At around ten that night I had him drive me to an area where I'd copped before. I knew of a little private Colombian coffee shop where I heard a lot of the drugs came from. This was a no-go zone. You didn't mess with the Colombians. An Irish guy, a bar owner in Queens, at about this time wound up in a bathtub of boiling water wearing his tongue as a tie for messing with the wrong Colombian girl. But I'd had a few drinks, and the urge to have a little blast of the white stuff took over all reason. I had the pilot park his Porsche about two blocks away and told him if I wasn't back in five minutes to disappear. I walked up the block and spotted the light on inside the coffee shop. I took a stroll past the window but the blinds were drawn and I couldn't see a thing. I turned and went back. I rapped the door a few times. There was a sudden silence inside. The door opened a crack and some Colombian guy about my age asked, "What the fuck do you want?"

"I just need to see you for a moment outside."

"Not now."

"Just for a second."

"Get lost, asshole."

I'm not exactly sure what happened to me between leaving London and coming to America, but somehow my fuse had shortened, and after five or six drinks I didn't have a fuse at all. I was involved in some kind of altercation at least once every couple of weeks. In most instances I would initiate the fight even if the odds were stacked impossibly against me. I might be in a bar by myself having a drink and decide that some guy was giving me attitude. I'd walk up and punch him in the face in front of all his friends, then get the shit kicked out of me and get tossed out of the bar. I actually relished it and miraculously never sustained any major injuries during those fights. I would walk away smiling. Even getting a beating felt like a victory. Perhaps it came from the fact that at about this time I'd started to do a lot of cocaine.

I shoved the door, sending him back a few feet, and followed him in.

"What the fuck did you call me?"

"Who the fuck is this guy?"

"What the fuck is going on here?"

"Jesus Christ, close the fucking door."

There was a volley of infuriated voices all around me. The young guy had the barrel of a massive gun about an inch from the end of my nose. I took a glance around as the door was slammed shut. There were maybe fifteen very dangerous-looking Colombians in the room; four of them sat at a table in the middle with stacks of cash and maybe ten kilos of cocaine. I'd burst into the middle of a major drug deal. This was not good.

The oldest guy at the table, a man with graying hair in a suit and dark glasses, raised his hands.

"What the fuck is this? Who the fuck is this asshole?"

"I'm sorry," I said. "I made a mistake. I shouldn't be here. I thought this was a coffee shop."

"You thought wrong, asshole," the old guy said.

"I'm sorry," I said. "I was just trying to get a cup of coffee."

"Take him outside and get rid of him," the old guy said, nodding to the kid with the cannon in my face.

The young guy grabbed me by the shoulder, spun me around, and pushed me to the door. Outside he followed me down the block, prodding me along with the gun. The street was deserted. About halfway down the block he stopped and or-

dered me to turn around. When I turned to face him he raised
the gun to my forehead.

"You think I should kill you?" he said. He didn't look much
older than I was, maybe twenty-two or -three. I looked into his
eyes and said nothing. I was perfectly calm. I didn't feel any fear
of him or his gun. "Open your mouth," he said. I opened my
mouth and he put the barrel of the gun in and rested it on my
tongue. All the time we kept staring at each other. If I were
going to kill myself, I thought, this is the kind of gun I'd use.
One that didn't make mistakes. A big handgun that would take
your head completely off with one shot. I was curious as to how
it would feel, if I would even have time to hear the shot. One
thing was certain: I wouldn't have any time to mull it over afterwards. My brains would be four blocks away. He repeated his
question. "You think I should blow your head off?" I just kept
staring at him, and then I saw it: fear. He was more scared than
I was. He'd never shot anybody and he didn't want to see my
brains all over the sidewalk in front of him. "OK, I'm going to
give you a chance," he said, taking the gun out of my mouth and
leveling it at me with two hands. "I want you to turn and run for
it. Maybe I shoot, maybe I don't." I stood for a moment, still
staring at him, and then turned and walked off down the block,
taking my cigarettes out and stopping just a few feet away with
my back to him to light a match. "Run, motherfucker," he
shouted. "You think I won't kill you?" When I walked around
the corner the pilot was still waiting.

"Well, how'd it go?"

"Fine," I said. "Let's go for a drink."

Less than a week later I was at it again on Bainbridge Avenue. I
was drunk and I wanted to go buy some coke. It was two in the

morning. I wrestled with the idea. I was disgusted with myself for not being able to get through a night without it. I had not been able to get drunk without taking cocaine for months now. Every night I was promising myself that this would be the night I would just get drunk, go home, and sleep it off. I left the bar and jumped into a gypsy cab.

"Woodlawn please, buddy."

"You got it."

"Cheers."

"Goin' home already?" My driver was a black guy. He was the darkest-skinned black guy I'd ever seen.

"Yeah. I'm done."

"There ain't no girls in that bar tonight."

"Yeah, there were a few."

"Yeah, I saw a few. Phew, they were lookin' good."

"Yeah, you know what, I've changed my mind. Make a right on Two-thirty-third and take me over to White Plains Road. I'm going to make a quick stop and then you can take me back to the bar again."

"I don't think you should go to White Plains Road at night, man."

"Just drive the car. I've got money." It was a Friday night; I had a full week's pay in cash in my pocket. I hadn't been back to my apartment since I'd left for work that morning.

"It's dangerous over there."

"Yeah, don't worry about it. I know where we're going."

"OK."

I had him turn onto White Plains Road and cruise along nice and slow, heading south under the elevated tracks. I scanned the sidewalks for a hookup. I'd been here before with a driver who knew the scene. I could do this by myself.

"I don't like this," my driver said.

"What the fuck, man, just drive. I'll pay you."

"No, I don't like it. It's dangerous. These people are dangerous. They've got guns, man." I ignored his pleas. I couldn't seem
to remember exactly where I had stopped before. I noticed
a crowd of guys standing on a street corner and told him to
pull over.

"Are you fucking crazy?" he said, and sped past them.

"I told you to pull over."

"You're crazy. I want my money."

"You're not getting a fucking penny until I get what I came
here for."

"Give me my money, man."

"Fuck you. You're not getting a penny. Turn this car around."
We'd now gone too far. We were down in an area I didn't recognize. There were no buildings, just empty lots. He abruptly
pulled the car over to the curb and turned to face me.

"You give me my money or I throw you out here."

"Fuck you." He jumped out of the front seat and before I
could lock the back door he was dragging me into the street. I
shook him loose and he stepped back a few feet.

"Now you give me my money."

"Fuck you. Try to take it."

"Fuck you."

"Fuck you." He ran at me, hitting me a good one on the side
of the face. I tore into him. We fought for a little and then he
backed off. And stood staring at me, his fists clenched.

"Give me my money, man."

"I'll give it to you when you take me home."

Then he looked over my shoulder and said, "Oh shit." He
looked genuinely frightened. He turned and jumped back into
the car. I looked behind me. There were five or six tall black figures just a few feet away. One of them spoke.

"What's goin' on here?" He spoke in a mocking tone. I knew
I was screwed. My driver had the motor started.

"It's nothing," he said. "We were just talking. Come on, let's go." I made a move for the car, but it was too late. One of the guys slammed the back door shut with his foot. Then he leaned into the driver's window.

"You should just go on and get out of here. We're going to take care of this." The driver gave me a last horrified glance and then he sped away. I was surrounded. They started laughing and pushing me.

"You made a wrong turn somewhere, white boy." This was not the evening I'd had in mind.

"I'll give you my wallet," I said, reaching for my back pocket. "Just take it and . . ." That's when I got the first punch in the mouth. It didn't stop. They all tore into me like a pack of wolves. I put my arms up in front of my face and kept stepping backwards. They were connecting pretty hard with my head, my ribs. My heel hit the curb and I fell flat on my back. One of them jumped on me, straddling me, and grabbed me by the hair with both of his fists. The others kicked from either side, my legs, my ribs. The one on my chest raised my head toward him by my hair and smashed my head down into the pavement. I swear I could feel the back of my head open and I remember thinking, "This is it. This is how you die."

He lifted my head and smashed it again; there was a crack and then a flash of white, the smell of sulfur as if somebody had just cracked a match inside my head. That's when I passed out.

When I woke up I was in my perfectly white bedroom. I was staring at the ceiling. It was definitely my room. White walls. White sheets. White dresser. Was I alive? I tried to sit up, but the pillow came with me. It was stuck to the back of my head. I put my hands up and carefully teased it away from my scalp. Then I sat up. I thought my head might explode. There was blood caked everywhere. The sunlight came in through the window. It was a beautiful Saturday morning. I could hear the telly in the living room. Ian was watching cartoons. How was this possible? I checked my pockets. My wallet was gone. My keys were not to be found. How did I get home? My head ached. But I was alive. I would never do drugs again. I swore it to God. I got up and walked into the living room. Ian was lying on the couch, watching cartoons. He glanced up, then his face froze.

"Colly, what the fuck happened?" He jumped up and grabbed me. "Who the fuck did this?" There were tears in his eyes. "Jesus Christ, are you alright?"

An hour later I was in McKeown's bar, tossing back vodka, spinning some elaborate story for the boys about how I'd been dragged out of a gypsy cab and mugged on my way home from Bainbridge. It was less ugly for me than the truth. To this day I still don't know how I got home. I had learned one valuable lesson: Don't carry your entire week's wages with you when you go looking for coke in the middle of the night.

It didn't take long for me to tire of the Irish bar scene around the Bronx. But it wasn't just the bar scene that was beginning to bore me. I had been in America for one year and I was fed up with my life. It was the same old cycle every week. I wasn't moving. I was making myself ill. Maybe I was homesick. Maybe I was just tired of one-night stands that didn't lead anywhere. I was sick of the drugs. Sick of the hangovers. In short, I was feeling good and sorry for myself. I was spending more and more time drinking alone.

One particular Sunday evening I spent hopping from bar to bar down Bainbridge Avenue. I wasn't in a hurry to go anywhere.

I wasn't even in a hurry to get drunk. I just didn't want to sit in one place long enough for anybody to bother me. All the damned bars were full. I wound up in a bar next to the Roaring Twenties called Sarsfields. It was the same deal there. Lots of people having a good time. I'd had just about as much as I could take of people having a good time. I took a seat about halfway up the bar and ordered a screwdriver, then I ordered another and another. Then I heard this girl's voice next to me.

"Can I buy you a drink?" I turned to see a beautiful, tall, strawberry-blond girl standing next to me.

"Do I look that pathetic?" I said. Maybe I could talk to her. She looked like Lauren Bacall in her prime and I was feeling like Humphrey Bogart at his worst.

"No, I just saw you sitting here by yourself and I thought I'd buy you a drink."

"OK. I'll have a screwdriver."

She didn't need to call the bartender. He was hovering nearby, waiting for her to speak.

"What'll it be, MaryAnn."

"Two screwdrivers."

He glanced at me unapprovingly and grudgingly splashed a little orange over some vodka and handed her the drinks. She handed one to me.

"Cheers."

"Cheers."

The guy next to me at the bar got up to leave and MaryAnn took his seat.

"So," I said.

"So."

"So your parents are Irish."

"Yip."

"Let me guess: Your father's from Cork and your mother's from Kerry."

"Nope."

"Ah . . . So who died?"

"What?"

"You look pretty down."

"Mmmm, I've been in a bit of a mood all weekend. I'm just not feeling very social."

"So you come to a crowded bar?"

"I've sort of been bar-hopping all evening, trying to avoid contact."

"I can leave you alone if you like."

"No, stay. I'm . . . a . . . you're . . . I owe you a drink."

"You don't owe me anything."

"OK. I'd like you to stay so I could buy you a drink."

"You sure you can handle it."

"I think I can handle that much."

"OK, but I can only stay for one more."

"You're leaving already?"

"I have a twelve o'clock curfew."

"What are you, in the military?"

"Nope."

"So what happens if you're not home by twelve?"

"I get grounded."

"Grounded? How old are you?"

"It's rude to ask. I'm old enough, but I live with my mother and it's her rules."

"Are you old enough to be in a bar?"

"Are you?"

"Just about."

"Well, then, me too."

After a couple of drinks I walked her outside to get a cab.

She was at least four or five inches taller than me. I didn't want her to leave. I could have talked with her all night long. I was falling for her already. We kissed and I asked her for her phone number.

"If you're here on Friday night maybe I'll think about it," she said, smiling as she got in the cab.

"I'll be here."

And I was there, and she did give me her phone number, and we started seeing each other every opportunity we could, unfortunately for her.

By this time I was pretty much out of control drinking and doing cocaine, though I wouldn't have admitted that. I was young. My hangovers were still manageable. I could still drink all night and go directly to work the next morning. Being Irish, it's always been difficult for me to gauge my drinking. It's hard to convince yourself that you have a problem when the Irish guys you're drinking with accuse you of getting soft if you lighten up, or of letting the American mentality get to you. It's hard to take being an alcoholic seriously when your fellow countrymen can and do drink more than you. The Irish have always prided themselves on being able to drink everyone else under the table. It's an ugly stereotype, I know, but it's a stereotype that deserves merit in a town like New York, where almost every bar is Irish. How many bars have you noticed with the Star of David rather than a shamrock above the door? How many Greek, German, Italian, French, or even Australian bars do you know in New York?

We were dating for about six months when MaryAnn asked me if I'd come with her to meet her family on one Saturday. She'd told them all about me—well, not all about me; she'd told them about the digestible elements of my lifestyle. Even MaryAnn didn't know about the drugs. Being Irish himself and a teetotaler, her father wasn't very keen on her dating me, as you

can imagine. Her family were meeting early in Van Cortlandt
Park. They had hired a photographer to take a family portrait.
Her five older sisters would be there, and her brother, the cop.
She even purchased a ticket for me to go with her and her sisters to a Rolling Stones concert the same day. I had been fore-
warned a week before not to get drunk on the Friday night
before the photo shoot so that I wouldn't show up with a hangover. MaryAnn had arranged to cook dinner for me at her new
apartment down on Bainbridge Avenue after work, then we
could stay in and have a quiet night watching a movie. It
seemed like a fairly simple, straightforward plan.

After work on that Friday all the boys decided to stop by
McKeown's for a few quick beers before going home to get
cleaned up. The place was mobbed as usual. It was one of those
typical summer evenings where all the stars seemed perfectly
aligned for a party. I called her around six o'clock to tell her I
was finishing my bottle of beer and coming straight over after I
made a quick stop at my apartment to shower and change.

"Dinner's going to be ready in half an hour. You were supposed to be here already."

"I can't show up in my work clothes to meet your folks for
the first time."

"But you weren't supposed to go drinking at all."

"I didn't have a choice. I was with the guys in the van and
they drove here first. They wouldn't let me go off until I'd had a
few beers."

"Please don't get drunk tonight."

"Am I drunk? I've had three beers. I told you to relax. I'll be
there in twenty minutes."

"OK, hurry."

"OK."

I called her again about an hour and a half later from
the bar.

"Listen, I'm sorry, this guy came in I haven't seen since London. He just stopped into the bar by pure chance. I had to stay . . ."

"I can't fucking believe you. You're drunk already."

"I've had maybe five or six beers. I'm fine. I'm sorry."

"I cooked you a beautiful dinner. I even bought something special to wear tonight."

"Just stick the dinner in the oven. I'll eat it when I get there."

"Forget it; it's destroyed now."

"It'll be fine. Don't worry, I'll eat it."

"You said you'd be here. You promised."

"What did you want me to do? I couldn't very well run out on the guy when I haven't seen him in over a year. These things happen. What would you do if you were in my shoes?"

"I'd tell my friend it was nice to see them and make plans to see them another night."

"Yeah, but you're a girl."

"I can't believe you're doing this. You're supposed to meet my family tomorrow morning."

"And I will. Don't worry so much. You need to lighten up a little. I swear, you Americans take everything so seriously."

"Take a cab now."

"I will—I'll get a cab in five minutes."

"Promise."

"Promise."

I didn't bother calling again until about eleven thirty. She was crying, and when I tried to calm her down she hung up on me. It was too late to worry about it; I'd just try to get back before one o'clock so I could still patch it up and get a night's sleep. I'd be in good shape for the morning.

When I left the Shamrock at eight the next morning I was still under the impression I could put it right. I had my gypsy cab pull over at a deli where I saw flowers for sale. It was the first time I'd ever bought flowers, but I'd seen it done in American movies and it seemed to work.

When she opened the door to her apartment she began to sob. I offered her the flowers.

"You're an asshole," she blurted. "I can't believe you did this to me."

"You're right. I'm an asshole. I'm sorry. Look, I bought you flowers."

"Are you serious?" She snatched the flowers from me, walked into the kitchen, and stuffed them into the garbage can. I followed her in and sat down in the living room.

"I'll take a shower. I'll clean up. It'll be fine."

"Have you seen yourself? You're still in your work clothes. You're drunk off your mind. You can barely walk straight. Do you honestly think I'm going to take you to see my family looking like this?"

"I said I was sorry. What do you want me to do?"

"You just don't get it, do you? I'm running late. I have to go."

"I think I'm just going to have a little nap here before I go home," I said.

"Do whatever you want. I don't give a shit anymore."

"I'm sorry. I know I'm an asshole. I love you."

She picked up her keys and left and I stretched out and went to sleep for a few hours. When she returned home that night I was drunk as a skunk with her roommate, Susan. We'd polished off a large bottle of vodka. This didn't go down well either, so I decided I'd better leave. I had to get home, shower, change, and meet the guys for a few beers. It was Saturday night, after all.

• • •

Then came the New York City Crackathon. Overnight it seemed the whole city had gone on a crash diet. Everywhere you looked were the faces of the walking dead. Skeletal panhandlers manned every stoplight from the Bronx to the Bowery, throwing themselves across the hood of every car, slopping dirty rags across your windshield and then threatening to rip your throat out with a claw hammer for a quarter. Driving through Harlem in the morning was like running the gauntlet. The cops, it seemed, just stopped ticketing people for running red lights down Martin Luther King Jr. Boulevard. How could you fine people who were running for their lives?

Crack permeated every phase of life. It was worse than cancer, or AIDS. For a time it seemed as if it would swallow the city whole. Petty crime was out of control. Cars were broken into so often that people stopped locking their doors to save the price of a new window. They weren't going to steal the car. Crack addicts didn't want cars. They were too bulky, too awkward to hide under your jacket. People put signs in their windows: NO CAR STEREO, NOTHING OF VALUE INSIDE. Muggings and bag snatchings became so commonplace, you hid your watch in your pocket. It was a problem nobody could ignore.

It wasn't just the black kids in Harlem or the Hispanic guys up in Washington Heights; it was rich white preppy schoolkids and Wall Street bankers. You were just as likely to get ripped off by a car full of New Jersey jocks on West End Avenue as you were to get threatened by a knife-wielding granny at a stoplight on First. The city was hyper with it.

After a while, real New Yorkers were getting wise to the fact that the only real threat from a crack addict was if he pulled out a blood-filled syringe. With its promise of AIDS, the syringe was more deadly than any Uzi. If they didn't have a syringe you could be fairly confident they didn't have a weapon. All weapons were being traded to the dealers for vials of crack. A knife could buy you another rock. A gun could keep you high for an hour, your sneakers another fifteen seconds.

Around about this time I started running a job for Con on 105th Street between First and Second Avenues. The building had previously been used as a school; now it was being turned into condos. We had a crew of about eighteen painters who were there most of the time. I was drinking and drugging heavily. The job was the most corrupt and dangerous job I'd ever worked. Everybody was working some sort of scam. Knife fights were a fairly common sight on the job. Everybody, it seemed, was carrying some kind of weapon. It was like the Wild West.

Truckloads of new kitchen cabinets were being unloaded in the front courtyard, carried into the building, and placed in each apartment for installation. They were no sooner set on the floor than they were lowered out the back windows of the building into waiting trucks on 104th Street. This sort of thing happened in plain sight of everybody. Nobody said a word. Palms were being greased. All the top guys were making money. Everybody else kept their mouths shut.

A black guy from the neighborhood was hired to stand guard at the front gate. Henry was in his fifties. He lived in a makeshift hut in the courtyard. He was on watch twenty-four hours a day. Henry was a real alcoholic. Unlike me. He drank cheap vodka out of plastic half-pint bottles. He always had one in his pocket. I think that's how they kept him there, a never-ending supply of cheap vodka. He was as mean as a rusty saw. He'd survived this long in the neighborhood; he had to be.

One morning we arrived for work and this black kid was lying in a pool of blood on the pavement less than ten feet from where we were driving our truck through the gates. I was told he'd been shot in the face. I was too nauseous with a hangover to look closely for myself. I'd seen guys who'd been shot in the face before, back home. It's an image you can do without.

A bunch of the workers stood around him smoking cigarettes, shooting the breeze, laughing, talking about last night's ball game. They were waiting for the cops to come along. They were glad for the diversion. I asked Henry what had happened. He shrugged. "You know, just some stupid kid shit." He slipped the bottle out of his pocket as we spoke and took a hit. "A life ain't nothing around here," he said. "Just one less mouth to feed, tha's all it is."

Two weeks later on the job, one of the drywallers stabbed his boss. The ambulance arrived and we watched him get stretchered out, bleeding from his gut. A week later, on a Friday evening, someone went into the main office on the first floor with a hood over his face and a sawed-off shotgun and stole about seventy thousand dollars in cash. The money was there to pay the wages. The rumor on the job was that the guys in the office knew who did it and that they were certain they would get him. But it was hard to tell who knew what anymore, there was so much corruption on the job. I'd half suspected one of our guys of the holdup.

This kid called Ramone had started smoking crack with his first paycheck. He'd show up for work wired out of his skull, begging for money to eat for the rest of the week. I let him stay because he was the fastest painter I had ever seen in my entire life. He could prime seventy door frames a day. He was like a machine. I don't know if it was the crack, but I joked about getting some for the rest of the crew to wake them up a bit. Ramone disappeared about the time of the robbery and never showed up for work again.

A week later Henry went missing. Someone said he'd been shot, but nobody seemed to really know what had happened. Nor did they care. One less mouth to feed. Tha's all it is.

• • •

I was growing tired of New York. Things were so bad at the time that you were literally taking your life in your own hands when you walked from the front of the building we were working in to the corner of the block to get a sandwich from the deli. To stay safe, a bunch of us would go together. The place was like a war zone. It was not unusual to hear gunfire before breakfast.

This wasn't the New York I had dreamed of. This was not the romantic city I had read about or seen in movies.

I was still seeing MaryAnn. She had eventually forgiven me for botching the family get-together for her. I'd been on my best behavior around her since. I was trying to be a better boyfriend. I wasn't sure if it was because I was in love with her or that I just couldn't stomach the idea of her being with somebody else if we did break up. I had this idea that if we could just somehow escape all this madness we'd be OK. Life had to be easier somewhere else. I'd always had this feeling that there was going to be so much more to my life. This was a dead-end situation. I had to get out. There had to be more to America than this. There just had to be.

Maybe I had just arrived in the wrong city. That was it. I hadn't gone far enough away from home. The East Coast was still too close to home. There were so many Irish in Woodlawn living on top of one another, I might as well have stayed at home. I had a cousin living in San Francisco. I told MaryAnn that I had to go. I'd go out to San Francisco and check it out and when I got set up I would come back and get her. She wasn't as keen on the idea as I was. She'd grown up in the Bronx, her entire family lived here, the friends she'd grown up with still lived right in her neighborhood, and . . . oh yeah, I was a no-good, unreliable, piece-of-shit drunk.

I called my cousin in San Francisco and she told me she had a spare bedroom and that I was welcome to stay with her and her boyfriend as long as I wanted. That was it. I bought a ticket a week later and flew to San Francisco. I didn't tell anybody I was going. I didn't give Con a week's notice. I just got my paycheck and fucked off.

There was nobody to meet me at the airport this time. I arrived sometime around ten at night. The moment I got off the plane, I knew I'd made the right decision.

I took a cab to my cousin's apartment in the Richmond District. I remember the feeling of relaxation I had on the ride from the airport. It was as if my body was decompressing. I rolled down the windows and let the warm California air wash over me. I'd survived New York. I should have been here all along. The cabdriver was in no hurry. He offered me a cigarette and rolled along at a relaxed pace. The Eagles played on the radio. I saw a palm tree for the first time.

The apartment was above a comic-book shop on Clement. Maura greeted me at the door with a hug. I hadn't seen her since high school. She hadn't changed a bit. She had the same enthusiastic bounce about her. She was a bright, bubbly girl with a short ginger bob. She was living with her French boyfriend, José. That was very Maura. Maura had been a cosmopolitan girl before she'd even left Beragh. They kept a tidy two-bedroom. José lounged on the couch with his legs crossed, a cigarette raised aloft between two delicate fingers like some 1920s Parisian hairdresser. He stood to greet me.

"*Bonjour, Colin.*"

"*Bonjour, José. Ça va?*"

"*Bon, tu parles français.*"

"*Oui.*"

"*Ah, très bien, très bien.*"

"*Et tu parles anglais?*"

"*Oui,* I mean, yes, I speak *un peu,* a little. Not good yet."

"That's good, because I don't know any more French."

José stared at me with a slight smile, then glanced at Maura, who began to laugh.

"I think you two will be able to communicate just fine."

"Ah. Oui, oui." Then José smiled as if he'd just had an epiphany and raised his bony finger toward the sky. "Welcome your humble abode."

Maura laughed. "That's 'Welcome to our humble abode,' José. I just taught him that before you arrived."

"Merci, José."

"Vino!" José declared, and he marched off to the kitchen.

"I heard that, bubba," I said.

We drank a little wine and Maura and José took me for a stroll down Clement to the Plough and the Stars, an Irish bar, to meet the locals. It was a Friday night and the place had a nice crowd. A traditional Irish band played in the corner. Maura introduced me to a few of her friends; there was a politician, a journalist, a real estate broker, a travel agent, a cabdriver, and Ellen the nanny, with the streak of blue through her blond hair, who after a few drinks invited me back to her place for a joint.

I woke in the morning to find myself in Ellen's bed. It was the first night I'd been out drinking in over a year that I hadn't gone off to buy coke or even had the urge. I'd had more fun without it. I decided there and then that I was done with cocaine. I was going to clean up my act. This was a fresh start. I was going to make a life for myself here. I was going to be a more responsible human being, goddamn it. I was going to be a better boyfriend to MaryAnn. After I left Ellen's apartment, that was. Ellen made us some coffee and brought it back to bed. She had to leave for work, so she walked me back to my apartment and kissed me good-bye. I was just coming up the stairs when I met Maura on the way out.

"Good morning." She grinned, raising an eyebrow as she passed me by.

"Good morning, Maura."

"Well, did you get a good feel for the place last night?"

"I did."

"Oh, you had a phone call this morning from New York. I told her you were gone out with José."

"Thanks, Maura."

I spent the morning making phone calls. I just picked up the yellow pages and started calling construction companies and floor-sanding businesses. By two o'clock I had a job arranged.

The thing about working construction was that the party never stopped, regardless of what coast you happened to be on. Most guys didn't do construction because they liked to work with their hands; they did it because you could show up every morning hungover and looking like shit and not have to worry about losing your job. You worked with a bunch of guys who liked to party just as hard as you did. Having a beer for breakfast was not frowned upon. Maybe I should say it was not frowned upon as much back then. Maybe I was just too out of it to notice anyone frowning.

Within two weeks I had enough money to fly back to New York to convince MaryAnn's parents that moving to San Francisco with me was the best thing for their daughter.

I arrived in New York on a Friday evening. I had not told her I was coming back to New York. I thought I would surprise her. I called her once I arrived in the terminal at JFK.

"Hey."

"Hey."

"What's going on?"

"Not much. I just got in from work."

"Yeah, how was that?"

"Good. What're you up to?"

"I'm just going out to dinner with Maura and José. They're waiting for me right now, actually."

"Great. You're always running. No time to talk. I hate this."

"Don't worry; as soon as I get the money, I'll come and get you."

"I won't hold my breath."

"Do hold your breath."

"You want me to die."

"You have no faith in me."

"I can't imagine why."

"Do you want me to come and get you or not?"

"I suppose so."

"OK, listen, I have to run; they're walking out the door right now. I'll call you soon."

"Whatever."

"Byeee."

"Yeah, bye."

I dashed outside and grabbed a cab from the airport to her father's apartment, where Mary Ann was now living. I arrived at about six o'clock with a bunch of flowers. This time I was sober.

MaryAnn answered the door in a pair of Daisy Duke shorts and a sweatshirt butchered *Flashdance* style. Her long strawberry-blond hair was tied up in a ponytail.

"Hi," I said, handing her the flowers. "See, I told you I'd come back to get you." She stared at the flowers and then back at me.

"But you just called . . ."

"From the airport. I wanted to surprise you." She put her hand to her mouth; she was shaking. I thought I sensed a hint of disappointment in her eyes. "I'm sorry, I should have called . . ."

"No," she said, throwing her arms around me. "I'm sorry. You just took me by surprise."

"I want you to come to San Francisco with me. I've bought you a ticket. We leave on Sunday evening."

"What?" she said, leaning away from me so that she could see my face. "Are you joking?"

"I have the tickets in my bag. I told you I was going to come back and get you when I was set up. Well, I'm set up. We have our own room in a nice apartment. I have steady work and I know how to get around already. You'll love it. Trust me."

"I don't know, Colin. My parents will never let me go."

"They can't stop you. You're over eighteen."

"Barely. I'm their youngest daughter."

"Don't worry. I'll talk to them."

"They'll kill you."

"They can't kill me. They love me."

"You're insane."

"Possibly."

MaryAnn's father arrived from work a short while later. I had no trouble deciphering Frank's reaction to seeing me once again next to his daughter on the couch as he came through his front door. He must have thought I was gone for good. His shoulders slumped automatically as he tightened his grip on the handle of the door.

"This is a surprise. Aren't you supposed to be in Australia or somewhere very far away?"

"San Francisco," I corrected him, not bothering to get up and shake his hand. "Yes, I was, but I had to come back for a few days."

"Oh, so you're leaving again?" he said, releasing the door handle, his shoulders snapping back into the upright position as the door closed behind him and came on into the room. "Great!

Well, it's good to see you again. What did you have to come back for?"

"Your daughter," I said, giving MaryAnn a big smile. She looked frightened.

"You came all the way back just to see her again. That's some trip."

"Actually, I came back to get MaryAnn. I have a ticket for her to come with me."

"A ticket to go where?" he said.

"San Francisco."

"Well, I don't know about that . . . she, ah . . . that's . . . ," he said, scratching the back of his head with a long bony finger. He glanced over his shoulder at the door as if he was looking for an escape route. "I should put the kettle on."

"I'm fine, thanks. I have to go meet my cousins for a few beers in a couple of minutes. Thanks just the same, but you go ahead."

"Well, we'll have to talk about this," he said, regaining his composure as he walked toward the kitchen, shaking his head. "I don't think this is such a good idea. MaryAnn's just getting settled into her new job. We'll probably have to take some time—"

"We've talked about it already," I said. "Before you came in. MaryAnn's coming with me. We leave on Sunday. I have to be back for work on Monday morning. I got a new job and—"

"You're leaving on Sunday?" He shook his head and looked at his daughter. "Well, as I say, we'll just have to talk about it. You're obviously free to do what you want, but—"

"I promise I'll take good care of her," I said. "We'll be living with my cousin Maura. It's a nice apartment. San Francisco's a nice town. You could come out and visit. You'd like it."

"I don't like anything outside New York," he said, slipping into a chair. He sat quietly for a few moments.

"She's too young," he said finally. "You're too young. It's too far away."

"It's a few hours on a plane. It's no farther away than Ireland. You came here when you were young," I said. "Maybe we'll only stay for a little while. Anyway, it's not my decision or yours; it's hers." We both looked at MaryAnn. Neither of us had stopped long enough to hear what she had to say on the subject.

"I'm going to go," she said, getting up to sit next to her father. "I want to see what it's like."

I got up and said I had to go meet my cousins. I said good-bye and told MaryAnn I'd call her in a little bit. She needed to be alone with her dad. My damage here was done.

The following night the family arranged a going-away party for us. All of her sisters and their husbands were gathered to say their good-byes. I stood in the corner of the room with a beer in my hand, praying for it to be over. It was obvious that nobody was thrilled about the idea of a family member leaving to go anywhere with me. I didn't blame them. Her older brother, Jason, a New York City cop whom I didn't get to see very often, arrived late. He was in uniform and he just wanted to stop by and wish his little sister the best. They hugged briefly and he whispered into her ear. Then he said he had to leave; his buddy was waiting in the squad car downstairs. I offered to shake his hand as he was leaving.

"No," he said. "I want you to come with me." We left the party on the fifth floor and he called the elevator.

"So you have a job out there?" he asked.

"Yes. Yes I do. It's a good job."

"You OK for money? You'll be able to take care of my little sister?"

"Yes. It's no problem. It pays well."

Ding. The elevator arrived. I offered Jason my hand once more.

"No, come down with me. You can come right back up again."

We both got in the elevator. Jason hit the button and the door closed. He turned toward me wearing a grave expression. He casually pulled back his jacket to reveal the gun on his belt. "MaryAnn's my baby sister," he started. He paused and rested his hand on the handle of his gun as if he was considering just shooting me right there. "I would be very unhappy if anything were ever to happen to her." He paused again. "Do you understand?"

"I understand, Jason." It was a small elevator and Jason was a good six inches taller than me and had his hand on a loaded gun. I understood perfectly. The elevator stopped and the doors opened. He offered me his hand, letting his jacket cover his gun again.

"Take care of my little sister."

"You got it, Jason."

I took the elevator back up to the apartment. Everyone but MaryAnn appeared a little disappointed to see that I was still alive. I grabbed another beer. This party was really shaping up.

Our arrival at the airport in San Francisco foreshadowed how things were going to go for the next year. As the plane touched the tarmac, MaryAnn was in hysterics.

"I don't want to go. I want to go home," she cried.

"Relax," I said. "You'll love it. You haven't even seen the place yet."

"I miss home. I want to go home." She was inconsolable.

"It's going to be OK. I promise."

Looking back on it now, I probably should have saved us both a lot of trouble and just let her go.

MaryAnn got a job as a temp in an office somewhere downtown. She wasn't real excited about it at first, but she grew to like a few of her workmates.

At night we would go to the Irish bars around the neighborhood, and at the weekends a bunch of us would get together and go boogie boarding, or maybe we'd rent a few cars and drive down to the wine country and get hammered, driving from wine tasting to wine tasting.

I started reading again. I'd always loved books, but since moving to America I had stopped reading completely. Reading was not a sport held in high esteem in the circles where I had been spending my time, and cocaine is not a reader-friendly drug. But in San Francisco I fell in love with books all over again. There was a bookstore on the next block down from my apartment. I spent hours browsing through the shelves, looking for a book jacket that interested me.

At that time I was reading Charles Bukowski and Robert B. Parker simultaneously. I read every single thing they had written. Bukowski was my hero; the talent, the heart, the fuck-it-all-to-hell attitude. I have never read another writer of our time whose work rang so true for me. Bukowski made me want to be a writer. Parker I devoured for his linguistic simplicity and his devotion to discipline. My own personality, I imagined, lay somewhere between the two, although at that time I had no idea what it was. I was lost. I honestly didn't know which end of me was up. I could not have pinpointed a single certain thing about myself; I could not have given you a straight, honest answer about anything. Who's your favorite band? I haven't a clue. What kind of clothes do you like to wear? I haven't a clue. What religious belief do you most identify with? I haven't a clue. Are you really in love? I haven't a clue. Who knows these things at twenty-three? I hadn't a clue. What would you like to be when you grow up? A writer. Ah, I see.

I'd come home from work at three in the afternoon. For about three hours every evening I had the apartment to myself before Maura, José, or MaryAnn came in. I could read for a few hours in silence, drink a six-pack to brace myself for their return. Those were peaceful afternoons; even the mice would come out from behind the radiator and play right next to me on the floor as I lay on the couch, reading. They seemed to understand that I was amused by their presence and that they were safe. Even when I stood up to get another beer they would stand cautiously but would not run for cover. The moment anyone else arrived home, they disappeared.

MaryAnn suddenly seemed happier. I, of course, assumed her newfound happiness had something to do with some guy she worked with. Josh. She talked about him constantly in glowing terms. The more I drank, the more handsome and charismatic Josh became. I had never seen the guy, but I could picture him vividly. I could see through his infectious good humor, his perfect physique, those pristine white shirts that he wore, the way he would hold her hand or gently move the hair back from her face when she cried to him about what a horrible boyfriend I was.

I was twenty-three years old and already I was distrustful of all men and women. I had already been with women who had boyfriends that they went home to and swore they would never cheat on. I had been with women who were married, women who were engaged to be married. I'd had girlfriends whom I'd loved who'd cheated on me, sometimes with my best friends. I trusted no one. I began to have fantasies about disappearing completely. Maybe I could move to Mexico and live in a shack somewhere by the ocean. I could be alone all the time and read.

I was good at being alone. I was happiest when people weren't around. It was becoming a problem.

Things were so bad between MaryAnn and me by Christmas that I decided the best solution would be to propose marriage. I didn't have enough money to make a huge deal about it. So I bought a ring in a jewelry store and stopped on the way home to buy flowers and a bottle of champagne. It was a Friday afternoon. Maura and José had gone out for the evening. When MaryAnn came home from work I had her sit down on the couch and, without further ado, I got down on one knee and popped the ring out of my pocket. There was that look again. The same one I'd seen when I'd surprised her by showing up at her door in New York. Her hands were shaking as I placed the ring on her finger and she shed the appropriate tears and gushed about how beautiful the ring was. I couldn't really tell if she was happy that I'd just asked her to spend the rest of her life with me or if she was overwhelmed by the fact that I'd managed to spend so much on a Christmas present for her. Girls do like nice jewelry.

"I have to call my mother," she said.

"Are you sure?"

"What do you mean, am I sure? We just got engaged. It's not a big secret, is it?"

"No, of course not. Why would it be?"

"I'm going to call my whole family and my friends."

"I'll pop the champagne," I said. I really needed a drink. "Here, these are for you as well." I handed her the flowers.

"Aren't you going to call your parents?"

"I'll tell them tomorrow when I call to wish them a happy Christmas."

"Aren't you going to call your cousins?"

"They'll find out soon enough."

"Aren't you excited about this?"

"Of course I'm excited, but I'm not a girl. Guys don't run around screaming that they just got engaged. My friends will find out soon enough. Here, have some champagne. We'll drink this and head down to the pub for a few drinks with Maura and José. I told them we might meet them later."

"But it's our special night. I want to stay home with you."

"OK, OK, no problem. I'll just go out and buy some more champagne and we'll stay at home."

The engagement ring was working; here we were, alone together in the same room for almost ten minutes, and we weren't killing each other. It was like a Christmas miracle.

The real gift that Christmas Eve was the one MaryAnn got for me.

"You want me to give you your gift now?" she said excitedly.

"No, it's OK. It can wait until tomorrow."

"No, I want to give it to you now. You should have something as well."

"But I have you for the rest of my life." The champagne was kicking in. It was beginning to feel like maybe this was the start of something beautiful.

"I have to give it to you now," she said excitedly, jumping off the couch and dashing into the bedroom. She came back with a neatly wrapped box and handed it to me, her face glowing with anticipation as I held it.

"Do you know what it is?"

"I have absolutely no idea," I admitted. "It weighs quite a bit. What did you get me?"

"Open it, you idiot."

"Did you get me a telephone book?"

"Open it."

I tore open the paper and there it was . . . my very first typewriter. An electric typewriter.

"Wow." I was honestly astounded. My heart was pounding.

It was the best gift I had ever received in my whole life. I was speechless.

"And look," she said nervously. "I even got you a book on how to teach yourself how to type properly and a sheaf of white paper so that you can begin right away."

My whole life, this was all I'd really wanted. I'd wanted someone to give me permission to be a writer. I hadn't realized this until this very moment; I needed somebody else to tell me I could do it. I needed somebody to believe I could do it. Since I was a little boy, this had been my dream. I'd been scribbling in notebooks silently my whole life. I'd mentioned on occasion that I felt like this was my true calling. Nobody had ever really taken me seriously. It was as if I had just been handed the key to my life.

"Why are you crying?" she said, stroking my face. "Don't you like it?"

"I love you, MaryAnn," I said. "This is the best gift I've ever received in my whole life. Will you marry me?"

"Yes."

We were truly happy for a few moments. It didn't last long.

By March I understood why women spent so much time agonizing over the construction of their engagement rings. I could finally comprehend some of the deeper mysteries of the female psyche regarding their attention to the mechanics of the ring: the width of the band, for example, or the setting of the stone, indeed the very idea of using a diamond to begin with, a rock so hard it will cut glass. I am no longer curious when I witness the innate response in a woman to examine a ring up close, whether it's just been handed to her as a declaration of love or it's merely being presented on an extended finger by a friend. It's quite simple: The ritual is to determine how much force the ring will bear when it's flung into a wall or into the middle of traffic. Will the setting hold the stone securely if it's bounced off a skull or a doorjamb? Will it withstand being dropkicked under the wheel of a bus? Is the rock big enough and bright enough to be spotted in the middle of a field of long grass, or, God forbid, the bottom of the ocean? These are the nuances that determine the true quality of an engagement ring, small enough to fit on a finger, bright enough to be photographed from outer space, and strong enough to permanently maim the one you love.

After Christmas I met John Byrne, or as he was known to his friends, the Burner. He was drinking alone in the Plough and the Stars one afternoon and I was next to him doing likewise. He was maybe forty-five to fifty years old, a tall, bony kind of a character with a sort of a comical face. You couldn't help smiling a little when you looked at him. We got to talking and it turned out that the Burner had been a woodworking teacher back in Galway and had packed it all in and moved to San Francisco, become a partner in a small bar. Now he had his own flooring company. In fact he *was* his own flooring company. He liked to work by himself. After about ten drinks I convinced him that he should expand and take me on as a work partner. He did. I had a new job.

I spent hours at the typewriter every day teaching myself how to type. I was somehow under the impression that if I could use a typewriter, I could write. But it was becoming apparent that what I could do was type. Writing was a different cart full of cabbages entirely, but I did take a poke at it nonetheless.

By late March MaryAnn and I decided the engagement had been a bad idea. We decided that it was time to call it quits. We were in a vicious cycle of horrible fights and earth-shattering sex. To quit cold turkey would require medication. I suggested that she move home to New York to give us some distance. It seemed like a great idea to me. She was furious.

"How about you go back to New York and I'll stay here," she said.

"Where would you stay? You can't stay here with me. We can't continue living together."

"I'll find somewhere."

"Where?"

"I don't know. Somewhere."

"Where would you stay?"

"I know some people."

"Who do you know?"

"People."

"You mean Josh."

"He's told me if I ever needed a place to stay . . ."

"Are you fucking serious? You're going back to New York."

"You can't tell me what to do."

"You had this planned all along."

"You're the one telling me I have to leave."

"Have you slept with him yet? Is that what this is about?"

"You're insane."

"You have, haven't you?"

"You know what? You're right. I fuck him every day on our lunch break."

"That motherfucker—I want you out of here. I'm going to buy you a ticket for New York. You're not going to move in with that fucking scumbag."

She gave me one of those stares and said nothing. I could fill in the blanks for myself.

That afternoon, after talking with MaryAnn, Maura decided that she would leave José also. Just like that, we were all single.

Less than one week later, on a Saturday morning, I drove MaryAnn to the airport and kissed her good-bye. She handed me the engagement ring and told me to keep it. I'd had it thrown at me many times but never handed to me like this. I was heartbroken. It wasn't yet nine in the morning and here we were, standing in a parking lot, staring at each other, and all I wanted to do right then was to take her in my arms and bring her home with me. I wanted to make everything alright again. I tried to get her to keep the ring, but she wouldn't take it. Looking at her now in the last moments, I could see the girl I fell in love with again. We held each other for a long time, then she turned and walked away. Maybe that's what I was in love with, the way she would walk away from me. She did have a magnificent ass.

Within forty-five minutes I was sitting in the Burner's bar over in Noe Valley having a screwdriver. Then I had another five or six. I arrived back to the apartment around two o'clock, nicely buzzed, and announced to José that the party was now on. The girls were gone; Maura had miraculously left San Francisco on exactly the same day. He was also just back from the airport. We were single again.

I was on a roll. I went on a three-month bender, day and night. When I needed money I would buy myself a six-pack and go to work with the Burner for a few days. He never complained about me drinking on the job. As long as the job got done and done right, he didn't interfere with my partying. In fact he seemed to enjoy it. He was more interested in the juicy details of my life than in how many square feet of flooring I installed. We'd quit work early and he'd insist on taking me to whatever bar was nearby. I might have some girl come by and meet us for a few drinks. Maybe we'd all jump into his old green work van and smoke a joint together. For a guy who spent most of his life teaching back in Galway, the Burner sure liked to party.

But things were spiraling out of control. My life had become a three-ring circus.

I got a phone call from MaryAnn saying that she had quit drinking completely. She had gotten help and was trying to convince me to do the same thing. Maybe we could still work it out. It wasn't too late yet.

"Have you met anybody since I left?" she asked.

"No."

"You haven't been with anybody in the last few months."

"No."

"You're lying."

"Why would I lie about that? We're not even together anymore."

"So you haven't been with anybody?"

"No. Have you?"

"No."

"Are you sure?"

"Yes."

"I don't believe you."

"I'm telling the truth. Why would I lie?"

The hangovers were getting worse. I was dying. I remember one morning in particular that was so bad that I was convinced I would die before lunchtime. I was scared. I didn't want to die. I'd been up for three days doing cocaine, drinking Bacardi and tequila and cheap red wine. My head hurt; my gut hurt. I couldn't think straight. I tried to eat some scrambled eggs, but they came straight back up. I called the Burner and told him I needed to see a doctor right away. He gave me the number of some guy he knew over by the Haight. It was the guy all the Irish went to see, our man in Frisco.

I dragged myself out to see him at lunchtime. There were pamphlets in the waiting room. DO YOU HAVE A DRINKING PROBLEM? ARE YOU AN ALCOHOLIC? I borrowed a pen from the receptionist and took the twenty-question quiz. I aced it. Apparently I was 100 percent alcoholic.

The doctor came out and called my name. I got up and

followed him into his office. He was a middle-aged Irish American guy with a round beer belly and a red drinker's nose.

"What seems to be the problem?" he said, checking my wrists, my neck glands, tongue, the usual stuff.

"I've been feeling sick a lot lately."

"Like what? Do you have the flu? An upset stomach? Explain your symptoms to me."

"Well, I can't keep any food down. I'm losing weight. I can't seem to think straight."

"How much weight have you lost?"

"I don't know, but I can feel it."

"Are you doing a lot of drugs?"

"I have a smoke once in a while, maybe a little coke."

"Cigarettes?"

"A pack a day, maybe a little more."

He ignored me for a minute as he counted off my pulse rate. He put his stethoscope up my shirt, checked the heart.

He listened to my lungs from behind. "Take a deep breath." He smelled like whiskey. There was an ashtray on his desk with four stubbed cigarettes.

"OK, young fella, take a seat." He moved around his desk and pulled out a bottle of Jameson from his desk drawer. He set up two plastic cups and poured a good healthy shot into each of them. "What part did you say you were from?"

"Tyrone."

"Ah, Tyrone among the bushes, eh."

"Something like that."

"Cheers. Sorry I don't have any Bushmills for you."

"Cheers, Doc."

We swallowed them and he tossed the plastic cups into a trash can next to his desk. I wondered if he gave all his patients this treatment or if he reserved his favoritism for the Irish.

"Right, here's my advice," he said, adopting a somewhat professional doctorly tone. "Cut back on the booze, you know, the vodka, tequila, brandy, that sort of stuff, start drinking more Guinness. A few pints of the black stuff every evening and no more white stuff up your nose, you'll be as right as rain in no time."

"And that's it—everything else is fine?"

"You're as strong as a horse." He smiled, standing to usher me out the door. "If you find yourself getting a little paranoid, I might cut back on the weed a bit too."

"Thanks, Doc," I said.

"You're welcome. You can settle up with the receptionist on the way out. Don't mention the drop of whiskey to her or she might try to charge you for that, too." He laughed and gave me a hearty slap on the back as I left his office.

"Next, please."

I was feeling better, I decided. Doc was right. I was just being silly. I was as strong as a horse, and that from the horse's mouth. I decided to celebrate with a drink. There was a bar nearby, the Pig and Whistle. An English place. Even this far from home, as an Irishman I still felt a tinge of guilt stepping inside. I took the doctor's orders and started on the Guinness. I drank about four or five pints right away. I'll be damned if the doc wasn't right; I did feel a little better.

By six o'clock that evening I was pretty hammered. I needed cocaine. I called my guy and had him meet me on Clement. By the time I got back to the apartment it was midnight and I was wired out of my skull. I woke José and told him to get a bag packed.

"What are you doing?" he grumbled.

"We're going to Los Angeles."

"It's one in the morning. Go to sleep."

"José, if you're not out of bed in ten seconds I'm going to get a bucket of water from the kitchen."

"I'm sleeping."

"Get a small bag packed; we might not be back for a few days. We're going to have a drink with Bukowski."

"Buck who?"

"He's a writer. I'll tell you all about it in the car. We're leaving here in five minutes. There's a line of coke for you on the coffee table—get it into you and hurry up."

"It's going to take us hours to drive there."

"We'll make it in six."

Six hours later we were lost in the desert somewhere. I'd finished the whiskey and cocaine a while back. We were almost out of gas. According to the thermometer glued to my dashboard it was over a hundred degrees already. Every time I tried to use the air conditioner the engine started to overheat. My tongue rattled around in my mouth like a chunk of tree bark. José was behind the wheel trying to keep his cool for both of us.

"I need booze," I said.

"You need water. And so do I."

"We're going to die out here, José."

"You might." He grinned.

"Let's find some desert rodents and squeeze the juice out of them."

"I'll keep my eyes peeled."

We were rolling that old Buick on fumes by the time we hit the next gas station about an hour later. It popped up like a mirage. A line of families had formed to fill containers at an outdoor water tap. I ran past them and sat down directly underneath it, letting the cold water wash over me. I tipped my head back and let it run into my mouth, lapping and whimpering at it like a stray dog. I opened my eyes to see that some of the parents had backed away, huddling their children close to them as they eyed me with a mixture of fear and disgust. I noticed José standing next to the car, laughing and shaking his head.

"We're about three hours from Los Angeles," José said as he examined a map he'd picked up inside.

"How is that possible? We've been driving for over seven hours."

"We must have taken a wrong turn. You think Bukowski's gone to bed yet?"

"He's probably passed out by now. I've got some friends I haven't seen for a while. We might as well go see them and have a drink now that we're down this far."

They were friends I'd lived with a few years before in London. That's one of the advantages of working in construction; you become part of a worldwide fraternity of drinkers and travelers. I could travel to almost any city in the world today, find the nearest Irish pub, and within hours have a job and a place to stay.

My friends in Los Angeles were easy enough to find. I had their address in my pocket. When we pulled up at about eleven that morning, Sean was coming out the front door of his building. I almost didn't recognize him. I hadn't seen him in four years. He could have been a stunt double for Tom Cruise: the thick crop of dark hair neatly trimmed, the Gucci shades, the sleeveless black T-shirt, and the impossibility of his pearly whites when he recognized me stepping out of the Buick, a cigarette hanging out of my face and a bottle of Corona in my hand, looking like something that had been dragged out of the desert.

"No way." He peeled off his glasses to make sure he was seeing right. "No fucking way. Broderick?"

"In the flesh. Whassup, numb-nuts?"

"No way," he said, starting to laugh and covering his face with his hands. "What the fuck are you doing here? How the fuck . . ."

Sean was from the same area as me back in Ireland. We both grew up just a few miles from Omagh. We lived far enough apart that I never met him until we wound up living in the same house in London. He now lived with our old housemates in Los Angeles. See what I mean? We sat on the steps outside his building in the sunshine, drinking Coronas as if it were all perfectly normal.

After José and I had cleaned up and showered, Sean took us to see the rest of the gang. They were all working together on the singer Phil Collins's house. Sean drove us there in his brand-new black five-liter Mustang.

The Collins house was like a compound hidden behind thick stone walls off a busy main drag. The entrance, two monstrous wrought-iron gates, led into an old country lane that ambled through a leafy wooded area, over a small bridge crossing a man-made stream. The stream ran throughout the property to a pump house somewhere, where it was filtered and rerouted on its circuitous path. The house itself was an old English Victorian mansion undergoing an enormous face-lift. There were workers everywhere, or lots of people who looked like they were dressed for work. Sean and the boys had been employed in the renovation for over three years already.

We tracked down the rest of the gang. Liam was smoking a large joint by the pool; Cathal was in deep discussion with an architect over some authentic English gargoyles that had been shipped in at enormous expense that morning. One had lost its hooked nose in transit, revealing it to be made of plaster of Paris. My cousin Nial, another of Sean's roommates, was fast asleep in the straw packaging that had accompanied it.

Once we had the gang assembled, we decided on a business

meeting to be held at Molly Malone's bar as quickly as the Mustang could whisk us there. So began three, or was it four or five, days of drinking and general debauchery. Others joined the circus before nightfall; there was a fellow named Brian Mallon, an American actor who spoke fluent Gaelic, and a pudgy little actor by the name of Jack McGee, who was in love with my cousin Nial's girlfriend. By day two I was living with a girl called Jasmine in a lavish apartment just off Wilshire Boulevard who insisted that her father should finance my drinking for the week. And so, armed with his credit card, we proceeded to party the week away. By day three I was drinking straight whiskey at the Whisky with Lemmy from Motörhead and Alice Cooper. Things were getting hazy. Jasmine had taken my passport and was threatening to destroy it if I didn't agree to stay. By day four I was sitting on Venice Beach at sunrise, sharing a bottle of wine with Jasmine. I remember that her makeup was smeared as if she had been crying. A tractor was combing the sand. I was cold. Sean was waiting for us nearby in the car with some girl he'd met. I didn't really know any of these people. I was six thousand miles from home. Nothing here was familiar. I hadn't seen José for two days. Apparently he was sleeping at Nial's place. I finished the bottle of wine and said I was tired and wanted to go home to sleep. I whispered to Sean the address of where I was staying with Jasmine and told him to have José pick me up there in about an hour. Back at the apartment I told Jasmine I was tired, and when she had fallen asleep I found my passport, left her a short note on the kitchen table, and slipped down the steps to the street. José, my old faithful, was waiting at the curb with the Buick. It was about eight thirty in the morning.

"I'm tired, José," I said, slipping into the backseat and covering myself with a blanket.

"We going to see Bukowski?"

"I think we'll have to do it another time. Just get me back to San Francisco. I need to sleep."

"You're going to kill yourself like this."

"I need to sleep. Try to keep the noise down."

The second we pulled up in front of our apartment on Clement I was ready for action. I was thirsty again.

"José, grab the bags and throw them in the apartment and I'll meet you in the pub."

"You're mad," he said, shaking his head in disbelief.

"You know what that is, José?"

"What?"

"Road rage. There's no other logical explanation. You've been driving for way too long. Maybe you should go upstairs and get some sleep."

"You've lost your mind."

"You're a good man, José. You're just very tired right now, so I'm going to ignore this despicable behavior. Good-bye, my friend."

I didn't know it at that moment, the moment I walked away and left José standing there, but this would be my last drinking binge for eight years.

It was foggy in San Francisco for the next ten days or so. Day and night the fog stayed. There was a series of bars, a long line of them, stretching out before me like a path straight to hell. There was a party with a bunch of strippers from the O'Farrell Theatre. I remember the manager of the club taking me down to the basement to see Artie Mitchell's ghost. It was shortly after Artie'd been murdered by his brother Jim. The strippers were crying in their drinks about Artie, Artie, what a great guy. The manager handed me a massive joint and pointed into the shadows and I said I saw Artie too, a vague shadow that flickered across the exposed brick wall of the basement. "He won't leave," they said. "He's still in the club." And we all raised our drinks to Artie. There was an FBI agent who drove me around for an afternoon visiting bars in and around Market searching for some boozehound who'd been robbing banks around town. There was a Jacuzzi party with a girl called Pat and six of her girlfriends. There was a midnight race through Golden Gate Park. Me and Pat in the Buick, drunk and high on mushrooms, doing over a hundred miles an hour with some terrified Asian kid we'd picked up at a bus stop screaming in the backseat. And then there was the end, in a lowlife hole-in-the-wall bar down in the Tenderloin, peanut shells and sawdust on the floor. I could have been on another planet, I felt so far away from home as I sat comforting an ancient black drag queen in a tiara who was convinced she was the Queen of England.

"You don't believe me," she sobbed.

"Of course I believe you. But you have to admit it's strange, us bumping into each other here in a bar like this. You being the Queen of England and all."

"You think I'm crazy, don't you."

"Why would I think that? You're the Queen of England and I'm an orangutan."

"What do you mean? Are you mocking me?" She had a wounded expression.

"No, I'm just saying you've got your cross to bear. I've got mine."

"You're an orangutan?" she asked cautiously. "Like the monkey?"

"Exactly—like the monkey."

"You're saying you're a monkey?"

"An orangutan. Yes. I'm an orangutan trapped inside a man's body."

"How do you know?"

"Have you ever gone to the zoo?"

"Please. I can't go to the zoo. I'm the Queen of England."

"Right, right. Well, if you ever saw an orangutan you'd know what I'm talking about. They have this raw, primitive approach to life. They eat, sleep, masturbate, scratch their armpits, and smell their fingers in public. They just do what they want when they want to and they don't give a damn what people think. That's me. I saw an orangutan take a shit one day in front of a whole crowd of people and then he just scooped it up in his hand and threw it at a family of Japanese tourists. A big piece of dung landed on this little guy's head and the orangutan went crazy. He was laughing so hard he almost fell off his rock. That's when I knew for sure I was an orangutan too."

"You want to throw shit at people."

"I can't. I'm trapped in this body. I have to hide my true self. I have to pretend I'm one of them or the real people will find out and lock me up in the nuthouse. Prisons and nuthouses are full of orangutans."

"I know how you feel."

"I knew you'd understand."

I finished my drink, gave Elizabeth a hug good-bye, adjusted her feather boa, and assured her that she was far better off where she was, that the imposter who had taken her place in Buckingham Palace was far more miserable than she was. I walked to the bus stop. I was surprisingly sober. Everything was suddenly clear to me.

I took the bus that night back up Geary and out to the Richmond District, home. Two flamboyant gay guys on the bus were gossiping and laughing with the driver up front, so I went all the way back to distance myself from the noise and sat in the last seat. There was no one else on the bus. It was midnight on a Sunday. I was done. Empty. There was nothing left to do. Nowhere else to go. I picked a white fluffy feather off my shirt and blew on it. I'd reached the bottom, a series of dark party rooms full of ghosts, confusion, and tears. I wanted to stick a fire hose into my mouth and blow the poison out of my system. I wanted to flush all the bile and toxic sewage into the street. I wanted to be clean again, to breathe. I wanted new clothes, a haircut, a nice meal, a clean bed with cool white sheets; I wanted to read a newspaper and drink a glass of ice water and call my parents. I wanted to see MaryAnn and tell her I was sorry, that I still loved her and that it was all over now, whatever it was that had had me was gone, I was somehow back now, ready to get on with my life. I was twenty-three years old. I was ready to hide the orangutan. I pulled a zipper of flesh over my orange coat. I was going to begin my life as a writer.

MY
AMERICAN
DREAM

I LEFT San Francisco six days after my run-in with the Queen of England. I packed my typewriter and a few items of clothing and had José drive me out to the airport. I handed him the keys to the Buick as a parting gift. He deserved to have some form of payment after the craziness I'd subjected him to. I told him I'd call him with a contact number once I got set up in New York. I never did; I haven't heard of him since. I didn't tell anybody else I was leaving. I just stopped answering the phone for the last week I was there. I had already decided to leave San Francisco behind. I was developing a real knack for leaving people behind.

I had talked to MaryAnn. She agreed to meet me at the airport in New York. We were getting back together. I promised I'd clean up my act. I'd even vowed to hit a few Alcoholics Anonymous meetings. What the hell! I was willing to give it a shot. I needed a fresh start.

I arrived at JFK early on a Sunday morning. MaryAnn had told me she would be there to greet me at the gate. I was giddy with excitement. There was so much I wanted to share with her. I had not had a drink for a whole week. I was like a live wire, all nervous energy. I was ready to jump out of my skin. There was so much to be excited about. The truth was that I was still detoxing.

This was the second time I had found myself at JFK ready

for a fresh start. Act two was about to begin. This time I was going to do it right. Unfortunately, there was no one there to meet me.

I found a pay phone and called MaryAnn's apartment. There was nobody home. I waited for an hour or so, thinking she must be stuck in traffic. Her sister June was a terrible driver. Maybe they got a flat. I called her mother. No, she hadn't seen MaryAnn either. In fact, she'd just talked to June and she hadn't said anything about going to the airport to pick me up. Another hour passed. Maybe she'd had an accident. Maybe she slipped and fell in the shower. That was it. She must have had a terrible accident. My God, MaryAnn could be dying that very second and there I was all the way out at JFK. It was time for action. I took a cab to my cousin's place in Woodlawn, which was actually my old apartment.

I dashed in the door and dropped my bags and went straight for the phone. A few of my cousins were sitting around watching a movie and drinking beer. I hadn't seen any of them in about a year. I barely even acknowledged them. They barely seemed to notice me. There was no time to waste. This was an emergency. I dialed her number once more on the off chance that maybe she could drag herself to the receiver. She picked up on the third ring.

"Hello."

"Hey. Are you OK?"

"Yeah, I'm fine."

"You are?"

"Yeah, why wouldn't I be?"

"Did you get my message?"

"I just got out of the shower."

"I've been calling you all day."

"Oh, you mean from earlier? Yeah, I got those messages when I came in."

"Oh. Did you go to the airport?"

"No."

"So where were you coming in from?"

"I stayed over at a friend's house."

"Ah. One of your girlfriends."

"No."

"No?"

"It's this guy I know."

"What guy?"

"This guy. He's Irish. His name's Damian. You'd like him."

"I'm sorry . . . you're just getting in from some guy's house . . . And you're just getting out of the shower? When did you go over to his house?"

"Last night a bunch of us went to the diner. And he asked me if I wanted to go watch a movie."

"What?"

"Don't start."

"What do you mean, don't start? I just stood at the airport for three hours waiting because you told me last night that you'd be there to meet me. Now you're telling me that you spent the night at some guy's apartment."

"We were watching a movie. I must have fallen asleep at some point. I didn't wake up until a little while ago."

"I can't fucking believe you—"

"I can't talk to you like this. You know speaking to me like this is a form of abuse. These are your issues. I'm hanging up now."

She hung up. What the fuck was this shit? Abuse? Issues? Who was this person? Is it wrong to say that if she'd been within arms' reach I would have strangled her to death? Well, I would have, without a moment's hesitation. I called her back immediately. She didn't pick up the phone. My cousin Frank nudged me on the way back from the kitchen. He handed me a can of beer.

"Welcome back, buddy."

"Cheers, Frank."

Her machine picked up. "If you'd like to leave a message you know what to do." I didn't know what to do, so I hung up. I set the beer down next to the phone without taking a sip and took off up 237th Street toward the park. I needed to go for a long walk to clear my head.

I made a deal with myself. From this moment on I would never allow a woman to rule my heart again. I would stay sober. I would focus on my work. I would become a great writer. I would live alone in a pristine apartment in Tribeca, date all the fresh young models of the day. I would disappear from MaryAnn's life forever. She would read about me in the *New Yorker* or *Vanity Fair* one day. She would read about the great writer I had become and would have to lock herself away in the bathroom of her double-wide to escape from her screaming kids and her hungry redneck husband banging on the door for his dinner as she muffled her sobs with a towel.

Or maybe not.

I did manage to stay sober. I got a job, a car, an apartment, some goldfish. I started going to AA meetings seven nights a week. It was the early nineties. It seemed everybody was getting sober. I got a sponsor and a home group. I read all the self-help books I could get my hands on. I created a whole new social circle. They were clean and proper; they didn't slur their words or piss their pants in public, or not as often. I had entered "program" life. At first glance the guys seemed like a fairly self-centered, egotistical bunch of posers in general, and the girls were hot and angry at their daddies. I donned my spiritual cloak and within no time at all I was hanging out with all the cool kids. I was climbing that twelve-step ladder to success.

The program was really a lot like school. Say the right things. Look a certain way. Wear the right clothes. The cool kids were going to like you. Unless of course you were really ugly; then you needed a parlor trick or two to get by. I knew a trick or two, plus I had the accent. Every group of recovering alcoholics needs an authentic Irish guy to lend the operation an air of legitimacy. Without the token Irish guy in your gang, you ran the risk of appearing like a bunch of miserable, lonely, whining old ladies. I know, I know, it's blasphemous talk. God's going to reach down and strike me in the kidneys. He's going to jaundice my liver for daring to mock the institution of sobriety. Well, let him. I can handle it.

The truth was, if there had been no hot girls at the meetings, I would have assumed immediately that I was in the wrong place. Sober girls are hot. And wherever there are hot chicks you're going to have a bunch of guys hanging around, posing. The meetings I was going to around the Bronx and Riverdale especially were like going to a cool bar every night, without the booze and drugs. And if you were nervous or insecure, well, it didn't matter—so was everybody else.

There was a different meeting spot for every night of the week. One cool thing about New York is the variety and sheer number of meetings to choose from every single day. You can start out with a morning meeting before you head off to work. Hit one at lunchtime in almost any part of the city, and then in the evening there are maybe a thousand different meetings in the five boroughs to choose from. It creates a great social replacement for the bar scene. You're walking into a room full of people with one very important factor in common. You all love to drink. Every single person in that room has some understanding of where you are coming from. It's a great way to never feel alone.

I was at a meeting in Riverdale one night and saw a bald-headed guy with a familiar face leaning against a pillar. He was standing by himself with his arms folded, surveying the room with what appeared to be a suppressed smirk. I walked over to say hello.

"I think we've met before," I said.

"Oh, that's possible."

"You were on Sixth Avenue a couple of years ago. Your car had broken down. I was with Con McCormack. Last time I saw you, you were headed for a drink."

"Mmmm, so that's how I wound up here?"

"You were in some shape that day. I think you'd just been released from jail in Boston."

"Mmmm. I suppose I was."

"My name's Colin."

"Tony."

"I almost didn't recognize you. You look well."

"Mmmm. I don't feel it. You wanna go get a cup of coffee? I'm getting distracted here by all this flesh."

"Let's go."

Seeing Tony there made me feel like maybe I was in the right place. If this lunatic was doing it, then I could too. We had a natural rapport right away. Nothing about my life shocked Tony. We just strolled away, talking about this and that. There was nowhere I couldn't take the conversation. Tony had been there, done that, stole the T-shirt, smoked the book, and jacked off at the movie. For the first time in my life I realized I was not alone. Here was somebody just like me. A fellow orangutan.

With me sober, MaryAnn and I shoved our anger aside and decided to give it another chance. We moved into a one-bedroom apartment just up from the train station at 242nd Street and Broadway. I redid the floors, painted the place, and bought all new furniture before we moved in. We had a nice view overlooking Van Cortlandt Park. My sponsor lived upstairs in the same building. I was sober but I still felt like shit. I was confused and angry and irritable. I felt like the program just wasn't working fast enough for me. I needed some real help, professional help. I needed a therapist. Besides, all the really cool people at the meetings seemed to have one. I felt left out. So after about six months of meetings, I made a few discreet inquiries and went to see my first therapist. It was, after all, the early nineties. If you weren't in analysis—well, then you just weren't with it.

I was referred to my first therapist by an Irish American thug called Mike whom I went to meetings with. This therapist was a tough guy. He dealt with a lot of construction workers, union labor. He sounded like the kind of no-nonsense guy I could relate to. I might have needed a therapist, but I didn't want no sissy boy. His name was Al, or as he was known in recovery circles, Big Al.

Big Al was Italian. He had an office in a typical brown brick residential building in Pelham. He was, as his name suggests, a big man. He was burly with a long mane of silver hair tied back in a ponytail. Al was a guy who'd been through the mill. He'd come up in the streets. He'd worked construction himself. He liked to remind me that he'd conquered his own demons; in fact, he gave me the distinct impression that he'd probably set their feet in cement, put a bullet in the back of their heads, and tossed them into the East River.

Al liked to do the talking. He might listen for the first five minutes or so, but then he was off telling stories. "You think that's bad, well, when I was on the juice . . . blah, blah, blah, blah, blah." I listened patiently to the stories of his wild days in the streets. I always had the feeling that maybe I should have been taking notes. I'd wait for a break or a segue to try to veer him back to what I wanted to talk about, but it was difficult work. After about seventy minutes or so I'd have to tell him that our time was up and that I was sorry but I really had to go. I'd write him a check and promise I'd come back and see him the same time next week.

I'd never been in therapy before. I felt lucky to have a guy who liked me so much that he would tell me all his stories. Listening to his horror stories made me feel like maybe I wasn't so screwed up after all. I would leave the session feeling relieved, thinking, "Well, I'm not as fucked up as Big Al, and he's a therapist. I must be OK." Therapy was working.

I wanted Big Al to help me with my relationship problems. I started to tell him about a specific incident that was bothering me.

"This is tough for me to talk about."

"Don't worry about it. Spit it out. Shoot."

"OK. Well, you know things have been difficult between MaryAnn and me lately. You know we've been fighting a lot—"

"I know how that feels. Boy do I know how that feels. I told you about my ex-wife, didn't I?"

"You mentioned her, but—"

"About when we were getting separated?"

"I . . . ah . . ."

"See, we were getting separated. We'd been fighting and bitching at each other like a couple of old queers. But this bitch, she wanted me to move out of the house, right?"

"Right."

"Like I was going to move."

"Mmmm."

"Like I was going to move out of my own goddamned house. Well, she pissed and she moaned and threatened to have me evicted. Have me evicted! Who the fuck did she think she was dealing with here? Hah? What am I, some fuckin' douchebag? Do I look like a fuckin' pushover to you?"

I shook my head.

"Well, I showed that cunt. I hired a twenty-dollar hooker off the corner of the block down here, black chick, sweetest ass you've ever seen. She's maybe eighteen, maybe, huge tits on this girl, and I take her right in my front living room and I have her sucking on my cock and I call my wife down. She's upstairs in bed, asleep. Well, I should have had a camera, because the look on her face—it was priceless. The next day she was gone. Bags packed, out the door. You know what I'm sayin'. You understand what I'm getting at. Sometimes you gotta do what you gotta do, hah? A man's gotta do what a man's gotta do."

"Right," I said, trying to change direction a little bit. "That's sage advice, Al, but you see, the problem is this: My girlfriend got harassed on the train the other day. Some scumbag pushed up against her from behind and, well, he must have upset her a lot, because she started crying the moment she came in from work. She told me he'd whispered something to her, but she won't tell me what it was. And I just can't get this bastard out of my head. I want to kill him, Al. I mean, I really think I might murder this guy."

"You know who this cocksucker is?"

"I had her point him out to me the next day when he got off the train. He gets off at the same stop as her in the evening and she sees him there in the morning sometimes."

"What's he look like?"

"He's got a suit on, but he looks like a real degenerate."

"Motherfucker."

"Here's the thing. I just don't think I can handle this guy walking around in my neighborhood like nothing happened."

"You think he should pay!"

"I want him dead."

Al narrowed his eyes and nodded, cracking his knuckles one by one as I continued. "I picture myself just grabbing his head and smashing it against the pavement until he's nothing but a bloody mess of pulp." Al continued to nod, one eyebrow now arched as if to signify that I was indeed on the right track. I felt proud of myself for making this breakthrough. Was I making progress?

"I'm going to tell you a little story," Al said, leaning forward a bit and lowering his voice so that I had to lean a little closer to hear him. "I was on vacation with my first wife." He paused and held a match to his cigar. "I haven't told you about her, have I?"

"Actually, Al, I'm sorry, but our time's up. We can pick it up here again next week."

"You're the boss."

The following afternoon I waited in a car just up from the train station, looking for the scumbag who'd touched my girlfriend. I had my Irish American buddy Mike with me in case things got out of hand. I jumped from the car and ran for him. Within seconds I had him by the throat and I was pummeling him. The guy dropped his briefcase and began to scream for help. People who were passing by looked on in shock. Before I knew what was going on, Mike grabbed me from behind and pulled me off the guy. He pointed to the car, wanting me to go and sit down. "You're a dead man," I shouted at him as I walked away. Mike grabbed the guy by the throat. I remember Mike removing a lollipop from his mouth as he leaned close to the guy and whispered something in his ear. Then he slapped him playfully, popped the lollipop back in his mouth, and sauntered back to the car, leaving the guy shaking against the wall. Those who were standing around put their heads down and moved away quietly.

"What did you say to him?" I asked as we drove away.

"Don't worry about it," he said around his lollipop. "He won't be bothering anybody on the train again."

I felt unimaginably better. There was reward in excavation. This had been my first real breakthrough in therapy. Self-analysis was working like a dream.

When things were running a little smoother a few weeks later, I called my older brother Michael and asked him if he'd like to bring his wife out to New York to stay with me for a vacation. I thought it might make up for the fact that I hadn't made it home for his wedding the previous year even though I was supposed to be his best man. I was drunk in San Francisco at the time. It was time to make amends.

I was working for an Irish flooring company when my brother and his wife, Caroline, arrived in New York. I gave them general instructions on how to use the train to get to Manhattan and explained that they would have to entertain themselves during the day because I was too busy at work to take any time off.

I was working for Big Pete Connolly, a bear of a man famous in Irish circles for his legendary appetite for money, booze, and ladies. Pete had quit drinking too, it being the early nineties and all, and had downscaled his operation to save himself from having a heart attack. Pete had a way of getting things done. He had a way of disarming you just when you were about to rip his throat out. And he was big with giving favors to those he trusted, so when he needed something done, it was almost impossible to refuse him without feeling guilty.

Recovering alcoholics like myself make great employees: low self-esteem, eager to please, never hungover, and usually trying to make up for lost time in the marketplace. That was me to a T. I planned to work hard for a little bit, then kick back and really get down to do some writing once I had a few dollars saved. In the meantime I would continue to take notes. Fill journals. That way, when the time was right, I would be ready to get started.

A few days after my brother and his wife arrived, I was sprinting around like a blind chicken. I was stressed out beyond belief trying to balance everybody's demands. My brother wanted me to take time off to spend time with him and his wife. MaryAnn went to stay with her sister for a few days while they were here. I had to find time to spend with her. My sponsor insisted that I make a meeting a day regardless of whatever else was going on in my life. And all Pete's employees had fucked off to go drinking for the week, leaving me to soldier on alone. Pete was driving me into the ground to keep up with an unbearable workload. I was exhausted and pissed off. Being sober was beginning to feel like a whole lot of work.

On Thursday morning I was near breaking point. I told Pete that I could work for that day but then I needed to take Friday off to spend some time with my brother. I just couldn't go on this way, I told him. "No problem," he said. "Sure. Why didn't you say something before? Take all the time you need. You're a great guy. I don't know what I'd do without you around here." As usual he had disarmed me at the last second. The fuse had been clipped.

It was a hot bastard of a day in the city. I remember driving down the Deegan past Yankee Stadium, listening to Howard Stern and grumbling to myself about having to lift these damned sanding machines by myself. I had to get out of this racket. I had a small bedroom floor to sand in a building on Seventy-ninth Street and Park Avenue. I'd knock it out as quickly as possible, one two three, bing bang boom, Bob's yer uncle and Fanny's yer aunt. I'd be done in no time and back to the Bronx, a shower and clean clothes, done for the long weekend.

The service entrance, it turned out, was down a steep set of stairs into the basement at the rear of the building. I asked the doorman, a portly red-gilled fellow in a green cap, if I could maybe sneak the machines in the front door. "Oh, no. We don't allow that here. You have to use the service entrance like everybody else." Hey, no pressure there, pudgeball. Don't get your shorts in a bunch. Asshole. I was in a mood, alright. I lugged the machines down the stairs and raced through the job, finishing by two thirty, a coat of sealer and one coat of polyurethane and out the door. That's what was known in the business as a Pete Connolly special. I stopped the elevator at the lobby on the way down and asked the doorman again if maybe I could just run the machines out the front door, real quick-like, lickety-split. "No. This lobby is for the use of tenants only. You'll have to use the service entrance like everybody else. We have rules here." I cursed him every step I lugged that big machine back up to the street and vowed never to let anybody talk me into lifting one of these sanders by myself ever again. It was enough to break your back.

I raced back to Yonkers to drop off the van, cutting off cars left and right on the Deegan all the way. Move it or lose it, asshole. Get that piece of shit out of my way, old-timer. Cigarette smoke belching out of my windows, heavy metal blaring out of the speakers. My pager started beeping just when I hit McLean Avenue. It was Pete's home number. Fuck. It was almost four o'clock. I was tempted to fling the pager under the wheels of a passing truck. It was a dangerous time of the day to return one of Pete's phone calls. It could mean only one thing: more work. I pulled over to the first pay phone I saw. I was just going to tell him the joke was over. No more. I was done.

"What's the story, Pete?"

"I know you're wrapping up early this evening. I just wanted to make sure you were alright for money."

"Yeah, I'm good, thanks."

"How's the brother and the little missus enjoying their stay?"

"Good, good. They like it."

"Good stuff. Good stuff. You're sure you don't need some running around cash? I have a few bob laying around up here at the house if you need it."

"No, really, I'm fine, thanks."

"Good stuff. So you're all wrapped up down there on that job? No problems?"

"As clean as a whistle, Pete."

"Yer some man for one man. Eh?"

"What?"

"I say, yer some man for one man."

"Right."

"Where are you now?"

"I'm just up here on McLean Avenue."

"Good man, sure yer as good as home. Maybe you'd just do me a wee favor there, Colin, would you just swing by the hardware store there and pick me up a couple of gallons of poly like a good man."

"Two gallons. Right. What sort of finish?"

"Good man. It's alright; I've called in the order already; it's not that much stuff, just a few bits and pieces, but you might as well get it there when you're passing by."

"Right."

"I'll see you in a few."

"Right."

"Hi."

"What?"

"I'll see you in a few." I could hear him trail off with a little laugh just as he was hanging up. He'd done it again. Nipped the fuse and gotten me to do another little favor, just like that. Pete loved this game. I could just picture him chortling away to himself up at the house. He lived for little moments like this.

I jumped back in the van and hightailed it down McLean Avenue, blowing the horn and waving to some Irish girls I knew who were out strutting around in their summer gear or lack thereof. They were on their way into Fibber Magee's. Goddamn, a cold beer would taste good just about now, to clear the dust out of my throat. I pulled an illegal U-turn in front of McKeown's bar and rolled the van into a parking spot between two parked cars, across the street from the hardware store. A girl in a tight denim miniskirt and a long shining mane of brown hair glided past me down the pavement; I discreetly glanced after her for just a few seconds. Those young Irish American girls were genetic freaks of nature. When I turned again there was a car coming up McLean at a fairly brisk pace, a red Camaro. I stepped back a little to let him pass before I crossed. He slowed suddenly, seeing me there between the parked car and the rear of the van, and he signaled with a wave of his hand for me to go ahead and cross the street in front of him. I gave him a quick wave of appreciation and hopped into the street. The moment I set foot in the street the lunatic gunned the Camaro and barreled straight for me. I reflexively jumped back and he raced by, missing the tips of my toes by inches, much to the delight of his big-haired girlfriend in the passenger seat. I recovered instantly and jumped into the street behind the Camaro with my middle finger up, screaming at him as he sped away, "You dirty fuckin' . . ." That's when I heard the screech directly behind me. I spun around just in time to see another car barreling down on me. It was too late to do anything. I automatically glanced down to see the front bumper connect with my kneecaps, sending me hurtling into the air. I remember every detail vividly. I came down on the front window with the side of my face and saw the face of the young black driver, his teeth clenched, his eyeballs about to pop out of his head. I bounced off the hood of the car and landed in the street in a ball, ducking my head as the front right tire came bearing down, stopping an inch or two away from my skull. I was alive.

I rolled flat onto my back and just lay there for a moment, letting it all settle in. There was a whirl of commotion all around me. I could hear a woman screaming; there were shouts; people were gathering around my head with their hands to their mouths. The young driver's face was there close to me. He looked terrified, probably wondering if he was going to get pummeled by an angry white mob. I tried to look down at my knees; I wasn't moving very well. I pictured the bone splintered under my jeans. I tried to move my legs, but I couldn't feel them. They had to be smashed.

A crowd had gathered over me, blocking out the warm bright sunshine over my head. Suddenly I felt a flash of humiliation. What the hell was I doing lying on my back in the middle of the street with everybody staring at me? I must look like an absolute fool. I made an attempt to sit up, but someone stopped me. I looked up. An Italian lady I recognized from the pizza parlor on the corner of the block had a hand on both of my shoulders and was pressing me down again, gently, to the ground, saying, "It's OK, hon. We've called the ambulance; you just relax. Stay where you are."

"But I think I'm alright."

"Sure you are, hon. But you just stay where you are and relax. It's going to be OK."

She was making me feel much better, mothering me like that, so I just lay back and stayed where I was. Then the cops were there. "OK, everybody just back up and give us some room here." A cop kneeled down beside me. "How you doin', kid?"

"Good."

"Good. You just relax. The paramedics are here. Is there

somebody you want me to call for you, to let them know where you are?"

"Yeah. Call the number on the side of the blue van parked right here."

The cop glanced up over my head. "The blue flooring van?"

"That's it. Tell Pete where I'm headed. He'll sort it out."

Then the paramedics were there next to me, on their knees, checking me. They rolled me onto a board or something and strapped me down tight to it. Strapping my legs and arms and my head so that I was unable to move a muscle. Then they lifted me into the back of an ambulance and, after a brief deliberation with the driver about traffic and distance, decided to take me to Lawrence Hospital in Bronxville. One of them approached me with a needle about as thick as a child's finger and without warning jammed it into the back of my hand. That's when I almost passed out.

"What the fuck are you doing?"

"We have to prep you."

"You think that's absolutely necessary?"

"Yes, it is."

"Jesus."

Then we were at the hospital. I was being fed into machines and pushed from here to there, poked, prodded, discussed, and then abandoned in a hallway, still strapped to the gurney.

A doctor came along eventually with a clipboard. "Mr. Broderick?" he said, giving me a professorial glance over his glasses.

"That's me."

"How are you feeling?"

"Good. Am I almost done here?"

"Are you feeling any pain anywhere? Any discomfort?"

"My legs are a little sore, my knees, but I think I could probably stand."

"Anywhere else?"

"No. I feel like I might have a bump on my head where I hit the window, but that's it."

"Right," he said, but he didn't look very convinced.

"What about your back? Any pain there?"

"No, my back's fine."

"OK," he said, letting it trail off as he went back to looking at his charts.

"Can I go home now?"

"I'm afraid you're going to be staying with us for a little while here at the hospital."

"I really think I'm OK, Doc."

"You've fractured two vertebrae."

"What does that mean?"

"You've broken your back in two places."

I laughed. "I think you picked up the wrong chart, Doc. My back is fine." He glanced at his chart again.

"You're Colin Broderick, right?"

"Yup, that's me alright, but my back's fine. No pain there at all."

He slipped his hand under the arch of my back and touched my spine with the tip of his finger. That's when I felt it. It's just as well they had me strapped down, because if they hadn't I'd have been hanging off the ceiling, upside down on all fours, screeching like a cat. I did let out an involuntary howl of pain as my whole body spasmed.

"I'm sorry, Mr. Broderick, but you're going to be here for a little while longer."

"Am I going to be OK? Is it bad?" I said when the spasm had relaxed enough for me to speak.

"It's serious. But we don't know everything yet."

"What do you mean, you don't know?"

"That's why you have to stay with us for a while. We need to see how things progress."

"You think I'll be able to go back to work soon?"

"I don't think you'll be going back to work for a very long time, Mr. Broderick."

"Will I be able to walk? Am I going to be paralyzed?"

"It's really too early to know any of these things."

"So it's possible?"

"I'm not going to lie to you. Yes, it's possible. Your back is in pretty bad shape. What I need you to do is try to relax and let's try to get you strong again. Can you do that?"

"Yes."

"OK. I'll send a nurse by with some painkillers and I'll see about getting you a room."

"Thanks, Doc."

They got me a bright room with a TV and a window and the nurse came in and gave me some painkillers. Within about forty minutes I'd settled in nicely, still strapped securely to the bed in case I attempted to jump up and perform an Irish jig to impress the nurses. Pete was there first. Tears in his eyes, promising he would make sure I got the best treatment possible. My brother and his wife came by to see me a little later on.

"Listen, if you didn't want to see us you could have just said so." Michael smiled, walking into the room.

"I thought this would be easier."

"It's effective. A little overly dramatic, but effective."

"Thanks, brother. It's my passive-aggressive side at work."

MaryAnn arrived with her sister and shed the appropriate tears. While she was there, the doctor came by and checked my legs and feet with a pin just to make sure I still had feeling in them. I asked him again if I would walk. He told me again that we'd just have to give it some time to see how things would go.

He explained that one of the vertebrae had been crushed almost flat on one side and that the one above it had also snapped straight across and was pretty badly crushed. The thing was to make sure I didn't move around and nip a spinal nerve with the cracked bone, if in fact that had not already happened. He told me I'd never work construction again. "Is that a promise?" I joked. But he didn't think it was funny. Then my nurse came by after everybody went away and had a little chat with me about the severity of the situation and how important it was that I did exactly what I was told. She explained her concern by telling me about another kid who'd had an accident very similar to mine in Yonkers just the previous week. He'd been hit by a car also. He also thought he could walk away from it. But there was no one at the scene to keep him pinned down, and when he stood up the cracked spine nipped some nerves and now he was paralyzed from the waist down. I thanked the nurse and stayed very still in my bed and thought long and hard about the pizza lady who'd quite possibly saved me from a similar outcome. God bless her.

I woke up sometime during the night covered in sweat and writhing in unbearable pain. I felt embarrassed about calling the night nurse, but the pain was so bad that my body was involuntarily straining to bend against the straps. I was afraid I would cause unnecessary damage. The nurse rushed in and, seeing how bad I was, she disappeared again as quickly as she had arrived and returned with a syringe. She shot me up and within moments I was better. She had cured me not just of my back pain but of every miniscule speck of discomfort I had ever felt. I had been cured of fear, of insecurity, of the future, of the past. I had been truly and utterly absolved of the burden of humanity. It was as if God himself, that old devil, had placed his big wet tongue at the base of my back and slowly licked the entire length of my spine up into my brain and washed me completely clean of the world. My whole body smiled and the only thing I could think was, "Oh my God, oh my God, oh . . . my . . . God . . ."

This is the reason people become addicts. We are all addicts at heart. Some people just haven't found the key that unlocks their heaven. For some it's ice cream, for others it's sex or heroin or religion. I, on the other hand, am like an old janitor. You can hear my bundle of keys jangling from a mile away.

It helped that my body had been clean of all other drugs and alcohol for about eight months. In fact, if you're planning on trying Demerol, that is exactly how I would advise you do it. Starve yourself of narcotics for a year or so, then break your back in a couple of places so that your pain is appropriately excruciating, then call your nurse to administer the entire scope of heaven through the tiny tip of that needle. Or don't.

After just four or five nights of euphoria I told the nurse that she had to stop giving me the Demerol. I said, "Even if I beg for it. Don't give it to me."

"It's that good, hah?"

"It's better than that good."

"Well, if you feel that way about it, you're smart to stop. I'll find you something else."

"Thanks."

"I could give you some Vicodin pills."

"Will they stop the pain?"

"They should."

"Sounds good."

They did work, of course, and just like that I added another key to my big old janitor's ring. This was a key I could hang on to and use from time to time if I was careful. There's nothing worse than being locked out in the cold. Jingle jangle.

About a week after I arrived at the hospital, the doctor was fairly sure that I wasn't going to be paralyzed as long as I kept doing exactly as I was told. He introduced me to some dude who was brought in to measure me up for a body brace. He was like a cross between a tailor and a mechanic. His job was to build me some kind of contraption that I could wear to hold my spine in place so that it might heal properly. He took some measurements and reappeared about a week later with the finished product. It was basically an aluminum cage with straps and pads that when fitted held the small of my back in a pad and pushed my chest out and my chin upright in an exaggerated pose of proper posture. Aluminum bars ran across my chest, my abdomen, around my sides, and down my back like a human cage. You could have tossed me off the roof of a building and I would have maintained perfect posture, even on impact.

I asked the doctor about leaving the hospital now that I was indestructible. He told me that if I could build up enough strength to walk up and down a flight of stairs, he would consider releasing me. But I would have to remain at home in my apartment in the horizontal position for the next few months.

For the next couple of weeks I spent a lot of time trying to climb in and out of bed and walk to the bathroom by myself. When I felt I was ready I asked the nurse to bring me into the stairwell so that I could begin training myself to walk up the stairs. The sooner I was better, the sooner I would be having sex again. That was the only motivation I needed. Being incapacitated had helped MaryAnn regain her feelings for me, even if the main feeling was pity.

Within a few days I had the staircase mastered. I could walk up one flight and back down again as long as I held on to the rail. The walk up hurt, but the walk down was excruciating. I knew I would have to grin and bear it under observation or there was no way I could convince them to let me go. When I felt I was ready I asked the doctor for my big chance. I was ready for my close-up. He consented reluctantly, trying to convince me that I really should just stay at the hospital until I was stronger. I wasn't having any of it. Sex awaited me.

The doctor came around early the next morning with a couple of assistants to observe my attempt to climb the stairs. I gritted my teeth and maintained as upright a posture as possible while I slowly took the climb and casually sauntered down again, my nurse by my side the entire time.

"Well?" I said as I stepped off the last step. "What do you think?"

"I think you're insane, young man. But that was a valiant performance and a deal's a deal. You have to promise me that if I let you out of here you'll do exactly what I tell you to do."

"I promise."

"OK. I'm keeping you here for three more days for observation and then I'm going to let you go. You know you can't have sex when you get out of here?"

"I know."

"I know what you're thinking, but you just can't do that."

"I know. It's not even an issue."

Three days later I was at home in my apartment having very carefully orchestrated sex. A few moments of great pleasure followed by the most excruciating pain I've ever felt. But it was worth it.

I was now a prisoner in my own apartment. A prisoner with a girlfriend who looked like Lauren Bacall, cable TV, and a never-ending supply of Vicodin. MaryAnn would help me dress and move around the apartment. Pete would come by with groceries three or four times a week, spend time with me, cook and clean. My cousin Frank would come by on his afternoons off and play board games with me, cook, and generally lift my spirits with his big laugh. My sober friends took the meetings to my apartment a couple of times a week.

One of my new sober friends during this time, Harold Van

Cleef, started to give me an education in literature. He'd arrive every week armed with a few more books for me to read and we'd smoke about a hundred cigarettes, devour a few pots of coffee, and talk about Hemingway and Fitzgerald, Dos Passos, and Gertrude Stein. I read van Gogh's letters to Theo and I popped Vicodin and dreamed of Paris in the twenties. Maybe I had just been born in the wrong period. I was at one of those stages in my nonwriting career where I spent my time dreaming of how successful I was meant to be. I was angry that no one had discovered me yet; meanwhile, I had yet to show anyone a single thing I had written. Not that I had written anything that warranted attention. But I was still angry.

My sponsor called me from upstairs and told me that when I was strong enough I could walk upstairs and see him. I guess this was his idea of tough love. Harry could be a heartless son of a bitch. That's why I liked him. I had to strive for his approval.

Within a matter of weeks I had developed a habit of about ten to fifteen Vicodin a day that I would consume with massive amounts of Coca-Cola and about two packs of cigarettes. But I didn't drink.

I grew increasingly jealous of MaryAnn. I would watch her dress to go out with her friends for the night and it would eat away at me. I couldn't even leave the apartment. I'd sit there in my body brace, watching her get ready for her night out. She liked to wear short skirts and low-cut tops. Not that there was anything she could have done to hide that body, but to see it walk out the door dressed like that was almost too much to bear.

It didn't help that she was also an incurable flirt. She liked to remind me that she'd always been a tomboy. She'd always been one of the boys. I'd tell her that I didn't know any boys who looked like that. She had few female friends. Guys would come by and pick her up outside the apartment in their little sports cars. I'd try to bite my tongue, knowing it was futile to ask her to change, but it was impossible.

"You couldn't just make my life easier and wear a pair of jeans when some guy is coming by to pick you up and take you out for the night?"

"Fuck you. You're such a control freak."

"You could at least wear a bra."

"You're such an insecure prick. It's my body. I'll show it if I want to."

"Fine. Fuck you."

"Fuck you too."

She'd slam the door and storm out. I'd go to the window and watch her disappear into some guy's car. She'd lean over and kiss the guy hello and maybe he'd wave up to me in the window before he sped away. Maybe she'd be home before midnight, maybe not. These were MaryAnn's sober guy friends. I was supposed to be cool with her having male friends now that we were all sober and healthy. I hated each and every one of them. But she loved the attention. I felt helpless. I wanted to break it off with her completely so that I wouldn't have to deal with the pain anymore. We were fighting constantly. We couldn't go forty-eight hours without a brawl. Then we'd make up and promise never to fight again. It was exhausting. It was worse than any drug or any drink. We'd wake up hungover from it and start all over again. "I love you." "I hate you." "I love you." Two emotional yo-yos trying to make a connection. We decided there was only one solution. We had to get married.

• • •

Three months had passed since my accident. I was somewhat mobile again. I was healthy enough to cause some trouble. I called the Yonkers courthouse and booked an appointment with a judge for a Saturday morning. We decided to tell only two people: my friend Eddie Kelly, who would be best man, and MaryAnn's friend Jennifer, her maid of honor. We swore them to secrecy. On the morning of our wedding, as MaryAnn was getting dressed, I dashed to the bathroom and fell to my knees in front of the bowl. I was as sick as a small hospital. The more I wretched, the more it tore at my back muscles. I threw up and moaned with the pain. "Are you sure you want to do this?" she asked, rushing in to hold my forehead as I heaved. "Of course I'm sure. It's just this damned medication; it has my stomach wrecked." I gathered myself and rinsed my face in the sink, tightened the bolts on my cage, and off we went to the court-house.

Afterwards we went for pizza and Jennifer insisted we all share a slice of chocolate pie. By three o'clock we were at home on the couch watching TV. It was a gray afternoon, and the clouds hung over Van Cortlandt Park so low and heavy that the sharp tips of the trees seemed to tear at their fat bellies till they cried. We cuddled under our blanket to the sound of the rain and fell asleep as husband and wife.

Nothing changed. The secrecy of our marriage only exacerbated our problems. The truth was, I knew that I had few friends among her family and I just didn't want them to know. She, of course, wanted to tell everybody. Now she really hated me.

By now I was able to run errands, take a walk in the park, go to a meeting every once in a while, or go sit in a café and drink coffee with my friends and talk about books, writers, politics, and girls.

The An Bael Bocht Café had just opened in Riverdale right next to Manhattan College. The café was owned by a guy from

Dublin called Dermot Burke. My friend Tony knew him quite well. We'd sit there and drink cappuccinos and watch the parade of beautiful college girls come and go all day.

A local poet named Rick Pernod started a poetry-reading series in the café around this time. It was an instantaneous success. Pernod was booking some of the top poets in the world to come to this little café in the Bronx. For a burgeoning writer it was a priceless experience. The little room would be packed shoulder to shoulder. I'd sit in the corner, high on codeine, with my cappuccino, smoking cigarettes and witnessing literary history in the making. Poets like Donald Hall, Stanley Kunitz, Nina Cassian, John Ashbery, Pierre Martory, Eamon Grennan, Gerald Stern, Paul Muldoon, Patricia Smith, Noelle Vial, and my personal favorite, Billy Collins. On a Tuesday night you had to arrive early to get in the door. I was always there early. MaryAnn didn't care much for poetry readings, so I'd go alone. We were spending less and less time in each other's company.

By Christmas it was apparent that the marriage just wasn't going to work. We had been married for only about five months. I was miserable. We fought constantly. If we weren't fighting we were making up. I couldn't think straight. The longer we were sober, the more apparent it became that we really didn't have that much in common. I wanted to go to poetry readings and used bookstores. MaryAnn wanted to go clothes shopping and disco dancing.

The truth was, it didn't matter what either of us did or didn't do. We were going to find fault with each other and the relationship regardless. I had an idea of who I wanted her to be and she had an idea of who she wanted me to be, but neither of us were those people. We were in love with an idea, a fantasy, and without the alcohol it was just impossible to believe in it any longer.

In the days between Christmas and New Year's Eve we

finally ran out of steam. On a Saturday night she came in late from a club and climbed into bed next to me, her hair still damp with sweat. I had been out to see a movie at the Angelika with Tony and had waited up for her to come home. Instead of screaming and shouting at each other, this time we just lay next to each other and talked calmly about how unhappy we had become together. We cared very deeply about each other, but we just didn't work together. It was going to be painful, but if we were to have any sanity or happiness in our future, we would have to separate and try to stay away from each other.

I moved out of the apartment the following morning with a suitcase full of clothes and a box of my books. I left her with a check to cover the next three or four months' rent; all the new furniture; and an agreement to pay any legal fees to cover the divorce. I didn't have enough self-esteem to realize I should have saved a little something for myself.

We had been married for about five months. No one in our families knew. A marriage that was not sanctioned by the Church would surely cause considerable discomfort to their Catholic morality. We had sinned.

The next morning I went to the An Bael Bocht Café and ordered a cappuccino. Tony came by and I told him that I was homeless. Within a few hours I was moved into a spare room in a house he was renting on a quiet street, behind the bank on Riverdale Avenue. My room was just big enough for a single bed and a small set of bookshelves. I unpacked my stuff, putting my clothes in a neat row along the wall, my books on the shelves. I stretched out on the small mattress and folded my hands behind my head. Here I was on the eve of my twenty-fifth birthday, in a small room; I owned almost nothing; my marriage was over. I was happy. I felt free for the first time in my adult life. Now I could make sober decisions about my life. I could write. *I could write.* I took out my notepad and a pen, thought about where I should begin, and fell fast asleep.

Of course it was all too simple. Too perfect. By Monday afternoon the storm was already brewing. I got a phone call from MaryAnn. She had told her sister about our secret wedding and impending divorce. Her sister was infuriated. She blamed me for coercing her innocent sister into this situation. She wanted blood. She encouraged MaryAnn to tell everyone what had happened. She wasn't going to let me get away with this.

"But we talked about this," I said in disbelief. "This was not only my decision. You wanted this also."

"I'm just telling you, if you run into her it's not going to be pleasant."

"What's she going to do, attack me in the street?"

"I'm just telling you it's not going to be good."

"I'm not married to your sister. It's none of her business."

"I'm just saying."

"Well, I don't give a shit what she thinks."

"OK."

"How're you doing?"

"I'm fine. You?"

"Good."

"Good."

"You started dating yet?" I ventured.

"That's none of your business anymore."

"I was just joking. We just broke up."

"Well, it's none of your business."

"You're dating somebody already?"

"I said it's none of your business."

"You're dating somebody?"

"What does it matter to you?"

"We're still married— It hasn't even been a week—"

"I can't listen to this anymore."

"You can't do this so soon. Who the fuck are you seeing?"

"Good-bye, Colin."

"Don't—" She'd hung up already.

Over that next week we talked a few more times. She told me that I should probably find another area to go to meetings in. Why should I move? I asked her. The problem was that we shared the same sober crowd and almost everybody, it seemed, was taking her side in our separation. I was blown away by this. I hadn't suspected that people would choose sides. Not sober people. Not these healthy people who were working their program. People I had known for over a year in sobriety now ignored me at meetings. I started feeling paranoid. What the hell was she saying about me in these meetings?

People I had considered very close friends were suddenly unreachable. Guys I had known and trusted as sober friends were now siding with her. Of course I didn't have her legs, but I'd expected better. The way they saw it, she was available now. It wasn't going to help their case if they were still hanging around with me. One friend actually came right out and told me to my face that he couldn't be around me anymore because she was single now and he'd always wanted to date her. This was his opportunity. He just couldn't pass it up. It was all very sober and proper, of course. He hoped I would understand. I did. Perfectly. I told him he was lower than a snake's balls and that he should go fuck himself.

I had been naïve, thinking that a bunch of drug addicts and alcoholics somehow transcended their true natures just because they weren't drinking. I was hurt and frustrated. I took the prescribed measures to deal with my feelings; I talked to my sponsor about it. Donnie said, "You know what you get when you take a drunk horse thief and sober him up?"

"What, oh Great One?"

"A sober horse thief."

He was right. People can change their ways; they can learn how to act and dress differently; they can reduce the odds of dying an early death or going to jail; but once a horse thief, always a horse thief. In the tradition of the great Western philosopher Popeye, We yis what we yis.

Of course, not all drunks are horse thieves. I still had Tony and a few others around to carry me through. Not that they wore halos. Some guys just have more class.

Just two weeks after I had moved out of our apartment I was an absolute basket case. I lay under the blanket in my small room like a wounded animal. I couldn't comprehend the pain. All week it was mounting. I heard rumors about where she was, who she was with. I'd lost friends or been forced to reevaluate my relationships with so many people that I was on the verge of just giving up on the lot of them. The whole ordeal had stolen the very last bit of moisture from my throat. I was bone dry. Wordless. I started going to meetings in Manhattan. I wanted to show up at a local meeting with a machine gun or a grenade. On Sunday morning I got another phone call from MaryAnn.

"I just wanted to let you know that my sister is going to break the news to our mother today. I think she's taking her to the café to tell her, so I wanted to warn you in case you were thinking of going there for breakfast."

"Great. One more place I can't go. She couldn't have taken her to a diner or somewhere."

"Oh, and I think you'd better call your parents in Ireland and tell them the full story as well."

"Why should I do that?"

"I think you should."

"Maybe I'm not ready for that just yet."

"Well, they might want to hear it coming from you first."

"What do you mean? How else would they hear it?"

She let me think about it for a moment in silence.

"She wouldn't! She doesn't even know my parents."

"I'm just saying you might want to let them know."

"Are you telling me that your sister is threatening to call my parents?"

"You might want to tell them soon."

"I can't believe this shit. I'm not friggin' married to your sister. What the hell does she think she's doing?"

"I can't talk to you when you're like this."

"Like what? Pissed—?"

She hung up. She was getting really good at that. I had to admire her, the way she could cut me out. I wasn't that strong yet. I had to tell my parents. Things had gone too far. They deserved to hear this from me. I lay there for a few minutes, waiting for God to give me some sign. As usual he didn't bother his ass. I dialed my home phone number. My mother picked up on the second ring.

"Mum."

"Colin, how are you?"

"Good. You?"

"Good. We just finished eating dinner."

"Good. Who's there?"

"It's just me and your father."

"Good."

"What is it?"

"I have some good news and some bad news. Which do you want first?"

"Oh. I hope it's not too bad."

"Well, good or bad?"

"Give me the good news."

"OK. I got married."

"What? You did not. To MaryAnn?"

"Yes, to MaryAnn."

"Ah, Colin, that's great news, you little shit. When did you get married?" I could hear my father laugh in the background. They both liked MaryAnn a lot. I had taken her back home to Ireland to meet them a year earlier. They both had said that it was like she was one of their own. Like she had always been a part of the family.

"About five months ago," I said.

"You got married five months ago. Why didn't you tell us?"

"It was a secret. We didn't tell anybody."

"Well, I'm delighted for you. How is MaryAnn? Is she there with you?"

"No, she's not here at the minute."

"She's OK?"

"Yeah, she's OK."

"Ah, Colin, that's great news. Sure it was bound to happen."

"Right."

"And what's this bad news?"

"We're getting divorced."

"What? Ah, Colin. No."

I could hear my dad in the background asking, "What is it now?" My mum answered him, "They're getting divorced." Then to me: "You're not serious, Colin?"

"I'm sorry, but yeah, I'm serious."

"Ah, Colin. What happened?"

"We were fighting a lot; we got married because we thought that would cure it and it didn't, so now we're getting divorced."

"Mmmm."

"You OK, Mum?"

"Mmmm. Here, your father wants to speak to you."

"Hello."

"Hello, Dad."

"What's going on?"

"I suppose you just heard the most of it. I got married a couple of months ago and now I'm getting divorced. That's about the height of it."

"No, Colin. That's not the height of it."

"What do you mean?"

"I said no. You can't do this."

"I'm afraid it's done, Dad."

"I'm telling you that you can't do this."

"I can—"

"No you can't."

"Listen, I didn't call to ask your permission. I'm telling you—"

"No, I'm telling you. You can't do this. You're not doing this."

"Hold on a second. It's none of your business—"

"It *is* my business and I'm telling you—"

"No, you're not. You're not fucking telling me a damned thing anymore. I'm telling you—"

"I'm telling you, Colin—"

"Stop fucking telling me!" I was screaming now. "I don't fucking care what you think. I'm a grown man. I don't need you to tell me anything. I need you to fucking listen. Can you fucking listen?"

"You can't talk to me like that—"

"Fuck you. Did you hear that, Dad? Fuck you."

"You can't—"

I slammed down the phone and screamed, "Fuck, fuck, fuck!"

I know. I know. I'm an asshole. My poor parents just finishing their Sunday dinner and I just drop this bombshell into their laps. What did I expect? Maybe that was exactly what I had expected. Maybe I'd set the whole thing up.

I collapsed on the bed. My brain was spinning in circles as if it had turned on itself. I was losing my mind. I *had* lost my mind. I felt as if I was trapped in some sort of psychological vortex. I was being pulled further and further into the abyss, and for the first time in my life, as I lay there, gripping my head, I considered suicide as an option. I understood suicide now completely. Anything would be better than this pain. Death would be a welcome relief from this pain. There was a tap on my bedroom door. It was Tony; he was carrying a mug of tea. He handed it to me.

"Are you OK?" He'd heard the conversation. The whole neighborhood had probably heard the conversation. I couldn't think straight. I couldn't make enough sense in my head to answer. Instead I read the writing on the side of the cup aloud.

"To thine own self be true."

"You just keep saying that," he said. "Just keep saying it. You'll be OK."

"I think—" I started, but I couldn't put two thoughts together to say anything coherent. I sat up and looked at him. "I've lost my mind, Tony," I blurted, and then it came in a torrent, a flood of tears that just wouldn't stop. I was reduced for the first time in my adult life to a big blubbery mess. Years of pus and mucus and salty bile poured out of me. Tony sat next to me on the bed and said nothing and I cried myself unconscious. When I woke up, the room was dark and I was alone. I felt a little better. My head no longer felt like it was going to explode. I could hear the TV downstairs. I went down to the living room. Tony was watching a movie.

"You feeling better?" he asked.

"A little. Thanks for the tea. That helped."

"It's going to be tough for a while," he said. "But you're not alone. That's not going to happen."

"Thanks, Tony. I think that was all I really needed to hear today."

I knew then that I'd survived it. Whatever *it* was. It was as if

I'd had a new pain gauge installed. I knew now that the engine wouldn't explode at eight thousand rpm. I had to accept that not everybody was going to be happy about the way I lived my life. They didn't need to be. I needed to be. I needed to be alright with the decisions I made about my life, or else I'd have nothing. Or maybe it just proved once again that I really did have the ability to be a no-good, selfish bastard. Most writers are, right?

Tony and I started working together. I needed to do something to get out of my head. I was sick of doctors and divorce lawyers. I needed to get out of Riverdale for a while. I was basically finished with physical therapy and I was feeling fairly strong again. I decided a little light painting work would be a good way to get back into the swing of things. We got transparent business cards printed up. They read, ENLIGHTENED DECORATORS. Our personal motto was, We're so enlightened we don't need to work, but we didn't put that on the business cards. Miraculously, people actually paid us to paint their apartments.

We were a good work team. We were meticulous about everything we did. We overpriced the jobs and worked them at our leisure. Our basic attitude was that we were sure we were worth the money, and if you didn't want our kind of job, then you were talking to the wrong guys. We wouldn't take a job that required us to go in and slap it on. There were plenty of other guys who were willing to do that kind of work. We were artists.

When we weren't painting we spent our time visiting museums, art exhibits in the Village, theatre performances, offbeat movies, concerts, coffee shops. I was truly exploring Manhattan for the first time. I started writing: short stories, poetry; I even signed up for acting classes at the Irish Arts Center. It was a great time for me, being exposed to so much art and realizing for the first time how much work I needed to do if I ever wanted to call myself a writer.

I was falling in love with the city: with Central Park on a Sunday afternoon, couples lounging in Strawberry Fields, corn-rows and daisy chains, a dog cooling itself in the fountain, boaters on the pond, disco-headed Rollerbladers, the smell of fresh horse manure, cut grass, and the occasional sweet perfume of a passing joint, break-dancers and bongo players, the tinny, tangy ping-pong ricochet of a summer salsa band, a lick of oily tanned skin, microminis, short shorts, hot dogs and lemonade, young German girls on the steps of the Met, mink stoles and do-rags, street art and candy floss, joggers, bikers, kite flyers, and sightseers. I could go on. I could tell you about Manhattan at night, the rolled-down-window cool of the place, heels so high I could cry, sequined hookers with razor-blade fingernails and fishing-hook tongues, neon, jazz, street hustlers, heroin heads, and supermodels. But I won't go on. Words don't do jus-tice to the whole big blue soupy feel of the place.

Back in the Bronx, two guys started a theatre company. Chris O'Neill had just moved to New York after a long-running stint in Ireland playing Michael on *The Riordans,* a popular weekly television program. He somehow managed to meet Jimmy Smallhorne, a local thespian from Dublin who'd recently com-pleted a run at the Irish Arts Center playing Bobby Sands. They were a match made in theatrical heaven. They had the appear-ance of two characters right out of a Beckett play, but on crack, maybe. All wiry hair and skulls right out of the Famine. They lived on a diet of caffeine and nicotine. Individually, they had the persistence and trajectory of a couple of long-range missiles. Together their energy was downright nuclear.

Tony and I knew Jimmy quite well. Jimmy had always been a sort of local guy you'd vote most likely to succeed. He was a captivating presence. His energy was infectious. He had the charisma of a madman. If Jimmy had organized a Kool-Aid party there wouldn't have been an empty seat in the house. So what he did with Chris was lease the old theater on Bainbridge Avenue in the Bronx. It was a glorious old theater with a huge stage, 250 seats, a marquee, and a box office. The plaster was cracked and the whole place needed a dusting. The Irish Bronx Theatre Company had found its home.

I had never been so excited about being a part of something in my whole life. I had never worked in theatre before. There was magic in the air. Tony and I helped out with fixing up the old theater, plastering and painting and repairing old light fixtures, taking down the old velvet curtains and draping them on the rear wall of the theater to soften the acoustics.

Jimmy and Chris cast the first play, *Da*, by Hugh Leonard, and set about rehearsing right away. Chris cast a young Dublin guy called Paul Ronan to play one of the leading roles. Paul had never acted before. He was a bartender Chris knew. He was easily persuaded. Paul and Jimmy became inseparable. Chris said Paul was a natural. Paul would show up with his little girl, Saoirse, and plop her down in a seat beside me so I could babysit while he rehearsed. I would sit for hours watching them work. I'd run out and get them tea and Irish candy bars to fuel them for another hour. I could have lived there. I sort of did at times.

"It's all in the details," Chris would say.

Chris would sit back in the theater, directing from his seat. Jimmy was onstage, handling the actors, living among them, pushing them on to get to the emotional core of the scene. "Let's do it again." Let's do it again. Let's do it again. Over and over. Night after night. Then they staged the sound effects and lighting and I was given the job of operating the lights. I sat in a booth in the back right-hand corner of the theater, where I could see everything. This was the best education in the world.

I asked Chris one night if he thought I should get into acting. We were sitting back in the theater after midnight, watching rehearsals. The actors were on a tea break. I told him I'd been taking some acting classes down at the Irish Arts Center.

"You want to be an actor?" he said with an exaggerated frown. Chris had a great face for frowning. It was a face that had been lived in, as leathery and wrinkled as a well-worn catcher's mitt.

"I was thinking about it. I love the theatre."

"Mmmm. I'm not saying you couldn't do it. In fact, maybe you should give it a try, but from what I've seen of you, you're an observer," he said. "My guess is you're a writer." I was surprised that he would make such an assumption. I'd never said a word to him about wanting to be a writer. "You never miss a thing. You have something nobody else in this room has."

"What's that?" I said. I was intrigued. I held Chris in very high regard; his opinion of me mattered a great deal.

"You have patience," he said. "My advice to you is: Continue to observe; take it all down. I have a feeling that you're the one who's going to record all this. Just keep writing."

"Thank you, Chris."

"You're welcome." He grinned that chinny grin of his. I almost wanted to pull him out of the chair and give him a bear hug.

Da opened to a packed house. When the seats ran out, people stood along the back wall of the theater and sat in the aisles to watch. When the lights went down at the end of the last act, the crowd rose to its feet in thunderous applause. A theatre company had been born. I had never fully understood the thrill of a live audience until then. So this was what all the big fuss was about. I was hooked.

A string of successful plays followed: *Peg O' My Heart, The Country Boy.* Paul Ronan continued to star in all of them. The crowds continued to show. Jimmy had me understudy a role in each of the plays in case one of the actors ever fell too ill to perform. They didn't. But he did give me my big chance one night to take the stage. It was during a run of Janet Noble's play, *Away Alone.* It was a play about Irish immigrants in the Bronx, appropriately enough. I had understudied the role of Paddy, but, as usual, I knew the play so well by then that I could have recited the entire thing backwards.

It was a Friday night. I had only been given a quick run-through of one or two of the scenes before the crowd started showing up, but I had watched the play every night. I was sure I could do a better job than the guy who'd been playing the role so far. I had actually tried out for the role originally but had lost it at the last call to Dave. A fact that we continued to rib each other about.

I was backstage moments before the show. The other actors, Kevin Dowling, Jimmy Cunningham, and Don Creedon, were telling me I'd be fine, to just relax. The beautiful Marion Quinn gave me a hug and whispered in my ear that I was in safe hands. Then I heard Jimmy Smallhorne take the stage.

"Welcome, welcome, welcome. It's a special night for us here at the theater. As you know, we've tried to create something here with this company that belongs to the people of this community. And in so doing, we make an effort to ensure that this theater is of the people and for the people. You are the reason we are here. In that vein I would like to announce that taking the stage tonight in the role of Paddy is a young man from the community who has never acted before, making his grand premiere here tonight for your pleasure. Your very own Colin Broderick." There was a thunderous applause, a few wolf whistles. Some Irish guy in the crowd shouted, "Broderick, you bollox."

I almost passed out. Marion shook her head in disbelief that he'd announced me at all, adding pressure to what was already one of the most nerve-racking experiences of my life. The music started and the play was under way. I listened to the noise of the crowd grow. A theater crowd, even in silence, emits a blanket of sound. I tried to tell myself that I could do this. I'd seen this play performed a thousand times before.

I readied myself for my entrance at the beginning of the second scene. What the fuck had I been thinking? I wanted to run away. I couldn't face this crowd. I stood behind the door that would take me onto the stage and I felt my knees might collapse beneath me. Then I heard my cue. I opened the door and stepped onto the stage. The crowd roared with applause. I was aware that some close friends of mine would recognize me, but I was not prepared for this. Two hundred and fifty people or so were focused entirely on me. I had to perform. The audience had before them a virgin of the stage. I felt they were poised to deflower me. The idea of taking them all on at once is something they can't teach you in an acting class. When you stand before the audience you are alone.

I crossed the stage to a makeshift counter to deliver my opening line. I took a seat on the stool and glanced at Jimmy Cunningham, who stood behind the counter shining a glass. I had a line to say to open the scene, and it was gone. My mind was blank. Not only could I not remember my line, I had lost the entire concept of the play. I looked at Jimmy with what I hoped was a nonverbal plea for help. Jimmy went on buffing the glass he was holding. I looked around behind me. There was no one else on the stage to come to my rescue. My heart was pounding. I could feel a sweat about to break on my forehead. The door was a long way away. I glanced back at Jimmy. He was now holding the glass up to inspect it in the light, avoiding eye contact with me completely. I was alone. I was responsible for the rest of the play. The play now hinged on what I would do over the next few moments. I could feel the audience; it was as if they were a part of me. I glanced around again for a brief instant and broke the fourth wall. I caught the eye of an old man seated in the front row. He was fixated on me. Riveted. He looked like he was about to come out of his seat onto the stage.

I'm going to have to apologize to the audience, I thought to myself. There was just no way out of it. I let out a small chortle and rubbed the leg of my jeans, getting ready to announce my failure. This couldn't be happening. I stood up and let out another small laugh. I actually shook my head in disbelief. A few people in the audience chuckled along with me. It was too hideous to comprehend. Then I said it. My first line. I looked at Jimmy, who seemed just as shocked as I was that it had finally come out of my mouth. He gave me his line and I was back from the brink. I gave him the next. I suddenly remembered everything. Now I had the audience right along with me for the ride. For one night and one night only they were mine. I owned them. By the second act I was prodding them for laughs where there normally were none. They were with me every step of the way. I had never felt more powerful, more in control. When the play ended and we took our curtain call, the other actors shoved me forward and applauded me as the crowd rose to its feet and cheered. I was electrified. I had found my new addiction.

The Irish Bronx Theatre Company was getting all kinds of attention. Articles appeared in nearly all the big New York newspapers about this new and exciting resurgence of theatre in the Bronx. The media always acts surprised when anything remotely artistic happens in the Bronx. Throw in an Irish accent and you're almost guaranteed a mini media frenzy for about two weeks. This kind of publicity has that sort of "Look, everybody, you're not going to believe this one" feel to it. It's the kind of story that gets tacked onto the end of the newsreel as if they've just discovered a three-legged tap-dancing dachshund or something.

Jimmy Smallhorne went on *Good Morning America*. He was invited to Gracie Mansion to have dinner with the mayor. Photographs from the dinner appeared in the papers and there were a couple of Jimmy and Mayor Dinkins. Jimmy was wearing a green suit that didn't fit very well. He came to my apartment just hours before the dinner and announced he had nothing to wear. The suit was the only one I had in my closet and it didn't fit me, either. In the photos, Dinkins had Jimmy's hand and he looked amused, maybe even a little wary, as if he wasn't quite sure what to make of him. Jimmy was laughing, covering his mouth with his hand so that there would be no pictures of his teeth. All of this attention was giving him a complex.

A reporter came by the theater one night to do a piece for a TV show called *Irish Eyes*. Her name was Lisa. She had a devious twinkle in her eye and the longest hair I had ever seen on a girl. I fetched her a cup of tea and sat with her while her cameraman ran around gathering footage of Chris and Jimmy at work directing rehearsals.

"I assume they came up with the name for the show after you showed up for the job?" I whispered. We were sitting a few rows back in the darkened theater. She was taking notes and sipping her tea.

"Why would they do that?" she said, turning to me. I smiled and squinted at her a little in the dark.

"Oh." She giggled. "No. That's nice of you to say."

"It must be fun?"

"If it wasn't I wouldn't do it."

"I'm envious. I want your job."

"Are you an actor?"

"You don't recognize me?"

"I don't know. Should I? I can't see very well in here." She stared at me again with a puzzled expression.

"I was Paddy in *Away Alone*."

"I don't think I saw that one."

"That's too bad; you missed a stellar performance."

"Oh, what else have you done?"

"That was it. One night as Paddy. I can't believe you missed it."

"You only did one night."

"That's all it took. I retired from the stage at the peak of my acting career."

"You're mad."

The Irish Bronx Theatre Company closed shop for the summer, and after a few weeks of working for *Irish Eyes*, reading the weekly newscast, and doing interviews including, most memorably, one with the great Richard Harris, the television show folded, along with my brief relationship with Lisa. My divorce was now final, so I was truly single again. I needed a vacation. I bought a white Trans Am with a T-top and against the advice of my mechanic took off on a little drive to see the country. I took a girl called Siobhan along for the ride.

Siobhan was an actress I had been working with in the theatre company at the time. We had become good friends, and when she heard that I was going to cross America she offered to share gas expenses and the driving if she could join me. I didn't find out until we were nearly in Chicago, on the first day of our trip, that the only driving she'd ever done was to steer a tractor through a hay field when she was five. I pulled off the highway onto a quiet road through a cornfield somewhere and tried to give her a few driving lessons. It became apparent fairly quickly that I was going to be doing the driving myself if we were going to have the car to get us home again. Thankfully, I love to drive.

In three weeks we covered seven thousand miles. We stayed on a pig farm in Omaha, Nebraska; raced another white Trans Am at over 130 miles per hour through Wyoming; stopped off in Salt Lake City; drove through Reno in the night; stayed in San Francisco for a few days; and then took the coast road down through Santa Cruz and Santa Barbara to Los Angeles, where we stayed with my friends for four or five days. Then we took off at midnight out through South Central, and by noon the next day we were sitting on the rim of the Grand Canyon. After that I didn't stop much. I was done. I was tired of sleeping in motels and driving every day; I just wanted to go to sleep in my own bed.

The last two days I drove nonstop back to New York. I took a different route through Texas, Tennessee, and back up the East Coast, home to New York. We arrived in the city after midnight and I remember going to my apartment and just sitting on the end of the bed and staring at the floor for about four hours. I was too shattered to even take off my shoes. But I had seen it. I had crossed the great nation from sea to sea. The whole country fit together better in my head now. It really was a big bastard of a country.

At this time, the Irish Bronx Theatre Company was preparing for the fall season with a musical scored by Jimmy's brother Stephen and featuring the singer Sheila O'Leary. Paul Ronan was already off to bigger and better things, playing the lead role in Kenneth Branagh's new play at the Irish Arts Center. Chris had been right about him; Paul was a natural. Chris was off to Boston to do a bit part as an IRA guy in a movie with Jeff Bridges and Tommy Lee Jones. The theatre company organized a series of music acts and one-man shows for the spring season: Black 47, Pierce Turner, and Malachy McCourt, among others. Jimmy decided that the time was right to snowball all this forward momentum into a movie about the Irish in the Bronx. Tony volunteered to finance the project now that he had two new bars up and running, Scratcher and Arlene's Grocery. I was designated the task of writing a book to coincide with the movie, a sort of background to how the whole thing had been put together. But somehow things fell apart over the next few months and Jimmy disappeared with the only real copy of the screenplay. The Bronx Irish Theatre Company had run its course. I felt deflated and hurt. There had been such a good buzz around the movie and now it was all over. The thought of a drink suddenly seemed appealing again.

I decided to refocus on my sobriety. I threw myself back into the program again, hitting meetings seven nights a week, and I stopped dating completely. Of course I never bothered to mention to the group that I was still popping Vicodin on occasion to take the edge off when things got too stressful.

A couple of weeks later I was in the café one evening for the poetry reading, drinking coffee with an acquaintance of mine. He had been watching a girl who had come in and was sitting near the door with her friend. He really wanted to ask her out on a date, but because she was sitting with a friend, he didn't want to approach her alone. I tried to convince him that she would be more impressed by his courage if he would just walk over there by himself, but he wouldn't listen. He wanted to drag me into the middle of it. I reluctantly agreed. They were both very attractive girls, but I was trying to stay single. It seemed to work better for me that way. I was beginning to feel that maybe women were more trouble than booze. Maybe that was my real problem. Maybe I wasn't really an alcoholic at all. Maybe . . .

"Now, now, Colin, that's your disease talking. Remember, your disease is insidious; it wants you to think you're not really an alcoholic. Your disease is out there doing push-ups. It's getting stronger and stronger all the time. It's a monster. It's getting ready to take you down."

"What? Push-ups? Is it jogging? Is it wearing a wife beater and a bandanna? Does it have a gun? What are you talking about? Shut up, for godsake."

I'm sorry. That was my new internal program voice at work. It's one of the side effects of too many twelve-step meetings. It's a bit like Tourette's syndrome, only the noise is in your head. Other people can't hear it.

We walked over and introduced ourselves and asked if we could join the girls at their table. I made sure to let him sit across from the girl he wanted to talk to. Her name was Brigitte. She was a schoolteacher. They were both teachers. Things didn't go quite according to plan. Less than two weeks later, Brigitte and I were living together and had set a wedding date for just two months away. I had met wife number two. My acquaintance never spoke to me again after that night. He felt I had foiled his big chance. Maybe I had. Maybe it would have been better for all of us if he'd just walked on over there by himself. But he was the one who had insisted I go along.

Tony had decided to quit the construction business altogether and focus on his new bars. Jimmy was still missing with the script. I decided to go back to school. Maybe a few years in college would sort me out. Brigitte encouraged me to enroll right away. I was reluctant at first. It's quite possible I had burned too many brain cells over the years. What if I couldn't afford it? The other kids in class might make fun of my accent. Brigitte bought me a new school bag, packed my lunch, and chased me out the door.

Brigitte came from a family that didn't believe in hesitating. Her father was a West Point military guy of German decent, a highly decorated Vietnam vet; for him, to hesitate meant death. After he had returned from the war, he taught literature at West Point for a decade or so. Then, upon retiring from the military, he moved the family to Atlanta, where he started purchasing real estate as a hobby as he put himself through law school. Once he passed the bar exam, Jerry set up his own law practice and quickly became one of the most notable attorneys in the region.

Brigitte's mother was no slouch either. Jacquelyn had grown up in Rye, New York, the daughter of a wealthy oil distributor. After raising her family she became a nurse and worked with AIDS patients in and around Atlanta, an occupation she certainly didn't need to do for the money. Brigitte, their eldest daughter, was a graduate of both Manhattanville and Sarah Lawrence colleges and equally as brilliant as her parents. She liked to remind me that a member of the Kennedy family (Caroline, I believe) spoke at her Manhattanville graduation. Her own life was very Kennedyesque. Summers at the little family place on the Cape, yachting with Grandpa, bike rides on Martha's Vineyard. Brigitte counted Sara Wilford, granddaughter of President Franklin Roosevelt, as one of her closest friends. I was a little intoxicated not only by her, but also by the backdrop her family circle had created. I decided I could use a little Camelot in my life. What was the worst that could happen? Assassination?

It was no surprise, then, that for the wedding, a church was reserved on the Rockefeller Estate in Westchester. An old white clapboard chapel right out of a New England fairy tale. This time around, Tony would act as my best man.

After she had already booked the church, retained the priest, and sent out the wedding invitations, Brigitte announced that she was a little concerned, that maybe we were rushing into this a little too quickly.

She wanted some reassurance. How was she to believe that this would be any different from the first time I'd gotten married? After all, I'd promised before God and witnesses and a representative of the State that I meant it the first time around as well. Hadn't I vowed to hang in there through sickness and health, till death do us part? I told her it was true that I had made that promise, but I was younger then; I was confused. I'd just been through a lot of trauma in my life, and I was newly sober. In fact, I assured her, a part of me knew deep down, from the very get-go, that I was making the wrong decision marrying MaryAnn. I told her about how I had been physically sick the morning of my first marriage because my body was reacting violently to the fact that it was being forced to swallow something, a lie, that it couldn't digest. I talked about the pain of that divorce and asked with indignation if she really believed I would want to ever subject myself to that kind of pain again.

"Well! Do you?"

"I suppose not."

"It's not too late to call it off if you're—"

"You don't want to get married."

"No. Are you crazy? I'm just saying. That's all."

I was a basket case the morning of that wedding too. Not only was I going to get married again, but I was also going to meet her family and friends, all 120 of them, in the parking lot of the church in the last few moments before I walked down the aisle.

Tony came by to pick me up at the apartment.

"You alright?" he asked the moment I flopped into the front seat.

"Yeah, I'm good. A little nervous."

"Mmmm."

"I'll be fine."

"Mmmm."

"I will. No, I'm good. Really."

"Mmmm."

We drove to Chappaqua. Brigitte had spent the night in her friend's house, but she had called to say she wanted to see me for a few moments before the ceremony. I know people say it's supposed to be an unlucky thing to do, but we weren't people.

They were all gathered in the kitchen of her friend's mansion, having a breakfast of strawberries and croissants, when Tony and I arrived. Edith Piaf was playing softly in the background. We were having a French-themed wedding. We had even reserved the French restaurant La Panetière in Rye for the reception. Brigitte took me aside and asked me how I was feeling. If I was still sure we were doing the right thing.

"Of course. And you?"

"Positive."

Tony helped himself to a few croissants and filled a little saucer with strawberries and cream.

"You should try to eat something," he said. "You'll feel better."

"Maybe you're right," I said. I nibbled on a few strawberries and managed to hurriedly down a cup of coffee. The moment I had done so I regretted it. I had a weird churning sensation in the pit of my stomach.

"Well, we should probably hit the road, Tony."

"Mmmm."

"You're going already?" Brigitte asked. "Are you sure you're OK?"

"Perfect, yip. Don't want to be late. Tony. Let's hit it." The churning had progressed into a heavy flipping sensation. I could feel a few beads of sweat beginning to form on my brow. I glanced toward the kitchen door. It was a long way back to the car. I could feel the coffee rising into my throat. Oh, no. Remain calm. There was a small toilet just off the kitchen; maybe I could reach that and casually close the door behind me. But I had already said I was leaving.

"Tony."

"Mmmm."

I stared at Tony, hoping for some flash of inspiration on his part to save me. Tony stared back at me blankly and popped another strawberry into his mouth. I ran for the bathroom door, putting my hand to my mouth, but it was too late. It came in a spurt before I reached the door. I fell to my knees in front of the bowl and let it come. I could hear Tony chuckle a little somewhere behind me as everyone else watched in silence. I took a quick glance behind me. There was Brigitte, with an expression of utter horror frozen on her face, in the middle of the kitchen floor.

"It's not what it looks—" I managed before I puked again.

"Mmmm," I heard Tony mumble.

I managed to shove the door closed with my foot before I released the remains of my stomach and my credibility into the bowl. I splashed some water on my face and braced myself for the fallout. Brigitte was sobbing. I put my arms around her and tried to console her. Everyone else who'd witnessed the show tried to make light of the situation, saying, "It's natural. It happens to everybody." Tony gnawed on another croissant. When I managed to catch his eye I gave him the SOS glance. I wasn't even married yet and already I was looking for an out. He casually picked another few strawberries and checked his watch.

"Wow, is that the time?" he said, not sounding astonished at all. "We should probably hit the road."

"You're right, Tony, we should get going."

"You don't want to marry me," Brigitte said.

"I do. Everything is fine. I should never have eaten the strawberries with coffee. That's all. I'm an idiot."

"Are you sure?"

"I'm positive."

I followed Tony out, down the driveway and past the other polished cars draped in red ribbons.

"Nice breakfast," Tony said.

"Delicious."

"Mmmm."

When we arrived at the church, the sun was glinting off the row of BMWs and Mercedeses and the crowd had already started to congregate in the little parking lot outside the church. The women clutched their Louis Vuitton purses to their chests, and adjusted their wide-brimmed hats to squint and frown at the big blue station wagon rolling into the parking lot. I urged Tony to drive on to the top of the parking lot to avoid having to deal with all these strangers right away. I searched the little groups of people for one of my own family members. There was not yet a single familiar face in the whole bunch.

"You're sure this is the right church, Tony?"

"Mmmm. Looks like the Kennedys have arrived."

"From the crackhouse to Camelot . . ."

"I think I'd prefer the crackhouse."

"How did this happen, Tony?"

"It's all a mystery to me, Col."

The surreal scene before me, the glittering clarity of it all, suddenly seemed farcical. How had this happened? Why was I here? Who was I here? Had I buried the orangutan so deeply that I'd smothered him altogether? If he were here right now he'd have a lot of fun with this crowd. This could be his finest moment.

"You alright?" Tony said as he pulled into a parking spot away from the crowd, toward the back of the parking lot.

"Yeah. I just need to take a little walk."

"Mmmm. A little one?"

"Yeah. Let's just look casual and take a stroll. Maybe they'll all just disappear."

We took a little stroll along a path that ran around the top of the little chapel, slightly shielded from the parking lot by a line of tall oak trees. When I felt I was far enough away from the crowd, I paused and told Tony to keep watch for me. Then I buckled over with my hands against the great oak and puked for about five minutes. Tony stood with his hand on my back as I heaved again and again. When I was done he handed me a big white handkerchief and a mint.

"You alright?"

"You know how I am around big crowds of people."

"Mmmm."

"What, Tony? Just say it."

"It's not too late."

"What?"

"We could leave."

"I can't, Tony."

"You could."

"Jesus, Tony."

"If you want to leave we can just walk back and get into the car and I'll just drive. You don't have to say anything to anybody. These things happen all the time. We'll just drive. Go away for a few days."

"I have to do this."

"You don't have to do anything you don't want to."

"I'm going to do it."

"You know I'm with you either way."

"I know, Tony." He put his arms around me and gave me a long bear hug, then we sauntered casually back down into the parking lot in silence. Do you, Colin Broderick, promise to renounce your inner orangutan from this day forth, so help you God? I do.

We were working on building a kitchen in the Scratcher about two months later, when Tony got a phone call from some guy who owned a bar up on Broadway in the Bronx. Sean had worked at the theater for a little while and had been one of the main performers in *The Risen People*. He told Tony he had received something from Jimmy Smallhorne in the mail that morning and that Tony should really come by and pick it up as soon as possible. We dropped our tools and headed for the Bronx immediately. Jimmy had resurfaced. There was no time to waste.

I sat in the car outside the bar and waited for Tony. I had been well warned at the AA meetings that bars were dangerous places. My disease could be in there right now, waiting for me behind the door with a lasso and a beer funnel. "Fuck you, ya big disease monster," I shouted at the bar. "You won't fool me so easy. I know you're in there." Luckily the windows of the car were rolled up and the stereo was blasting pretty loudly, so no one heard me.

Tony came out a few minutes later and tossed a script into my lap. It was the finished script for *2by4*, the movie. I flipped through it as he drove away, reading a snippet here and a snippet there.

"Wow," I said. "I can't believe it's done."

"Mmmm."

"Does he know where Jimmy is?"

"Did you read the first page?"

I closed it over again and stared at the cover: *2by4*, a screenplay, written by Jimmy Smallhorne and Terry McGoff.

"Who the fuck is Terry McGoff?"

"I have no idea."

"Didn't you help write this thing? How the fuck did Sean get it?"

"Jimmy met him yesterday in the city and gave it to him and told him he had a part for him."

"What did Sean say?"

"He's thinking about it."

"So that's it?"

"Mmmm."

"It's over?"

"Mmmm."

We didn't speak again for the rest of the ride home. I felt like I'd taken a good one in the gut. I kept looking down at the front page of the script in my lap to reread the names. It was Jimmy's movie now, and neither Tony nor I had anything to do with it. Welcome to the movie business.

I settled into married life. This wasn't so bad. I got a decent lump-sum settlement from my worker's compensation for the accident and decided to use the money to make a fresh financial start for both of us. Right away I took about ten grand and paid off Brigitte's credit card debts and back rent so we could apply for a mortgage. It turned out that my new wife had a few financial skeletons in her closet that I had not been fully aware of while we were dating for two weeks. Her parents had cut her off from the source, so it was my responsibility now. We started looking around for a house we could afford, a house we could grow in. A place we could always have. We settled on a nice solid brown brick house on a quiet tree-lined street close to the city line. It had a backyard, a two-car garage, and a front lawn the size of a postage stamp. I gutted the kitchen down to the bare plaster and floor beams and installed everything brand new. I tore down walls, built arches, ripped up the old carpets, and refinished all the oak flooring. I stripped off decades of wallpaper and plastered and painted the whole place anew. I hung new light fixtures and blinds and bought an enormous couch so that I could kick back and relax once it was all done.

For the first time, I had a room I could use as a study. I set up a desk and bookshelves. Finally, somewhere I could close the door on the world and get some writing done. I bought a pure-bred black Labrador puppy and named her Molly. We got rid of Brigitte's beat-up old Toyota Corolla and bought her a baby blue Toyota 4x4 that I paid for in cash to minimize our monthly overhead. I kept my old Honda. The stage was set. I was living the American Dream.

I signed up for classes at Lehman College so that I could study with my latest literary hero, poet Billy Collins. I started working on a degree in English literature. In the meantime I was able to close the door of my study and set about writing my first novel, *Church End*, based loosely on my experiences of the two years I'd spent living in London before I came to the States. I was finally writing something.

I also started a small literary magazine I called *Everyman*.

I'd started sending out poems and short stories of my own and the rejection slips had started to arrive. I became disappointed and angry. What the hell did the *Paris Review* know about what the people wanted? I put out the word that I was looking for material to publish in my own magazine, one that wasn't pretentious. It was going to be a magazine for writers from the area who had not yet had the experience of seeing their work in print. Not having had the experience myself as yet, I could understand the validation that lay in seeing your own work in print for the first time. It's difficult for most new writers to come out of the literary closet. Most of us need someone else to say it for us, that we are indeed writers. It seems a little egotistical to bestow the title upon yourself. It's easier if you have something in print to prove it. Something you haven't gone out and paid to have printed.

I had three hundred copies of the first magazine printed and sold it at the An Bael Bocht Café, at Tony's bar the Scratcher on Fifth Street, and at a few other random stores. All three hundred copies were gone within a week and material started pouring in right away for the next issue. I had no option but to continue. I decided the magazine should be a quarterly. It was only thirty pages long, but I was very particular about how it looked. And the truth was, I'd really only intended it to be a little hobby. For the next issue I decided to limit the publication to five hundred copies. All of a sudden the magazine was getting mentioned in all the local newspapers. *The Irish Voice* even sent a photographer to complement the interview they published of me. *Newsday* showed up at the café and ran a piece about the burgeoning cultural scene in the Bronx.

I managed to cough up my first novel in a three-week writing frenzy. It was like a fur ball that had been stuck in the back of my throat. I hacked it up and spat it onto the desk next to my computer. It looked, read, and smelled like a fur ball, but I'd done it. I had actually written a novel. I sent it off to a few publishers right away. I was in a panic. I had to get a book published as quickly as possible. Brigitte wanted a baby.

We had only been married a few months. I had just started attending college. I'd just finished the bulk of the work on our new house and moved in. I was still dealing with puppy poop and puddles on the rugs. I had literally just been able to sit down and actually write for the first time in my life, and now she wanted a baby.

This was not good news at all. In the short time we did have together before we'd been married, I had made it clear that I wasn't ready for a family. Absolutely no babies. I wanted to write. The only way I was going to be a writer was to write. I felt like I was so far behind. I was twenty-six years old and I had done nothing with my life. I was just beginning. I needed to close the world out and focus. I had so much work to do. A baby would mean sleepless nights and diapers and doctors and schools and . . . I DON'T WANT A BABY.

She wanted a baby.

After six months or so, when she wasn't pregnant with quintuplets, she was frantic. That's when the fertility nightmare began. She needed a fertility expert. Not just any fertility expert. The best fertility expert money could buy. My money. She found one in Westchester. I think his name was God. He was the Creator, after all. You didn't just go see him, you were chosen. God was very expensive. He had his own clinic in Westchester and dealt with only the monetarily blessed. Miracles were far from free at the Suck You Dry Clinic. Brigitte armed herself with her prayer book—I mean checkbook—and went off to worship at his feet. I thought that might keep her happy for another while and maybe now I could get some writing done. I was wrong. God had summoned me to his clinic also. I didn't want to go. This was getting out of hand.

I decided it was time for therapist number two.

I was referred to William through another sober friend. I was done with the tough-guy thing. I wanted a therapist who didn't take up the entire hour telling me horror stories about himself. I was getting enough of that at the meetings.

My new therapist worked out of a downtown office, on the seventeenth floor of a building on Twenty-third Street. I felt I'd made the right decision the moment I stepped off the elevator and saw the receptionist behind her desk, busy scheduling an appointment. A couple of very depressed-looking patients were thumbing through health magazines in the waiting room. One pencil-thin woman was chewing on her thumbnail like it was a beef jerky. This was more like it. This also made it easier to part with a hundred dollars an hour. With Big Al, I used to catch myself staring at his latest gold chain, thinking, "I just paid for that. I should stay at home for a few weeks and buy one for myself."

The receptionist directed me to the last office on the left down a long corridor. I knocked lightly. No response. I knocked again a little louder.

"Come in. Come in," a voice called. I entered. The door, strangely enough, opened toward me into the hallway. The office was not much bigger than a broom closet. There was just enough room for two fairly comfortable-looking but small chairs and a table lamp that sat on the floor in the corner. There obviously wasn't enough room for a desk to sit it on. William stood up to greet me. I shook his hand, but it was so cramped in there that we had to sit immediately to avoid rubbing up against one another. We shuffled our legs around so that our knees weren't touching. It occurred to me that if William were to leave the office now for any reason, he would have to either climb over my lap or have me exit first. I instinctively tried to slide my chair back a little, but it was already tight up against the wall.

When we had settled, I glanced around as you would upon entering any room, to take in the furnishings and give sufficient pause before entering into conversation. There was nothing to look at. There were no windows, no pictures adorning the gray walls. There was William with his ashen face, graying disheveled hair and stubble, wearing a grubby gray sports jacket. He looked as if he had just been awakened from a long sleep. God knows how long he'd been in here. The air smelled a little suspect. I didn't notice a vent anywhere. Maybe it was underneath one of the chairs. Then I had a thought: Maybe this really *was* just a broom closet. Maybe I had knocked on the wrong door. Perhaps this guy before me was the janitor.

"You are William?" I ventured, just to make sure.

"Yes." He smiled. He had a pleasant face, like a house cat you might imagine being stroked in the lap of an old woman in a cottage somewhere off in the woods. "You'll have to excuse the lack of space. They're working on getting me a bigger office here," he said, picking up on the uncertainty in my voice. That's good, I thought. At least he's intuitive, considerate even, and he doesn't look like he's ever killed anybody with his bare hands. Yes, this was fine, I decided. So what if we were in a broom closet. Maybe they really were going to fix him up in a big office of his own. Either way, I was staying.

"This seems fine," I said. "It's cozy."

William let out a little chuckle. "Yes it is," he said. "It's cozy. So tell me a little bit about yourself."

"Where should I start?"

"Anywhere," he said, settling in as if for a cross-Atlantic flight, folding his arms across his chest and putting his foot up on the wall. "The beginning."

"My childhood?" This was exciting. I hadn't told Big Al anything, really. I'd never had the chance.

"Yeah, start there and just talk."

I did. I started to talk. And I talked and I talked and I talked and I talked. William nodded occasionally, and once in a while his head jumped a little as if he had just fallen asleep. He'd adjust himself and give me a look with that cat face of his that told me he was listening and that I should go on. After an hour or so there was a tap on the door. He glanced at his watch. His next patient had arrived.

"Same time next week?" I said, standing to leave and opening the door.

"I'll be here." I didn't doubt it for a second. The next patient shuffled aside to let me out. She was at least 250 pounds and she was lugging two large plastic bags that seemed at a glance to be filled with groceries. A big bag of Cheetos hung precariously out of the neck of one of them. I wanted to stick around to see how she was going to manage squeezing in next to William in the closet. I could hear her rustling and panting as I walked away up the corridor, but I thought it would be rude to turn around and stare. By the time I reached the reception area and glanced around again she had managed to squeeze herself into the janitor's closet and close the door behind her. I felt a great sense of relief after my first session. I was lighter somehow. I was going to tell William everything, I decided. I felt right away as if I could trust him with anything. It was fitting that we should meet in a broom closet to sweep away all this old mess.

Jimmy made his movie. It was Jimmy's movie now, complete with a lavish ten-minute gay sex scene choreographed by, and starring, Jimmy. Thankfully it didn't resemble the movie as we had originally imagined it. It made it a little easier to move on from the disappointment of not being involved with it through production.

Paul Ronan, meanwhile, had landed his first big movie role playing Brad Pitt's sidekick in a movie called *The Devil's Own*, also starring Harrison Ford.

And Chris O'Neill was off to perform at an Irish festival in Palm Beach, Florida. The night before his show he fell ill. His temperature spiked and within hours he was in a coma. The doctors couldn't figure out what was wrong. They guessed that it might be some crazy bacterial infection. Chris never left the hospital. He passed away at about five in the morning on April 15, 1997. He was fifty-one years old. At his bedside when he passed were his daughter, Aisling, and Paul Ronan.

After much debate, I was summoned to the office of the Creator in Westchester. He wanted to see me alone. I was totally against it at the time. It's a difficult decision to make even if you want to have a baby, but if you're really hoping not to have one it's hell. The waiting room at the clinic was like a nursery. Four or five women were there reading fertility books. Surprisingly enough, most of them had brought their small children. Maybe that's not surprising. It was surprising to me that they had children and they wanted more. I searched the kids' faces as they played to see if any of them bore any resemblance to one another. I was distrustful of the doctor with his little baby factory. What if he was the father of all these little monsters? How hard could it be? I was summoned into his office and was surprised to find a Woody Allen–type character behind a humongous desk in his corner office. Maybe he just made the desk appear humongous because he was so small. He looked a lot like Woody Allen, glasses and all, only much sharper. He had the appearance of a man who scrubbed himself clean fifty times a day. He had an unnatural glow about him. He had the aura of a man who created babies for a living. I understood now. This was why these women worshipped him. I crossed my legs uneasily.

"Well, Mr. Broderick," he said, leaning back in his throne, clasping his hands. "Are we ready to make a baby?"

"Listen, you seem like a really nice guy," I said. "But I'm married."

"Right," he said with a straight face. I guess he'd heard them all before. "What we need to do today is take some tests, and then we'll reschedule another appointment for next week and we can sit down with the results and discuss our options. How does that sound to you?"

"Sounds great," I lied.

"OK, so if you'll just go back to the waiting room," he said, getting up and walking me to the door of his office, "one of the nurses will be with you in a moment."

"Thanks."

Mmmm. Nurses? Tests? This was beginning to sound like it might be fun. I went back to the waiting room and read an article about breastfeeding. Two of the women in the waiting room now had their nannies with them. There must have been seven or eight well-dressed, attractive, wealthy white women and a handful of little Gap babies. I tried not to dwell on the fact that I was the only man in the room.

The nurse behind the desk stood up from behind the counter and called my name, glancing around the waiting room as if there was a possibility that one of these women had the first name Colin. I approached as she held out a clear plastic cup with a blue lid.

"Here you go," she said. Now I understood. She was just trying to attract everybody's attention. "I'm going to need a sample of your sperm. You can just bring it back to me when you're finished."

"When I'm finished?"

"Yes. You can use the bathroom here on the right. There should be a magazine in there if you need some help."

"I see." I wanted to ask her if maybe she could speak up a little, as I was quite sure there had to be a few women in Staten Island who hadn't quite caught all that. I took a quick look around at the room full of ladies. It was obvious that everybody had heard, but they were polite enough not to stare.

The door to the bathroom was just to the right of the receptionist's work station, just as she'd said. Nice. Discreet. I sauntered on in as casually as I could manage and locked the door behind me. I set the plastic cup on the sink and sat down on the toilet. I could still hear the women talking in the waiting room. Their conversation seemed forced now, a little louder even, as if they were trying to cover for me. They were sitting less than ten feet away. And now I was supposed to jack off into a cup and then go back out there and hand my man juice to the nurse in front of everybody. I considered just packing it in right there. I didn't want to do this in the first place. I really didn't want a baby. I was here because I wanted peace and quiet in my home so that I could get some writing done. If I didn't get this done I'd never hear the end of it. I'd never get any writing done.

Maybe I was just being selfish. But this just didn't feel natural. What the hell was I doing in there? What was I doing? Oh my God, now I'd wasted time obsessing about it and all those women were out there still waiting for me to perform. I pictured them out there glancing at their watches, whispering to each other, straining to hear any trace of me manhandling myself. I'd really gotten myself into it this time. I had to get busy.

Sure enough, there on a shelf above the toilet was a magazine. I took it down and was turned off right away by the fact that it had lost its cover. This was not going to be easy. The corners of the pages were dog-eared. This little puppy had been through the mill. I could storm out, waving the magazine, and scream, "This is an outrage! You expect me to work with this?" like a French actor with a bad script. I could fling it onto the coffee table in the middle of the small waiting room and storm out the door, muttering something about how this was an insult to my talent. I was wasting more time. I had to get it together. How long had I been in there already? What if someone out there was waiting to use the bathroom? What if I couldn't perform? I had to escape. There was no window. I eyed the small air vent in the ceiling. If I could just manage to somehow dislocate both my shoulders and crush my pelvis with the toilet seat, I just might be able to squeeze myself through it. Focus. Focus. You're in here now; deal with it. The only way out is in your pants. Get it out and get on with it. There you go—

I washed up and gave myself a grin in the mirror. Who's the man? You're the man. No, you're the man. No, you're the man. I waltzed out with my little cup. I was James Bond twirling a martini glass. Shaken, not stirred. All the ladies seemed more relaxed. We'd done it. Was it good for you, ladies? I handed Miss Moneypenny the cup. She seemed happy with my work. I suppressed a smile as she handed me a card with my mission for next week. Did she just flutter her eyelashes? I felt like maybe we should all have a cigarette or something before I left.

My college education was drifting along nicely. I adapted well to student life. I liked having the name of a college in my repertoire. It took the edge off at parties, especially since I had a wife in the education field. "So where did you study?" was a commonly asked question in the circle I moved in now. "Lehman College, old bean, and you?"

I took some art history and tried my hand at painting some nude models. I realized quickly that I was not a painter. You'd have to be a born artist to be able to see beauty in some of these models. There's nothing more sobering than having to gaze upon the hairy sack of some washed-up, overweight middle-aged beast on all fours with his asshole pointing in your direction.

I took literature classes. And what I learned was that writers have always been a little or a lot mad. I wrote a few articles for the college paper and became more and more convinced that I should just stay at home and write. What did I need a degree for, anyway?

I kept going because I got a chance to work with Billy Collins. His class was entertainment for me. Here was one of my favorite poets, in the flesh. One of the greats of our time, babbling away, filling up the space, giving his little professorial performance for his younger fans, dropping his little nuggets of advice here and there, amusing us with his dry wit, his razor-sharp observations. Every class was like witnessing a small performance. All the pretty young writers were there, perched on the edge of their seats, starry-eyed and eager for any smidgen of his approval. I was among them, though not so pretty.

Billy became my official mentor while I was at college. I was required to have a mentor for my program, so I asked Billy because I knew he wouldn't bother me. I took his class every semester for about three years. And what I learned from him, apart from how many lines were in a stanza and how many syllables were in a haiku and that hot chicks really do dig poets, was that all great writing is rewriting. It's work.

"Odds are you're not going to write a masterpiece at two in

the morning all drunk on red wine with a candle going," he would say each semester. "It's all very romantic, of course, but what you're probably going to wake up with is a dull hangover and some unintelligible scrawl in your notebook. Writing is work. To write you must rewrite. You must be willing to sacrifice your darlings. Rip it apart, throw some of it out—throw it all out if you have to—and rewrite. I'm not saying you'll never write a great poem in one clean swipe, but the odds are you won't. Write. Rewrite. Write. Rewrite. Work."

I often wondered how he had the patience for it at all. Some of the drivel he had to put up with. Ninety percent of it was drivel; the rest of it was mediocre bullshit. But he was patient with even the worst of us, always managing to find some kind word of encouragement. And it taught me a lesson. The bottom line was this: The writers came to class as writers. Nobody becomes a writer in class. You can tear it all to pieces all you want, dismantle it and catalogue it and put it back together if that's what you're into, analyze it all to hell, but you never get any closer to the answer. The greats are born with magic, and there's nothing to be done about it.

After three years I was still taking his class, the same class. I wasn't even sure why anymore. Other than that it was entertainment and it was an easy three credits and a nice way to spend the afternoon. I wasn't even sure if I wanted to be at college anymore. Everybody at school seemed to have a plan. Everybody was going somewhere. I felt like I was playing along, passing time. I couldn't imagine a situation where I would ever need a college degree to get what I wanted out of life.

I met Billy in the corridor at the end of the third year and he took me by the shoulder and led me into his little office. It was the end of the fall semester. We were just breaking for Christmas. The hallways were full of dirty puddles of melted snow and students in big coats and wool caps. He turned the lock on his door and pulled out a bottle of red wine from behind his desk, along with two clean glasses. The snow was falling past his window on the second floor and he was bundled in a dark tweed jacket and a red wool scarf. The budget at Lehman never allowed for heating in the winter months.

"Well, Colin, I think we've come to the end here," he said, rummaging around for a corkscrew.

"You don't think I should take your class anymore." I'd known it was coming. I'd been hanging around waiting for him to chase me out for a long time now. Like a first-time parachutist in the open door of a plane. I was just looking for a shove. There'd been a moment when we were handing in our final assignments just a couple of days before when I'd realized I wouldn't be back to his class.

The rest of the students had filed out and I had waited to talk to him about something or other. But there was another student, a girl, a dancer, who had his attention first. She had long brown curly hair and she wore black stretch pants to class and wrote fairly decent poetry about how much she loved sex and dancing. She had complimented me on my poetry a few times in class and gushed about how much she liked my accent. I would look at Billy and roll my eyes.

When I walked up next to Billy she was saying, ". . . so, you know, I might not be able to come back and pick up these poems, but if you could mail them to me with your suggestions, that would be great. I'll just give you my address and my phone number in case there's any problems." She had smiled at Billy, then at me, as we stood next to each other, listening intently.

"Actually, I'll just write it out to both of you," she said, giving me a smile. "In case you want to talk about poetry sometime." Then she leaned over his desk and began to write out her details for us, letting her loose top fall open, revealing her tiny little dancer's breasts. She had our attention completely now. I had looked at Billy and Billy had looked at me as she continued talking for some time with her head down so as to retain our attention for as long as possible. Billy and I continued to stare at each other forcefully, avoiding the obvious temptation before us. As if we had been handed an unspoken moral challenge. We were both married men. We had both met each other's wives.

When she glanced up we were both grinning. "Did I miss something?" She smiled, quite obviously aware of the fact that she was still very much on display.

"It was nothing," Billy said. "Just something I remembered."

"Oh," she said, and continued to scribble.

But something had happened. I had overstayed my welcome. This was Billy's class. It was his show. He was the poet they came to see. She finished writing, handed each of us a card as if she were the teacher giving us our holiday writing assignments, and disappeared out of the classroom.

"There's nothing more I can teach you. I'm cutting you loose. You're on your own, kid," Billy said, glancing up at me from behind his desk.

"You're finally kicking me out of your class?" I said.

"I'm booting you out."

"That's it?"

"That's it. Just go off and write. I can't teach you any more. You know everything I can tell you. Go off and write." He was still foraging through his drawers, looking for something to open the bottle with.

"I can't have any wine," I said.

"No?" He had just located a cheap plastic corkscrew. He looked a little surprised.

"I've been off it for a few years."

"That's fine. I just thought we'd celebrate." He put the bottle down.

"It's tempting. Believe me. But I can't. Not right now. But

thanks." I stood up to leave. He stood up and gave me his hand across the table.

"I'm glad it was my class you stumbled into. It could have been anybody's."

"No. I don't think it could have been. . . . It's the accent, isn't it?" I said.

"What do you mean, it's the accent?"

"Well, you're a pretty good poet and all, but you just couldn't compete with the accent."

"Go on. Get out of my office." He laughed. "Before I throw you out."

I left, cursing myself down the hall and all the way home, and years later I'm still cursing myself on occasion for not sharing that bottle of wine with him in his office that day. There are some drinks, like beautiful women, you'll always wish you had taken when you had the opportunity.

I went home and finished the novel I was working on, *The Blue Store*. It's the story of a boy growing up in a small Irish town with his mother. His name is Elvis. His father was an Irish Elvis impersonator who had come through town years before and had a one-night stand with his mother. After his mother dies suddenly of cancer, he decides to go in search of his real father. He travels to New York and Las Vegas, following stories of his father like crumbs dropped in the forest.

I spent about a year working on the manuscript. Surely this one would get published. If it didn't, then I obviously wasn't meant to write at all. This would be the decider. I printed up a few copies and posted them off to a few random addresses I found in *Poets and Writers* magazine. Part of me expected them to come beating down my door with the Nobel Prize. The other part of me, the more insightful part, knew that I was worthless and that I would go to my grave without the slightest recognition for my efforts.

When I didn't hear anything back from the publishing houses after three or four weeks, I decided I needed to take drastic measures. I had just read a novel by a new Irish writer, Colum McCann. The novel was called *Songdogs* and it gave me the fleeting impression that perhaps Irish literature wasn't completely dead after all. It was April of 1998, and McCann was reading from his new book, *This Side of Brightness,* down at the Union Square Barnes & Noble. I would just go and introduce myself and give him a copy of my novel. McCann would then alert the media that I had arrived. It was a simple plan. I had done the work. It was time to be rewarded.

It was a cold, wet April night. Couples huddled under umbrellas along Union Square. The bars and cafés were crowded with that too-cool-for-school crew that always seemed to have everything, as they twirled their fine French wine in the windows and slipped the flesh of an artichoke between their perfectly puffed lips. Everyone was a model; everyone had a movie deal they'd just signed; everyone had that book they'd been working on and that wine . . . my God, why does wine look so beautiful being tipped back in a glass? Even Christ had to use up one of his miracles at the wedding, turning the water into wine when they ran short. I wonder if God told him off about that one later on: "Dude, that's not what I gave you these powers for. This doesn't look good. Next time just send someone to the liquor store."

There was an enormous crowd gathered for the reading on the fourth floor of the store. I stood in the back and listened as he read a few snippets from the new book. The crowd applauded excitedly. I picked up a copy and waited until I was sure that I was the last person on the line to have my book signed. I had a copy of my own manuscript along with me. The closer I got to him the more ridiculous the idea appeared to me. I really could be an idiot sometimes. I handed him my copy of his book.

"Last but not least," he said. "What's your name?"

"Colin. You could sign it to Colin."

"You're Irish?"

"Yeah."

"Where're ye from?"

"Tyrone."

"Are you here long, Colin?"

"Long enough."

"There you go," he said, snapping the book shut and handing it to me. "Thanks for coming down, Colin."

"No problem. I really enjoyed the reading. Actually, I really enjoyed your first book, *Songdogs;* that's why I came to see you. You see, I wrote this book myself and I was just wondering if maybe you could read it for me and let me know what you think."

"You're a writer."

"I'm trying."

"I'd love to read it. I'll tell you what I'll do. I'll give you my home address and you send it to me there and I'll take a look at it. That way I don't have to carry it around with me right now."

"Really?"

"Yeah, here you go," he said, handing me his address and home phone number. "What are you up to right now?"

"I was just going to head on home."

"You want to go to a party?"

"A party?"

"Yeah, they're throwing a party for me down at this place on St. Mark's place called St. Dymphna's. You know it?"

"Yeah, Jerome O'Connor owns that place. He's a friend of mine." I'd worked with Jerome quite a bit over the years. Jerome had his own construction business back then, specializing in high-end music studios around midtown. Tony and I had taken care of a lot of his painting.

"Great. I'll see you there."

"Thanks. I really appreciate this."

"Always good to meet a fellow writer."

I drove on down to St. Dymphna's bar and found a parking space right outside. The place was just a stone's throw from Tompkins Square Park. The area had cleaned up a lot in the ten years since I'd first arrived, but it still had an edge to it. A couple of straggle-headed grungers huddled in a doorway out of the rain, puffing on a fat spliff. I was half tempted to go ask them for a draw, but I could just imagine the paranoia I'd have to deal with, not having had a smoke myself for so many years.

The bar was packed. As soon as I entered I waded through the crowd down to the end of the bar to see if I could find McCann. Jerome was there at the end of the bar, pouring a pint of Guinness.

"Jesus, look what the cat dragged in," he said in that thick Cork accent of his, reaching over the bar to take my hand. "What's happening? I haven't seen you for a while."

"Yeah, I heard there was free booze."

"I think you must be mistaking this place for somewhere else." He laughed.

"Right."

"What are you having?"

"A soda."

"You're still on the dry?"

"Seven years or so?"

"You're not getting thirsty yet?"

"I am, actually. I ordered a soda about ten minutes ago and would you believe I'm still waiting for it."

He laughed and went off to get me a soda. I squeezed my way into a small space at the end of the bar.

I hated standing around in bars when I wasn't drinking. Everybody else always seemed to be having more fun than I was. Drinkers always think they're funnier than they are. They talk louder than they need to, they laugh louder than they should, they smile more than they should, they develop an inflated air of superiority. In short, they become Americans. They find you boring if you're not as excited as they are about the most mundane shit. Drinkers in general are on a constant mission to elevate the mundane to dizzying heights. When I'm not drinking I find it's better if I avoid drinkers.

I had just started on my glass of soda when I noticed a familiar face approaching me. It was Jimmy Smallhorne. I hadn't seen him since his big disappearing act.

"Jaysus, is that you, Broderick, ya little bollox."

"I'm a bollox? You're some cocksucker."

"You might be right."

"It's good to see you, Jimmy."

"It's good to see you, too." He put his arms around me and we gave each other a warm hug. It *was* good to see him. It was always good to see Jimmy. He is one of those rare people who always puts a smile on my face.

Just then a cheer rose up through the crowd. McCann had arrived. He made his way through, getting his back slapped as he went. He came all the way up the bar until he spotted Jimmy and me and he came right over and gave Jimmy a hug.

"How's it goin', man? It's great to see you," Jimmy said. I should have figured Colum would know Jimmy. Everybody knew Jimmy.

"It's good to see you, too," McCann said, still holding Jimmy in an arm lock. He looked at me and then back at Jimmy with an inquisitive grin. "You know this guy?"

"Jaysus, yeah, this is me auld pal Colin. We used to work in the theatre together. How the fuck do you know him?"

"I just met him an hour ago and invited him to the party. He just finished writing a book."

"What? Ya didn't mention that, ya bollox."

"I didn't have time."

"Jaysus. Congratulations, man. That's fuckin' great, that is." Jimmy gave me another hug. "I always knew you had a book in you."

Just then a tall gray-haired man with a peaked tweed cap nudged his way in between Jimmy and Colum.

"Congratulations," he said, taking Colum's hand. "I haven't had a chance to read it yet. But it's on my desk."

"Wow, thanks very much, John," Colum said. "I really appreciate you coming out tonight. It means a lot to me."

"Oh, it's no bother at all. I wish I could stay, but I have a more pressing engagement to take care of." He winked and held up his whiskey glass in a minor toast before finishing the last swallow. He'd had a few already and he was in merry form, flashing a big friendly grin. He had the kind of face I hoped to have as a seventy-year-old if I was still kicking around. An old man with a boy's face, a few soft wrinkles, and an air of familiarity that you can't quite put your finger on. He had a baby's skin and a reckless hungry twinkle in his eyes. There was the savage spirit of an orangutan still lurking in there.

"Do you know who that is?" Jimmy whispered to me.

"Naw."

"That's John Montague, the poet."

"No way."

"That's him." I'd heard about John Montague my whole life. John Montague had grown up about a half mile from my grandparents' house. I had gone to school with some of his younger relatives. I'd heard my father talk about a poem he'd written called "The Wild Dog Rose" about an old woman who'd lived next door to my father when he was a boy. The poem depicts the brutal rape of the old woman in her seventies. It had been the sort of savage secret a community buried back then out of shame until Montague had dug up its bones and courageously displayed them on the altar of the page for all to see. I felt a tinge of guilt that here was the great man in person and I'd never read a single word he'd written. I'd always assumed he was dead.

"Excuse me, you lot," a girl shouted. "Hey." We looked around. The girl was pointing a camera our way. "Yeah, you lot. Push together for the picture." Jimmy looped his arm around my shoulder and dragged me in, Colum stood on my other side, and Montague towered over us from behind.

"Say cheese or something," she said.

"Cheese or something," we all said together.

Somebody handed Montague another glass of whiskey. A few more people were shoving their way into the corner where we stood. It was getting a little too claustrophobic for comfort.

"Come on," Jimmy said. "Let's get outside for a smoke."

"Sounds good."

We shoved our way out through the throng. It was pouring outside. We backed up underneath the awning and lit up a couple of smokes.

"I suppose you think I'm an awful bollox," Jimmy said in a thick Dublin dialect that only an Irishman could understand. It was something all us Irish guys did when we were around each other. The accent came back, sometimes stronger than it ever was to begin with.

"I've thought about it," I said.

"I know it's probably hard to believe, but I had to do what I had to do. It was the only way I could get the movie made."

"Yeah, I know."

"You do?"

"Yeah, I do know."

"You're not pissed?"

"Naw. It was a load of shite anyway. I'm delighted I'm in no way associated with it."

"Ya bollox."

The door opened and out came John Montague, propped under each arm by a couple of very attractive younger women. The women left him standing with us for a moment under the awning while they dashed out into the rain, trying to hail a cab.

"How're ye, John?" Jimmy started. "It looks like those two girls might be in trouble tonight, what?"

"At my age I think the only one in any danger here is me." He laughed.

"I wouldn't be too sure about that." Jimmy laughed. "What part of the North are you from, John?"

"You'll never guess where I'm from," he said.

"Ah, let me see, is it Antrim?"

"Not a chance."

"Jaysus, I should know this."

"You'll never guess where I'm from," he said again, more pleased with himself now at having eluded Jimmy. He dug his fists down into the bottom of the pockets of his coat and tipped his head back at a defiant angle.

"I know where you're from," I said.

"Where? Where am I from?"

"You're from a little place called Redargen in County Tyrone."

"Who the fuck are you?" he shot back, startled as if he'd just been tracked down by a hit man.

"I'm a neighbor of yours from Altamuskin."

"Well, for fucksake," he said, blessing himself and raising his face to the sky. "What's your name?"

"Colin Broderick."

"Jaysus Christ." He paused, searching my face for a moment. "Johnny and Mary Broderick of Redargen?"

"That's my grandparents."

"Well, fuck me! Are they still around?"

"No, they both passed away."

"Well, come here with me for a minute. I have something I'm goin' to tell you."

"John, come on, are you ready to go?" one of the girls shouted as a cab pulled up to the curb and the other girl opened the door.

"Go on, jump in. I'll be there in a minute." He led me away from Jimmy and turned to me in the rain. "I got a piece of news today that I've been saving. I haven't shared it with another soul."

"What is it?"

He leaned over and whispered in my ear.

"I just found out this evening that I'm to be the poet laureate of Ireland, and you, young man, are the first to know."

"I didn't know they had a poet laureate in Ireland."

"Apparently I'm the first."

"Are you serious?"

"I'm as serious as cancer. You are the first to know. I wasn't going to tell anybody today."

About a week later I received a long letter from Colum McCann about how much he liked the book and about how he really thought I could write, but this was not the book that would get published. He was right. It was pure shite. I threw it on the shelf, on top of the other one I'd written. What did it matter? It had given me one memorable night out.

Now that I didn't have the Collins class to look forward to every week, I was bored with school. Then, during the following semester, one of my English literature professors took me aside and suggested that I should quit school altogether and go write full-time.

"I've read your essays. I think you should go out there and

give this thing a try. If you don't have your degree to fall back on you'll try harder. Don't teach," he warned me. "Not until much later."

I felt honored and baffled by the suggestion. I brought it up with William on my next visit to the broom closet.

"Well, what do *you* think you should do?" he said.

"I don't know, William; that's why I'm asking you."

"Well, it's something you should think about."

"William, I've *been* thinking about it. Now I'm asking you to think about it. I've done all the talking in here for months. You've said nothing." He dropped his feet off the wall and straightened himself in his chair, suddenly startled that I'd challenged him.

"This is your time." He continued trying to sound professional. "I'd like to hear your thoughts on it."

"I want some answers," I said, relieved that I'd finally had the sense to say what I was really thinking. "I'm paying you for help here. I've got some problems in my life right now and I need some answers. I don't have the answers myself or I wouldn't be stuck in this broom closet once a week listening to you snore for forty minutes."

"I do not snore," he said, his eyes opening fully for the first time since I'd been seeing him.

"You snore a little bit, William."

He looked hurt. But he was wide-awake now and the only way out of that closet was over the top of me.

"I want to know what your thoughts are about my marriage," I continued. "I've told you I'm not happy about this whole baby thing and you've said nothing."

"It's a difficult issue," he said nervously, rubbing the palms of his hands on the legs of his pants.

"I know, William; I've got that part; that's why I'm here. The question is, what do I do about it?"

"Well, maybe you need to tell your wife what you've told me—"

"I've told her a thousand times already. She doesn't care."

"Well, then you need to ask yourself, 'What is it that I want for myself?' "

"I don't want a baby—that's for sure."

"Well, that's a start." William glanced at the door and then pulled back the sleeve of his jacket to check his watch. "I'm afraid we'll have to end it there. But this is great. You've done really great work here today."

"I didn't do anything."

"You did. And we'll pick it up right here again when you come back next week."

I shook my head and stood to leave. William gave me an awkward smile. I went out and closed the door behind me. There was no grocery lady to squeeze past today. I pictured her on a couch eating ice cream out of a carton in front of a television somewhere with a cat sleeping against her leg. I walked past the elevators to use the bathroom before leaving the building. When I came out a moment later, William was standing by the elevator door. He looked surprised to see me. I'd never seen him outside of the closet before. He looked smaller suddenly. Even more sickly than usual. I noticed a small tear in the arm of the right sleeve of his rumpled jacket and a food stain on his tie just beneath his chin.

"You're on your way home early tonight, William," I said as the elevator arrived. I suddenly felt sad that I knew nothing of this man I shared a janitor's closet with once a week.

"I am," he said, standing back to let me on first.

I took his clipped answer to mean he didn't want to talk. The doors closed and it was just the two of us for the ride down.

"It's bigger than your office in here," I said. He managed a tight smile. I cut straight to the chase. "You married yourself,

William?" He took a deep breath and released it slowly before answering.

"No," he said finally.

"Divorced?" I continued.

"Divorced," he said. The doors opened and we stepped out. When we reached the street I stopped and offered him my hand. As we shook I said, "Have a nice night, William." Then he went one way and I went another. I never saw or spoke to William again.

Tony called to tell me he was drinking again. Ever since I'd gotten married to Brigitte we'd spent less and less time together. He was always busy now with the new bars downtown and with some new girl he'd been seeing. "It's just a glass of wine every now and then," he assured me. "It's working for me because I have it under control. I'm just at a good place in my life now and I deserve a glass of wine every now and then. I just wanted you to know. It's not for everybody." I wished him the best with it and asked him to be careful. What could I say? I'd been high on codeine for years.

I decided to quit school for a while and find myself a new profession. This time I decided I'd try something completely different. I had a friend who owned an employment agency in Manhattan. She set me up with an interview for a mid-level office position at a bank.

The following Monday morning, wearing a new dark gray suit, white shirt, and very impressive black-and-gold tie, I was strolling into a huge office building on the corner of Fifty-seventh and Lexington Avenue with a copy of the *Wall Street Journal* tucked under my arm as a prop.

Inside in the lobby I tried to appear nonchalant as a throng of suits waited for a bank of elevators. It was a far cry from a Monday morning on the construction site.

When I entered the office for my interview I encountered the boss, slumped in his big leather chair like some massive coronary. A blob of a man, all jowls and folds, with a napkin tucked into his shirt collar, shoving a humongous breakfast hero into his face.

"Humphsha sheat." I understood. I sat down.

He continued to eat. He moved some papers around on his desk with a pudgy, ketchup-smeared slab of meat that I assumed was his hand. He set the sandwich down and splashed some coffee into the enormous hole on the front of his head, and from it erupted a monstrous belch. This was no orangutan. This shuffling, sexless delicatessen would last maybe five minutes in the jungle before being trampled by a small herd of rhinoceroses.

"You're the new guy they just sent over?" He was back to speaking English.

"Colin, yes, that's me."

"Much experience working in banks, Colin?"

"Yes, sir. I've worked in banks most of my life. Since I was a little boy, actually. My father was a banker and his father before him."

"Really. That's impressive. I detect an accent there. We have a few of you English guys with us here at the bank." I was tempted to let it slide, as he seemed pleased with the fact that I was English. But I didn't want the job that badly.

"Actually I'm Irish. Northern Ireland. County Tyrone."

"You know this is an English bank."

"No, I didn't know that."

"Really? I'm surprised you hadn't heard of it. Yes, a very famous bank until some fool over there gambled all the bank's money and lost it."

"Sounds like the work of an Englishman, alright," I said. He managed a laugh at this. His enormous body jiggled with the strain of it, sending little shock waves through the floor, vibrating the windows.

"Well, we bought it, so it's ours now. We have a handful of their guys over here helping us with the transition. Maybe you can keep an eye on them out there for me."

"I'll keep my eyes peeled for any gambling."

"You do that." He hit the button on his intercom system. "George, get your ass in here."

"You're familiar with PowerPoint, Excel, Word . . ."

"I've used them all at one time or another," I lied. The truth was I didn't even know what he was talking about. "No problem."

"Of course you have." There was a light tap on the door and George breezed in. "Ah, George, you lazy bastard. Where have you been hiding out all morning?"

"In the men's bathroom, asleep in one of the stalls."

"I see. Well, this is Colin. He's starting with us today, so maybe you'd take him out there and show him to his desk. Good luck to you, Colin."

"Thank you, sir."

"Sir! Did you hear that, George? That's how I want to be referred to from now on."

"Yes, sir. Absolutely, sir. I'd be delighted, sir."

As I stood up to leave, Jabba lifted the hero and launched about another eight inches of it into his face.

"Dunphshma artananawarsh outhair," he said. I nodded and ran it through my internal translation computer as we left his office. "Don't you be starting any wars out there," I believe is what he said.

I followed George to my new work station, a six-by-six cubicle in the middle of the office space. I was surrounded by a sea of little cubicles. The walls were low enough that when you stood up you could see everybody else, but when you sat you were all alone. I had a desk and a computer and a swivel chair.

"Well, this is it," George said. "You can just get yourself set up here and I'll go get your confirms."

"Great," I said. What the hell are confirms? And what exactly was I supposed to do to set up? I put my newspaper next to my computer on my desk. I adjusted the keyboard so that it was lined up nicely with the front of the computer. Right. Well, the setting-up seemed to be all taken care of.

After a few minutes of chewing on the end of my pen, I decided that maybe I should at least get the old computer up and running. I searched high and low for a button, but I couldn't find a damn thing. I was beginning to panic. What if he came back and realized that I couldn't even turn on a computer? This called for drastic measures. I stood up and stretched myself and glanced at the guy in the adjoining cubicle. He was deeply immersed in his computer screen, tapping away. He looked like somebody I could beat up if I had to, a real dork.

"Hey," I said quietly, leaning over the cubicle wall a little to catch his attention. I didn't want to alert the whole office. He looked up.

"Hey."

"I'm the new guy. Colin."

"Oh, hey, Colin. How's it goin'?" He beamed a big toothy grin. This was definitely my guy. "Welcome to hell. The name's Eric."

"Thanks, Eric. How long you been stuck in here?"

"Oh, three years or so now."

"Cool."

"Yeah, it's alright."

"Cool."

"You getting settled in there alright?"

"Yeah, good. George just went off to get me the confirms; he'll be back in a minute."

"Oh, you're on confirms. That's a drag."

"Yup. What're ya gonna do? Somebody's gotta do them."

"Yup. They sure do. You're Irish, hah?"

"Oh yeah, as Irish as Paddy's pig."

"Paddy's pig," he said, laughing. "That's a good one. I haven't heard that one before. I gotta remember that one for my friend Margaret. She's gonna love that one."

"Yeah, it's a good one, alright. Listen, Eric, I have a little problem here with my computer. I wonder if maybe I could trouble you for a second."

"Sure. No problem." Eric was out of his seat in a flash and running around to my cubicle.

"What's the problem?"

"I can't switch it on."

Eric laughed a hearty laugh. "You are a funny guy. I can't switch it on. Is it broken?" He reached in behind the computer and switched it on. "Look, it's working fine now."

"Ah, so it is. What do I do with it now?"

"What do you mean?"

"I mean I have no idea what to do, Eric. I lied my way in here."

"What?"

"I have no idea what I'm doing."

"You really didn't know how to switch on the computer, did you?"

"Not a clue. And I'm going to need somebody to help me through the first couple of days here if I'm going to survive this thing." I looked over his shoulder. George was on his way back with a huge stack of papers.

"You have no idea what to do?" Eric was grinning.

"None."

"You just lied your way in here?"

"I work construction, Eric. I need this job." George was back. He plonked a stack of papers, almost a foot deep, onto the desk next to my computer.

"So you've met our new guy here?" he said to Eric.

"Yeah, sure did."

"Well, if you have any questions Eric can answer them for you. I'm going out for a coffee."

"Thanks, George."

I assured Eric that if he could just show me how everything worked one time, I'd take it from there. This was more excitement than Eric had seen in the office in the three years he'd been working there. He was more than glad to be a part of it.

The work was mindless. By day three I had a routine going. I would spend the first half of the day sorting through all the confirmed stock purchases for the previous day's trading. I would dump almost the entire stack of paper into the garbage can and take a small handful of the confirms with me to our other office over on Madison Avenue after lunchtime, where I would spend a couple of hours filing them away. The Madison Avenue branch of the office was where all the stock purchases and trading actually took place. I would then spend the rest of the afternoon working as part of a team documenting and confirming all the new trades that had been made that day. It was here that I got to witness the drama of high-pressure trading firsthand. It was a cesspool of greed, manipulation, overinflated egos, backstabbing, and deceit, and that was just the cleaning ladies.

The last forty-five minutes of the trading day were the most fun to witness. The approach of the closing bell would send the traders into a frenzy. Men screaming at the tops of their lungs. I witnessed telephones being ripped out and flung across the room. Tables were overturned. Chairs were thrown against the wall. It's hard to believe, but all this behavior seemed perfectly normal after one day among the traders. It was just part of the job, an acceptable side effect of being responsible for the loss or gain of millions of dollars in an instant. The female traders had had all the soft edges rubbed off them. They bore the hard masculine features of a suit of armor. There was no room for sensitivity here. This was kill or be killed.

I sat at a computer in the corner of the room. There were ten of us at a long table. Five computers back to back. We were the Confirms Crew. Whatever trades were made, we documented them. It was mindless, repetitive work filling out the same onscreen form over and over again all day.

Within a week I was up to speed with the rest of the crew. Two weeks in and I was offered a full-time position with the bank. It was a decent package with benefits and bonuses. I turned it down. I felt like an imposter. I spent my days observing the behavior of the other workers. I soon realized there was no room for creative thought or originality in this environment. The traders were given some creative license to scream and shout and blow off steam. But that was it. The rest of us were expected to behave with the efficiency and the personality of a steel cog in the great machinery of the bank. I could wear an orange tie or different-colored socks if I wanted to get whacky.

The crew I worked with had the collective IQ of a hayseed. They never complained about having to sit there day after day, week after week, year after year. Nobody talked about their personal lives. They stared at their screens and drank coffee, and once in a while one of the girls would cry and apologize because she was having her period. They were excited for a moment when they realized I was Irish. They wanted to know all the usual bullshit: Did I like corned beef and cabbage? Had I ever seen a leprechaun? Was St. Patrick the patron saint of alcoholics?

My cell phone was vibrating in my pocket. It was Brigitte; I had to be in Westchester at the doctor's office within the next twenty-five minutes. A serving of my baby batter was required, like, ten minutes ago. I made some excuse at the office and drove like a lunatic up the West Side Highway, obsessing about the absurdity of my situation, the lines of that Talking Heads song ringing constantly in my ears.

> This is not my beautiful house . . .
> This is not my beautiful wife . . .
> My God! What have I done?

Maybe this was how normal people lived their lives. It certainly appeared normal. Maybe I wasn't normal. "Now, Colin, that's your disease talking. It wants you to believe you're not normal. It wants you to think you're different from everybody else, but you're not. You're a garden-variety drunk. That's all you are."

When I arrived in Westchester, Miss Moneypenny greeted me with a plastic cup. Gone was the romance. Not even a kiss hello.

"I need you to take this and fill it. Your wife's in with the doctor already."

"Fill it?"

"Do what you can. When you're done I'll take it in to the doctor."

The waiting room was full, as usual. That didn't bother me very much this time, but it didn't make me feel any easier, either. Just the previous night in bed I had begged my wife to stop this course of action. It just didn't seem right to me to have someone else involved in this process. This other guy was going to give my wife a baby. And she believed he could do it. Maybe they didn't need me at all. The whole thing just felt unnatural, clinical. Sex between us had become a mechanical operation. My

gut kept telling me that it was a dangerous game we were playing. The truth is that I just didn't want a baby. I was being
forced into it. I could have said no, and I did constantly, but in
the end I always gave in because it was going to cost me my
marriage. I'd already been divorced once. Another divorce might
kill my parents. Perhaps my apprehension was just a refusal to
grow up and accept responsibility. Brigitte didn't care to discuss
my dilemma: She wanted a baby and nothing and nobody was
going to stop her.

"What if I go against my gut on this and our baby is born
with a deformity?" I had asked her.

"That could happen anyway, under any circumstances."

"Yes, but if I feel this way about it now and then I go ahead
with this thing and then our baby's born with something wrong
with it I might be resentful about it for the rest of my life for not
sticking to my guns. Do you understand?"

"You're just being childish."

"That's not it. You don't understand."

"You can't tell me I can't have a baby. That would destroy
me. Is that what you want?"

"No, but there are two of us here. I'm going to have to live
with this for the rest of my life."

"You're almost thirty years old—"

"Yeah, and you're thirty-seven."

"You knew I was seven years older than you when we got
married. I don't have much time left here, Colin. It's now or
never. The longer we wait the worse it gets. Don't you care
about me? Don't you love me?"

I took my plastic cup to the bathroom to see if I couldn't
whip up a little miracle. Somebody had removed the magazine
with the nurse fantasy and replaced it with one of the more
popular glossy men's magazines. I was surprisingly upset over
this little turn of events. Had the nurse taken it away? Had

some other poor husband taken it as a keepsake of this special moment? Something to show his boy before he went off to college. I sat down and opened the glossy. I found an article about ostrich farming that caught my attention. I was still reading it about five minutes later when someone tried the door. It was time to get to work. I flipped through until I found a picture of a naked Uma Thurman taken on a beach somewhere.

Perhaps I was being too sore on this whole baby-making business. This wasn't such a bad way to spend an afternoon: alone in a bathroom in Westchester, masturbating to pictures of beautiful actresses while an attractive nurse waited nearby for my sperm.

I handed the cup to the secretary. She barely glanced in my direction as she reached for it and continued on with whatever conversation she was having on the phone. I was reduced to this. A baby-batter machine. I left the office feeling empty and weak. I reached my car in the parking lot and stared at the flat little nondescript building. It seemed a perfect representation of everything that was wrong with my life. It was bland, characterless, the kind of building you could pass by every day of your life and never even notice that it was there. My wife was in that building somewhere with her legs up in stirrups. I felt nauseous. Here we were in the same building for the purpose of making a baby and we didn't even get to see each other. The only man present at the conception of our child would be her doctor. I couldn't have a child like this. Maybe it was OK for other people, but not for me. I decided that I would never do this again, regardless of what happened to the marriage. Divorce couldn't be more miserable than this.

I drove home at over 110 miles an hour on the West Side Highway, weaving through traffic. By the time I reached my block I was shaking from the adrenaline. I was going to explode.

Something would have to give, and soon. I made myself a peanut butter and jelly sandwich and curled up on the couch with my dog, Molly.

When Brigitte got home she informed me that she wanted to adopt a baby.

"Fine," I said.

"You mean it."

"Does it matter if I mean it?"

"Great. I've started looking into it. I met a woman at the clinic today who gave me the address of this adoption agency on Park Avenue. They're supposed to be the best in the city."

"Sounds great."

"So where do you want to adopt from? She told me we should probably stay away from Russia right now, because there have been some real horror stories about the doctors passing off really sick babies as healthy. I was thinking maybe South America."

"Yeah, South America sounds brilliant."

"Great. So I've already called them, so we have an appointment next Friday at their office. You think maybe you can get out of work?"

"Sure."

"Oh, and Barbara and Ken are coming here for dinner tomorrow night."

"Who?"

"You remember, Barbara and Ken from Larchmont. We had dinner at their house a month ago."

"Oh God."

"Well, it's our turn to cook."

"Oh Jesus—"

"What? You and Ken seemed to get along well the last time you saw him. He works in a bank, too, remember."

"I remember."

"They're coming at eight thirty. I was thinking maybe we could make that chicken cacciatore that you like."

"Sounds wonderful."

"Are you OK?"

"Yeah, I'm just tired."

"I'm really excited about this adoption thing. I think this is going to be the answer for us."

"That's good. I think I'm going to go and write for a little bit."

"OK, well, I'm off to bed."

"Good night."

"Good night."

I grabbed a can of Coke and went to my office, where I had the Vicodin stashed. I popped a couple and switched on the computer. I had three doctors whom I saw regularly now. One in Larchmont, one in Bronxville, and one in Inwood. Whenever I needed a new stash of pills I would hit all three doctors on the same day, complain about my back pain, and voilà, each one of them would write me a prescription for thirty Vicodin or some form of hydrocodone with a refill. That's 180 pills in one fell swoop. I'd visit three different pharmacies within a couple of hours of each other and I'd have enough shit to keep me high every night for about a month. I was now a fully fledged pharmaceutical junkie.

Three or four Vicodin, I'd been told by an ex-junkie friend of mine, has the equivalent effect of a small dose of heroin. He warned me that any more than six of them in one mouthful might be enough to put me to sleep forever. But I didn't pop pills the way I drank. I could pace myself all night. I usually limited myself to about six or eight over the space of a night, and when I was really beginning to nod off I went to bed and slept it off.

I had stopped going to meetings completely by now. Sober people bored me half to death. Almost everything bored me half to death. I was sleepwalking through my life. I daydreamed of running away. Just disappearing from everybody. Maybe I'd start over again in South America or Spain. I'd change my name. Not even my own family would know how to find me. I could do it. I'd written two novels already. Both rejected by publishers. I'd stopped going to college before completing my degree. I'd stopped writing poetry. I'd stopped writing reviews for the Irish newspapers. I'd stopped living.

I had been in love with the idea of being a writer. I loved the romance of it. But it was time I faced it: I was a bore. I was a typical married guy with a nice house in the suburbs, a black Labrador, and a drug problem. I had to get used to the fact that this was my life. That this was how it would be until I died or through some freak accident my wife died. I know it sounds horrible, but yes, I did fantasize about her untimely demise. I'd appear appropriately heartbroken publicly, of course, and I would feel bad, but secretly a part of me would rejoice. I'd thank God for bailing me out. Rather than wait for divine intervention to change my life, I finally decided to do something about it myself. I quit my job.

For a couple of years now, I'd been spending most of my weekend mornings at the Annex Antique Fair at Twenty-sixth and Sixth, the largest street fair in the country. I went primarily to browse for used books, but it was also a great way to spend the morning alone. You just never knew what you might stumble upon in an old cardboard box shoved under a foldout table at seven in the morning.

The winter mornings were the best, cruising alone down the

West Side Highway. The brittle light on the Hudson, the shadowy curtain of gray rock they call the Palisades, drawn on a sleeping New Jersey. Manhattan a cool grid of blocks quiet as a library, a billion stacked stories banked for now under lock and key. And for an instant she was mine, not another car on the road, not another living soul in sight, the whole glistening mass like a ghost city I'd just happened upon, perched there, at the last stop on the edge of a vast plane.

The serious dealers were already there, of course, shuffling from stall to stall, scanning rows of books at lightning speed, scowling at anyone who entered their peripheral line of vision like a wild dog guarding a bone. It was like the literary version of Mad Max, where the only hope for survival was an original signed copy of *Ulysses*. They were a dangerous bunch, liable to stab you in the spine with a ballpoint pen over a dog-eared paperback copy of *Gravity's Rainbow*, but they'd gotten used to seeing me sniff around and I knew not to get too close.

After about an hour the initial burst of scavenging was over. If there was a signed copy of *The Grapes of Wrath* hidden in the bottom of a box anywhere within a four-block radius, it was gone. You could bank on that.

By eight o'clock the fever would subside and the second phase would begin. The same stalls were revisited. There was a nice hardcover copy of *A Moveable Feast* you'd noticed earlier. Not an original first, but it had a clean dust jacket. You didn't take it the first time around because the guy was asking about fifteen bucks more than you wanted to pay. But now you'd go back and if it was still there you'd take a closer look. You'd have more time now to haggle with the bastard. There'd be no pressure to beat the crowd.

By nine o'clock it was all over for the serious collector. The work was done. There was not a book left that you couldn't find in any decent used bookstore for a similar price. There were no exceptions to this rule. Ever. The collectors who roam the Annex are unbeatable. They have been prowling there for years. They can smell a rare book wedged at the bottom of a cardboard box in the back of a truck from about a half a city block. Early morning book collecting is not for the faint of heart. This is New York City we're talking about here, after all.

By nine I was usually back home, stretched out on the couch with Molly, trying to steal another hour or two of early morning weekend sleep. Brigitte would still be asleep or off to Sunday morning mass up on Riverdale Avenue. We were passing each other in our lives now like two clichés passing in the night.

After a couple of years of this I had amassed quite a collection of books. During the week I tried to hit as many thrift stores as possible. I was always on the hunt. It had become an obsession. I had maybe a couple thousand books stacked and boxed in my basement den. I needed a bookstore. It was the natural progression of my book disease. My new disease needed a home.

After I quit the bank, I started scouting around the neighborhood for a suitable location. It didn't take me long to find it. A small store on Mosholu Avenue just half a block from Broadway. I drove by a few times and sat across the street to think about it. I didn't know anything about the retail business. I'd never worked in a bookstore or a coffeehouse, but I'd been to plenty of them and it didn't look that difficult.

It was a Saturday evening. I scribbled down the number and came home to make the call.

When I came through the door I noticed the light blinking on my answering machine. I hit the button and headed for the kitchen to grab a can of soda from the refrigerator. I stopped, hearing my mother's voice.

"I just wanted to let you know that we're all OK. Everybody is accounted for, thank God. Well, I'll talk to you later. I'm sure we'll be up late, if you want to give us a call. Bye-bye. Love you."

My heart started to race. Whatever had happened, it was big enough that she wanted to warn me about it before I saw it. I knew the tone in my mother's voice spelled trouble. I picked up the phone receiver and the remote control for the television at the same time. I started scanning through the news channels as I dialed my home phone number in Ireland. And there it was on CNN. A massive car bomb had ripped through the small town of Omagh, fifty miles east of Belfast. Omagh was our local town. We lived fifteen miles away. That's where my family had done our shopping every weekend since I was a child. My mother picked up the phone on the second ring.

"Holy fuck," I said, dropping into the armchair, seeing the first images of the destruction up on the screen.

"You got my message, I take it," my mother said.

"Who's dead?"

"We don't know yet."

"How many?"

"A lot."

"How many's a lot?"

"It's hard to say—maybe thirty. There were a lot of people badly hurt, too."

"What the hell happened?"

"I don't know."

"I thought this shit was over."

"Somebody didn't think it was over."

"Where were you?"

"We were in Omagh doing the shopping. We heard that there was a bomb scare up the town and we left. We just got in the car and were headed out the Dublin Road and we saw the two Donnelly girls from up the road here lookin' for a ride home. Yer father pulled over to give them a lift and they had just opened the back door of the car to get in when it went off . . ." I could hear my mother take a deep breath and hold it.

"How far away were you?"

"We were very close, maybe a hundred yards or so."

"Jesus."

"It was horrible."

"Did you see it?"

"Your father turned the car around and went back over to see if maybe we could do something, and then when we got there he just turned the car and drove straight home. It was an awful mess, Colin. My God, what a mess—"

"Is he OK? You're probably still in shock."

"We'll be alright. You're cousin Roisin was right next to the car when it exploded."

"Is she alive?"

"Yes, she's fine. She was in here just a couple of minutes ago." My cousin Roisin is like a sister to me. She was basically raised in our house after her mother died when she was a child. "Her daddy took her to the hospital. She had a piece of shrapnel removed from her leg and they let her go on home."

"What do you mean, shrapnel?"

"It was a piece of metal from the car that exploded."

"She was that close?"

"It's a miracle she's alive at all. The people standing right next to her were blown away."

"Who was killed?"

"We don't know yet. It's too soon."

"Who hasn't come home?"

"We're not sure. You hear things, but nobody knows. It's too soon."

"Who?"

"There's a girl from Beragh, Avril Grimes, who's still missing."

"Avril. Avril Grimes who stayed in our house?"

"Aye, she was with her mother and her wee daughter shopping and nobody has heard from them since. It doesn't look good."

"Avril Grimes?"

"Aye. You remember Avril?" I did remember Avril. Her face flashed across my mind. She had been one of the first girls I had ever kissed. We had been boyfriend and girlfriend briefly when I was about fourteen years old. She had jet black hair and thick dark eyebrows and a smile that could melt snow off a shovel.

"She's seven months pregnant with twins, the poor girl."

"No."

"Everybody's still praying that she's got mixed up at the hospital, but . . ."

"Jesus Christ."

"Have you seen it on the news over there yet?"

"I'm watching it right now."

"I don't even know what to say—" I could hear my mother's voice cracking.

"Don't say anything," I said. "Try to get some rest. I'll call tomorrow and we'll talk then."

"Right. Away you go."

"Good night, Mum."

"Good night, Colin. Love you."

"I love you too."

Thirty-one people were killed in the Omagh bombing on the fifteenth of August, 1998. That's including Avril's mother, her eighteen-month-old daughter, and her unborn twins. Over three hundred others were seriously injured. After thirty years of war, a single event had finally changed the course of history. Things would never be the same again.

The following Monday I called the number posted in the window of the store and I arranged to meet the owner. I needed something to change direction in my life. I was going to open a used bookstore–coffee shop. I didn't know the first thing about the business, but I could figure it out as I went along. Sometimes too much information is a bad thing. I signed the lease.

I ripped the place apart and rebuilt it over the next couple of months. My buddy Bill, my new AA sponsor, came by to see the place. We had a cup of coffee and he hinted that he would like to be a part of something like this. We decided to become partners. I figured this way I would have somebody I could trust to help me run the place.

I built bookshelves and a bar, refinished the floors, painted the place, fixed some new lighting, put in a bunch of chairs and tables. I called the coffee and soda companies to come in and hook me up with refrigerators and coffee machines. I put a cash register on the counter and stuck an advertisement in the *Riverdale Press* announcing our grand opening. I was all set to go.

I was working one Saturday evening, cleaning the inside of the big front window of the store. The evening had turned gray. People held their faces to the breeze. Leaves tumbled along down the avenue toward Van Cortlandt Park. Across the street a girl stepped out the front door of a house and walked down the short path toward the front gate. I froze. She closed the gate behind her and sailed across the avenue, her long, honey brown hair rising behind her in the wind. She was wearing a long black coat with a white scarf tucked in around her neck, and before she reached the other side of the street I knew I had fallen in love with her.

She disappeared into the convenience store next door and I waited anxiously for her to reappear and pass by my window. I'd smile and wave. She would stop and smile back. We'd live happily ever after.

She came out of the store a few minutes later and paused to light a cigarette. I casually buffed the window with a dry rag as she passed by just a few feet from my face. She didn't look American. She had high cheekbones and a graceful European air about her. She didn't flinch as she passed by. She just sailed on down the street until I lost sight of her

I finished cleaning up for the evening and went home carrying a heavy sadness. The tectonic plates of my heart had shifted ever so slightly, setting in motion a minute earthquake that would eventually rip my heart from top to bottom like a wet bag.

Molly followed me downstairs to my lair and watched me quietly as I put an old Miles Davis album on the deck and sat down at my computer to work on the play I had started writing about my miserable life. I called it *Father Who*. I had stopped popping Vicodin now completely. It had quite simply stopped making me feel better. The couple in the play I was writing were in trouble; she wanted a child, he didn't. He was having an affair. I stared at the screen and rubbed my face in frustration. It was almost finished. I just couldn't find the ending. How was it going to end?

The Guitar and Pen coffee shop/used bookstore opened on a Friday evening in the late fall. All our friends came and some strangers stopped by. For eight hours I made coffee and small talk and posed for photographs and quietly wondered what the hell I had gone and started now. The place was a hit. Everybody loved it. Bill talked to some friends of his who had a band and they agreed to come by once a week and put on a show.

My friend the poet Elizabeth Bassford organized a reading series for children on Saturday mornings. A local artist, Caroline Di Shaw, came by and we hung our first art exhibition of her work. We started booking famous poets and novelists to read on Tuesday nights. The *Daily News* came by with a photographer and they ran a full-page article on the place under the headline, CAFÉ SET TO GET BORO OUT OF ITS BOOKBIND. I had created a monster.

About a month after I opened the place, I saw her again. I was by myself in the café. It was a bitterly cold night in the Bronx. There wasn't a sinner in the place but myself. I was working on an ending for my play and listening to Al Green when she came through the door. She was wearing the same black coat and the same white wool scarf. She was just as beautiful as she had been when I had seen her before. She walked past me with a smile so delicate that it only happened beneath the surface of her skin. A subtle shift in the tissue that lay beneath that porcelain veil. I understood immediately that this moment had been written somewhere, the way things sometimes are. I quite simply didn't stand a chance.

I got up and moved around behind the counter so that she would know that I worked there. She unbuttoned her coat and laid it over the back of a chair and then put the scarf on top. She was wearing a soft pink sweater and I had to divert my gaze so as not to scare her into running for the street. She sat at a table a few feet away from the counter with her back to me and took out a notebook from the black bag that she carried and began to write. She had not spoken a word.

I watched her for a few minutes as she continued. She could have been alone in her bedroom for all the attention she gave to her current surroundings. Maybe she expected table service. I armed myself with a pen and a notebook and made my way over to her table to take her order. I was terrified and the terror sent sparks of excitement through my whole body. The orangutan was getting restless.

"Hi," I said.

"Hi," she said as she looked up from her notebook and gave me a smile as sad as a dead bird. I sat down at the table across from her.

"My name's Colin," I said.

"I'm Oksana."

"Hi, Oksana."

"Hi, Colin."

"I've seen you before."

"I live across the street."

"I saw you come out of that house."

"That's where I live."

"That's good—that you don't have too far to go—that it's just across the street."

"It's lucky for me. I love bookstores and coffee shops."

"You do?"

"I could live in here."

"Me too. I've thought of putting a mattress down in the back here so I can just sleep in here at night."

"I'd love that," she said.

I was just picturing the two of us curled up on a mattress down on the floor amid all the old books when the door opened and Brigitte walked in. She stood in the half-opened door and stared at me for an instant. I stared back. I must have appeared startled. I was startled. Her expression told me that I may as well have been curled up on a mattress with Oksana. In the six years we had been together there had never been an awkward moment between us involving another party. A moment like this. A moment where it was so blatantly obvious that something had occurred. Even though nothing had occurred. It had occurred.

"Could I speak to you outside for a moment?" she said.

"Sure." I stood up. "Excuse me for a moment," I said to Oksana, who never even glanced in the direction of the door but instead returned to her notebook and her writing.

"Sure," she said.

Outside I tried to take Brigitte in my arms, but she froze against me.

"What was that in there?" she said.

"What?"

"Who is that girl?"

"She's just some customer. Her name's Oksana. She just walked in two seconds before you arrived. She lives right across the street."

"What were you talking about?"

"What do you mean, what were we talking about? She just came in. I was introducing myself. She's a customer. Customers come in and out all day. I talk to a hundred different people every day."

"I don't like this."

"What do you mean, you don't like it? It's a coffee shop. People come here to talk and hang out. It's the nature of the business."

"I don't like it."

"There's nothing to worry about. Relax. Are you just on your way home?"

"Yes. I just thought I'd stop by and say hello."

"Good. I'm glad you did. Listen, I'll close early. Just as soon as I get her out of here. It's dead tonight anyway. OK?"

"OK. Don't be too late."

I had been caught red-handed. Caught with my pants down around my ankles. This was the way it was supposed to go down. Nothing was going to stop it. I went back inside and checked the coffeepots, being careful to steer clear of Oksana in case Brigitte was watching from the dark side of the street.

"Would you like a cup of hot chocolate?" I asked her.

"That sounds great," she said without lifting her head to look around at me. She knew what had happened. Women know these things. Whatever had just happened had also happened between Brigitte and Oksana. I made her a cup of hot chocolate and brought it to her table. We were still alone. Of course there would not be another customer tonight. I sat down again across from her.

"Was that your wife?" she asked, looking up from her notebook with an expression that said she understood what had happened.

"Yes. That was my wife."

"Is she OK?"

"Yes, she's fine."

"She seemed upset."

"I suppose she was a little bit."

"Because of me?"

"Something like that."

"It's really warm in here," she said, and she crossed her arms, pinching the bottom of her pink sweater on opposite sides and pulling it slowly off over her head. Her small white T-shirt rode up her belly just beneath her breasts before she adjusted it and placed the sweater next to her scarf. I could picture the fights, the tears, the accusations, the divorce papers, Brigitte's parents flying in from Georgia to confront me. I was going to have to find an apartment. A lot of people were going to be very upset.

"So what do you do?" I asked, resigning myself to the fact that there was no way this was going to stop, because I didn't want it to stop. I wanted it to go on. I needed this to go on.

"I'm still in school," she said.

"College?" I asked hopefully.

"High school," she said.

"I see. Do you mind me asking how old you are?"

"Almost eighteen."

"You're seventeen."

"I'll be eighteen soon."

I got up casually and placed my chair back under the table. "Well, if you need anything else, just let me know. I'll let you get back to your writing."

She didn't say anything. She sighed and gave me a disappointed smirk. I gave her one back.

Over the next couple of weeks she came back in almost every day. She never asked for anything. She'd write in her notebook and wait for me to carry her hot chocolate to her table. On the couple of occasions I found myself alone with her again, I discovered that she'd been born in Russia. She'd moved to the States with her parents when she was twelve years old. Both her parents worked for the U.N. She was an only child. She loved to read and said she would write a book one day when she was ready. She had a boyfriend. A local guy. Another Russian. A reckless blond boy with a reputation, as handsome a young man as I have ever seen in my entire life. He stopped by to meet with her once or twice in the café and she ignored him and smiled at me over his shoulder. He drank coffee and stared at her with the reverence of a young monk.

I went home at night and poured my thoughts of her into my diary. I did not dare talk about this to anyone. She was just a girl. Twenty years my wife's junior. She was a high school student. She had a boyfriend who liked to think he was dangerous, which can be just as dangerous as the real thing. I would just have to forget about her. There was no possible way this could happen. But something had happened. Something had moved within me. Something that had been close to death had stirred. Something that I had almost forgotten lay within me. The beast was stirring. I thought about what William had asked me the last time I'd been to see him. "What is it that you want for yourself?" What did I really want for myself?

Oksana brought her parents by the café to hear the Romanian poet Nina Cassian read one Tuesday night. They were stunningly handsome as a couple. It was easy to see where Oksana got her looks. They stayed around after the reading to talk to the poet. I took out a bottle of Stoli that I kept under the counter and poured them a few shots. Nina lifted the candle from the table and held it up to illuminate her face and joked with them about its triangular shape. Oksana sat next to me and held her leg firmly against mine under the table. Nina said something that made Oksana blush. I had been distracted for a moment and had missed it completely.

"I'm sorry, I missed that," I said, noting Oksana's discomfort. Her mother laughed and her father egged her on to tell me.

"What did she say?" I asked. Nina had a mischievous grin as she waited for Oksana's answer.

"She said . . . she thinks we're together." Her father laughed. Nina smiled and shook her head.

"That's not what she said, Oksana," her mother scolded. "She said, 'You two make a beautiful couple.' And she wanted to know how long you've been in love."

Nina was really smiling now. She was kind enough to move things along quickly once she had achieved her mischief. She lifted her shot glass in the air with her long bony fingers and toasted the table in Russian.

Eight years without a drink and I could still taste that vodka as it ran down her throat.

Bill was there that night, watching me from across the room. After everybody had left, we locked up and spent a little while cleaning the place together. Then we sat for a while in the empty café, drinking tea. We had known each other for a few years now. He knew my wife. They had become friends. He would take her out to dinner occasionally if I was working. He was also still my sponsor. He had noticed what was going on with Oksana. He'd commented on it once or twice over the past few weeks but only in passing. Subtle hints that he was aware of how tricky the situation was becoming. He wanted to talk to me about it.

"It's tricky," I told him.

"What's tricky about it?"

"You know. It's tricky."

"You're married, Colin. You guys are in the process of adopting a baby."

"I know. I'm just miserable. You know that. I never wanted a baby. She's obsessed with the idea."

"What are you going to do about it?"

"It's just not that simple. On one hand I feel like she has the right to have this child. On the other, I just don't want a baby and I hate her for it."

"What about this other girl?"

"What about her?"

"Have you done anything there yet?"

"No. Are you crazy?"

"But you're thinking about it."

"It's hard not to."

"Maybe you should ask her to stop coming in here. I'll do it if you like."

"Can I trust you with a secret?"

"You have to ask that at this point?"

"Yeah."

"What is it?"

"I've fallen in love with her."

"Are you sure?"

"I'm positive."

"You're sure you're not just trying to sabotage everything here. You've got all this stuff going for you right now. This could cause a lot of trouble. She's very young. People are going to be pissed off."

"I haven't decided to do anything right now. It's just wrecking my head. I can't think straight. I only think of her. I know it seems like I just want to run away from my life, but that's just it, I do want to run away from my life. That's exactly what I want to do."

"Brigitte's a great girl . . ."

"Fuck . . . of course she's a great girl. That what's so screwed up about the whole thing. You take her if she's such a great girl. You guys would be great together."

"What are you gonna do?"

"I don't know. I haven't decided yet. But something's gonna happen; I know that, and it's too late for someone not to get hurt. People are going to be hurt. That's just the way it's happening."

"Are you gonna drink?"

"Jesus, do I look like I'm gonna drink?"

"Maybe. I don't know. I'm still your sponsor. I'm just saying maybe you should think about that."

"I'm not going to drink. I have enough problems on my plate."

"That's good. So no matter what happens, everything will be OK."

"Right."

"She is cute."

"Yeah, she sure is," I said.

"She have any friends for me?"

"Right. We'll go on a double date. Thanks, Bill."

"Hey, what are friends for?"

• • •

Owning a café-bookstore had always seemed like such a romantic idea to me. I had envisioned dust motes drifting lightly in the sun rays, the aromatic blend of fresh coffee and old books, a little Dvořák on the stereo, a few seasoned bibliophiles lounging around, quietly immersed in their own poetic ecstasies. The reality was a little less utopian.

After a month I am in a state of exhaustion. We open at seven thirty in the morning and we don't close until eleven on weeknights, two at the weekends. Either Bill or I would be there at any given time of the day. The place isn't making enough money to hire extra help. So basically I am working more than sixty hours a week in the store for next to nothing. Then, on my time off I have to search for more books to keep the shelves stocked with fresh finds. Seven days a week, every week. It never lets up. Someone has to pick up the fresh bagels and the muffins. There's a problem with the track lighting, somebody's flushed their T-shirt down the toilet again and flooded the bathroom, an old woman has crapped in her pants and destroyed one of the seats. The police are called because the music is too loud. I have to take my car to the garage again, the dog to the vet. My wife reads my journal and is waiting for me when I come home from work with it opened to the page where I say that I have fallen helplessly in love with a teenager. The same teenager she's had her suspicions about all along. I try to deny it, but she informs me that it's too late, my good buddy Bill, my business partner, my AA sponsor, has already confirmed that it's true. I take a seat and try to comprehend the magnitude of his deceit.

I decide to take this opportunity to I tell her how I really feel. I tell her that I'm unhappy in the marriage and that I want a divorce. She hopes I rot in hell. So I move to the couch in the basement.

Within a week Bill and I have parted company. He has apologized for his indiscretion but I can't look at him anymore without wanting to rip out his throat. He comes by when I'm not there and takes his few personal items, then has me served with papers seeking half the business. I tear up the papers and throw them in the trash can. I have never seen him or spoken to him since.

The adoption agency has called; they have a child for us in South America. She's almost two years old. We are to fly immediately to meet her and take her back to the States. Brigitte tells me that this is the last thing she wants me to do for her. She cannot do it alone. The agency wouldn't allow it. She needs a husband. I agree to go along.

We agree that when I come back I will find an apartment somewhere nearby and we will work something out so that we can take care of the child together.

Three days before we fly to Ecuador I find out that Brigitte has emptied my bank accounts, sold the stocks I had purchased, and maxed the credit cards that were in my name. I'm suddenly about forty thousand dollars in the hole. I am completely broke. I have to call Tony to borrow money for gas. She won't lend me twenty dollars of my own money. My friend who's a lawyer begs me not to go through with the adoption process. He tells me that I'll lose everything. I know he's right, but I feel guilty about falling in love with someone else, so I go along as a form of penance.

My friend steps in and takes care of the business while I'm gone. The poet Rick Pernod and I decide to become business partners and make a fresh go of it at the café.

I tell Oksana that I am in love with her, and she tells me she will be waiting for me when I return from Ecuador.

Brigitte and I travel to Ecuador. My daughter is a beautiful, healthy two-year-old, and I cry the moment I take her in my arms. I had never expected to fall in love with her instantaneously. She is the most beautiful child I have ever seen in my entire life. I look into her eyes and I know her and she knows me.

I return from Ecuador a few days early, as agreed, to set up my own apartment and prepare for my daughter's return.

Oksana and Rick are waiting for me at the airport. I am an emotional basket case.

I borrow money from Tony and rent a one-bedroom apartment in Riverdale, up on the Parkway. I buy a new bed and move a few personal items out of the house.

Brigitte returns from Ecuador with our daughter. She refuses to let me see her, just as my lawyer had predicted. She hires an expensive lawyer of her own and announces she wants full custody. After a brief struggle and the advice of two other attorneys, I relent. I give her everything. The house, the money, Molly, and our daughter. She moves away and I have not seen or heard from her since.

I have an apartment in Riverdale that I can't afford. I have a ten-year-old car in need of repair. I'm completely broke. My credit is destroyed. The coffee shop is barely paying its own bills.

I close the café on a Friday night after I have signed the divorce papers. I lock the doors. Oksana has gone out for the night with some friends of hers. I am alone. I turn down the lights and take out a bottle of absinthe someone sent Rick and me as a gift from Prague. It's the real deal. The illegal stuff with the wormwood. We were saving it for special customers.

I pour a small glass of it. I dip a spoonful of sugar into it, remove it again and then light the absinthe-soaked sugar. It burns with a blue-green flame. I haven't tasted alcohol in eight years. I will have one drink just to see what it tastes like. I want to drink again. I don't want to be a drunk. I've just decided that I'm going to have a few drinks every once in a while. I deserve it after all I've been through. The flame is hypnotic. As it dances I picture van Gogh in Arles, Joyce in Paris, Hemingway in Spain. I was meant to drink. Why should I deny myself this right? I was born to drink. I drop the spoon into the glass and stir. I take it in my fist and smell its sharp menthol fumes. I lift the glass and my arm almost doesn't want to bend. I force it. It hits my lips and I don't stop until the glass is empty. My eyes water. I set the glass down and brace myself. My throat burns. A hot flame runs all the way to my gut. I'm still alive. That tasted good. I think I'll have one more. Just one. After three I decide I'd better just take the bottle home with me. I don't want to get drunk and then have to drive home. I take the scenic route home through Fieldston. There's something familiar about myself that I can't quite put my finger on, but I like it. I go home and finish the entire bottle. I'm thirty-one years old. I'm broke. I'm divorced for the second time. I have a teenage girlfriend. I'm drinking again.

IT'S
DRINKING
AGAIN

SEE, I'm not an alcoholic. I just drank a bottle of absinthe and I'm fine. You people are crazy. Alcoholic! Ha. Jesus, it's nice to be drinking again. I'm Irish; I'm a writer; who the fuck did I think I was kidding? So I was young and a little confused. Quitting drinking at the age of twenty-three! I can't believe I have denied myself this pleasure for eight whole years. Never again! I will never put myself through the misery of being sober ever again. Sober life sucks ass. It's no wonder all my cousins stopped inviting me to their little parties. What a bore I was. And those muscle cramps in my gut, gone. Gone. They were stress-related. I was all bunched up. I was a tightwad miserable fuck. All I needed was a good drink to relax. My God, I feel like an idiot. How? How could I have been so stupid? AA! Jesus. What a bunch of dry old farts. What a miserable, despicable collection of rejects. What a sad, pathetic little family of losers. What they need is a good drink. Every last one of them. I cannot believe I associated myself with those people for eight whole years. My family must have thought I'd lost my mind. I can't wait to have a few drinks with the lads again. Or a nice bottle of beer with the old man next time I'm home. Jesus, I can't wait. Drink like a grown-up. You know what? I'm glad I went to AA. I'm glad I went through a couple of therapists. It was not a complete waste. At least now I know myself. I will always be able to monitor my own drinking. If my drinking begins to cause problems, I'll check myself. I just have to keep an eye on it. If it gets out of hand, if I find myself crossing any lines, I'll just pull it together, knock it on the head for a week or two. God knows that shouldn't be a problem. I didn't drink for eight years. A week or two is a joke. If I watch it, if I'm careful, I'll be able to enjoy this luxury for the rest of my life. I am so damned happy I could cry. Thank you, God, for giving me this beautiful opportunity to drink again. I promise you I will continue to pray. I will keep the twelve steps in mind and continue to live a good, responsible life. All I have to do is keep my drinking under control. It's that simple.

TWO WEEKS LATER

It was one in the morning on a hot Friday night. I was sitting in the dark by the open window, watching the traffic roll by on the Henry Hudson Parkway. There's something about the sound of passing traffic that normally soothes me, but it just wasn't working on this particular night. Nothing was working. I'd finished the two bottles of wine and started in on the vodka. Oksana was gone. We'd had one of those boozed-up fights the previous night that makes *Who's Afraid of Virginia Woolf?* look like a children's fairy tale. She had stormed out, saying she was going back to live at home with her parents. Again. I was glad she was gone. I needed time to think. Everything was happening so fast I could barely keep up with it all. I was just out of a six-year marriage. My café-bookstore was closing. I was broke and back working construction. I needed a smoke. A nice fat joint would sort me right out. That had always worked before. I'd just go get myself a nice little dime bag of weed. Just enough to take the edge off. I'd come home, turn the lights down, listen to some Floyd. Chill the fuck out. Just like the old days. I'd just have another little glass of vodka for the road. God, it was good to be drinking again.

I took a ride in my old Honda Civic to White Plains Road. The same area where I'd been beaten and left for dead ten years before. It was time to give it another shot. Surely it was more civilized now.

I spotted a few guys hanging out near the old street corner. They looked cool. I was good at this. I have a real feel for people. I can sense danger a mile away. One of the guys, a young black kid, gave me the nod. I nodded back. I was in business. He flipped his head left to right a couple of times, checking for cops, and waved me onto the side street. I made the turn and pulled in at a hydrant. I left the car running and stepped out to greet him as he walked toward me.

I leaned against the front fender and folded my arms nonchalantly. I wanted him to know that I was cool, that we were the same, he and I. We were both cut from the same cloth. I'd done a little dealing myself back in the day, in London. I knew the scene: a lot of posturing, head-nodding, grunting, tough-guy shit. I could almost taste the weed already. Eight years without a smoke. This was going to be great. The kid was moving toward me, crossing the street at a brisk pace. And now that I could see him up close, he looked a little crazed. Maybe I'd misjudged this motherfucker. I'd had a lot to drink. It was too late anyway. I was just going to have to roll with it and hope for the best. Maybe I shouldn't have pulled onto this side street. Maybe I shouldn't have gotten out of my car. Maybe I shouldn't have left my apartment. Maybe . . . He had a knife in his hand. He must have pulled it from his waistband. I definitely didn't see that coming. Fuck.

"Give me your wallet, muthafucka." He had stopped about an arm's length away and he held the knife toward me. It was a big knife. Shiny. "Give me your muthafuckin' wallet, asshole."

"Fuck you," my mouth said.

"What d'you say to me, mutherfucker? You wanna die? Give me the muthafuckin' wallet."

"Go fuck yourself." There it was again. That mouth of mine sure did have a life of its own. He swiped the knife across my middle. I managed to pull back just a fraction without making a big to-do about it. He'd missed. Maybe he meant to miss.

"Give me the wallet, man," he continued. He looked a little perplexed now, as if this was just way too much work. He was obviously used to a little more cooperation than this. "You want to die?" he said.

"You're not getting my fucking wallet, asshole," my mouth said with great confidence. He swiped again. This time he was pissed. He slashed the knife across my throat in a wild swing.

"Give me the wallet!" he shouted. "You want to die here?" I casually reached my left hand to my neck and rubbed my fingers across my throat. I held my hand up to my face and looked at the thin streak of blood across my fingers. He'd cut me alright, but barely. It was only a nick across my Adam's apple. No big deal. He really was pushing it, this kid.

"OK. I'll tell you what I'm going to do," I said, pausing to collect myself. It was time for some diplomacy here. This was beginning to get serious. I was going to have to calm down and negotiate. Treat him like a businessman. That's it. Give the guy a little respect. They love a little negotiation, these guys. They want to feel like they're being heard. That's cool. I could roll with that. "I'm going to take my wallet out and I'm going to hand you the cash. But I keep the wallet—" Slash. There he was with that knife again. This time he connected. I lifted my right arm and sure enough there was a huge gash running across my arm between my elbow and my hand. It was wide open. I could see a white wall of flesh. It was deep. This kid was a tough negotiator, no doubt about it. I actually laughed a little. He'd really taken me by surprise with that one. It was time to wrap this thing up before things got out of hand.

"OK," I said, holding my arm up so that he could get a good look at the cut. "If you put that knife near me one more time, I'm going to take it off you and shove it up your fucking ass."

"Are you fuckin' crazy, man . . ."

"I'm going to take my wallet out and give you the cash," I said, reaching for my wallet. "I'm going to give you the cash and I'm going to keep the wallet." I had the wallet out. I opened it and he waited, shifting nervously from foot to foot while I removed the cash. There was maybe two hundred dollars in there. I handed it to him. "Now go fuck yourself, asshole."

He grabbed the cash from my hand and ran off up the side street. When he was about twenty feet away he turned and shouted, "You're fuckin' crazy, man. You need fuckin' help."

"Fuck you, tough guy," I shouted after him. It was then that I noticed that a few guys had gathered across the street. They made their way toward me. I was in no hurry to go anywhere at this point. I put my wallet back in my pocket as they gathered around. There were maybe four or five of them. Young black kids.

"He cut you, man?" one of them asked.

I held up my arm so that they could see.

"Fuck, man," he said, taking a good look at it. "He fucked you up pretty good, huh?"

"Yeah, he's a real tough guy. He a friend of yours?"

"Naw, man," one of the other kids said. "We don't know that guy." They were all huddled around, inspecting my arm. It did look pretty bad. I felt alright about it somehow. It didn't hurt too badly.

"Any of you guys got a smoke I could bum?" I asked. A

couple of them dug into their pockets. One of them handed me a smoke, another held out a light for me. "Well, guys, it's been real, but I gotta get myself to a hospital."

I got back in the Honda and searched around until I found a plastic bag on the passenger-side floor and placed it behind the stick shift between the two seats to catch the blood from my arm. The guys gathered around the car and watched me as I placed it just right. "This muthafucka's crazy," one of the kids said, laughing.

I was going to have to find a new spot for weed, I decided. White Plains Road was now officially off-limits.

At the hospital I gave them a false name and told the doctor I'd cut myself cooking a chicken. He eyed me with a look of tired skepticism, jotted something on his clipboard, and sauntered off out of the room, scratching his head without another word, leaving the nurse to patch me up. Apparently he'd heard that one before. He didn't want to hear the truth any more than I wanted to tell it. I'd had enough fun for one night without having to deal with the cops as well.

Two hours and fifteen stitches later I was back home on my couch with a large tumbler of vodka. The sun was coming up as I finally hit bed. I had to drink half the bottle to put me to sleep. The birds were already chirping in the trees outside my window. "You're an asshole," they were singing cheerfully. "You're a big fat waste of space," another one squawked. I got up and closed the curtains on them, fuckin' birds. What the fuck did they know? Goddamned pain-in-the-ass chirping motherfuckers. Go bug somebody else. Tomorrow was going to be a long day.

When I showed Oksana the stitched gash on my arm the next day, she slapped my face and burst into tears. I guess I deserved it. The blood had caked and blackened around the stitches, making it look a lot worse than it was. I told her an edited version of the story, minimizing my role in the whole scenario as much as possible. I told her that the guy had grabbed my arm through the open window and cut me when I tried to hand him my cash. It didn't help things much.

I poured us a couple of large glasses of red wine and promised her nothing like that would ever happen again. That did the trick. I was just going to have to be more careful from now on.

I was glad that something so violent had happened so soon. It had really opened my eyes to the dangers involved in drinking again. I could now see clearly where I had crossed the line. I should never have gotten into the car in the first place. I should have just gone to bed. It was a stupid mistake, but there was no point in getting my pants in a bunch about it.

It just wouldn't happen again. I was sure of it. I had to be careful. I had to keep this beautiful gift of drinking in my life. There was no way I was going back to those goddamned church basement meetings. No siree. I was done with that chapter, thank you very much.

Alcoholics Anonymous! Ha. Who could have ever dreamed up such an outfit? An American, of course. Bill W. What a wanker. Typical: an armchair philosopher; a lazy, good-for-nothing couch bum who couldn't do it by himself. He couldn't just tighten up a wee bit. Pull up his bootstraps and get on with his life like an Irishman. He couldn't just cut back a bit when things got out of hand with his drinking. No, no, of course not. That would take effort, self-control, discipline. It might mean work. God forbid. Talk about your stereotypical Yank. If the work was in the bed they'd sleep on the floor. Work? Not on your nelly. Not in this country. But if you'd like to sit down and have a chat about it, well, then, that was a different thing entirely. They'd be lined up around the block for that alright, in deck chairs, of course, with the portable TV and a cooler of refreshments, just in case. Oh, no, old Bill couldn't just stop;

instead he had to dream up some little egomaniacal, cocka-
mamie cult to absolve himself of all his drinking sins and spoil it
for everybody else. Well, fuck you, Bill W. Why couldn't you
have kept your big yapper shut? I will never, I repeat: never, as-
sociate myself with that bunch of brainwashed buffoons ever
again. Not so long as there's a breath in my body. My poor family. I can't imagine the embarrassment I must have caused them.
"Oh, our boy Colin's had to get help with his drinking. He's
an alcoholic." The shame. What utter humiliation. My God.
Brainwashed. That's what I was. Brainwashed. There was no
other logical explanation. Keep coming back. It works if you
work it. Keep it simple, stupid. Oh, yeah, well I've got a slogan
for you pal. Go fuck yourself. Boy, was it good to be drinking
again.

Things were good between Oksana and me again in no time.
She liked the idea that I had been stabbed, that I had a scar. It
was her scar. She owned it the way she owned everything about
me. I was hers and she was mine.

I was working construction again, but it was different from
before. I was a finish carpenter now. I was moving up in the
work chain. The work was cleaner and the cash was much better. I was working with a crew of guys installing baseboard and
door trim on a job up in Westchester. We had about four hundred apartments to do. It was easy work once you got the hang
of it. We worked in crews of two. One guy did the measuring
and nailing and the other took care of the cuts. We now had laborers to handle all of the rough stuff. My days of lugging
sheets of plywood and floor-sanding machines up and down
flights of stairs were over. I left work in the evening as clean as

the moment I walked through the door that morning. Now, this was the life.

On Friday evenings the tool belts were discarded and the gang box was bolted shut a good half hour early. Once we had those checks in our hands we were history. Irish lads working in every corner of the city were on the move and their destination was Woodlawn. It was a race straight to the Tara Hill Bar on Katonah Avenue to cash those checks. By five o'clock the place would be jumping, AC/DC on the jukebox, a line of quarters backed up on the pool table, a cold beer in every fist, the occasional group of cheeky-faced Irish American girls stopping by to flirt with the boys. The lads still in their work clothes, dusty from the day, some tanned from a day's sweat in the sun, tying one on before we all went our separate ways for the weekend. I was back. No, I wasn't back; I had never been here before. It had never been this good. I was no longer a newbie, fresh-faced and green off the boat. I had survived in this town for twelve years now, while others had chickened out, gone home, or gone mad. That was an accomplishment in itself. This was living. Beer had never tasted so good as it did on those evenings. We had earned it. We had suffered through the hangovers early in the week and managed to bash out another five days' work. We were the men. You couldn't take it away from us. We deserved this. For a fleeting crystallized moment, as those first few crisp beers rushed to our heads, we were the kings of Katonah Avenue.

I would usually stay for only about five or six bottles before I said my good-byes. I lived in Riverdale, another fifteen-minute drive away. I had to be careful. I couldn't afford to get caught drunk driving. I needed my transportation for work. I'd heard enough horror stories over the years that I did go to meetings to know that drunk driving was something I would never do.

On my way home I would stop at the liquor store. Oksana

was too young to go to a bar, so I would stock up enough booze and movie rentals to keep us going for the weekend and we'd just hole up for two days until it was time for me to go back to work. A half-gallon of good vodka, one decent bottle of red wine, two magnums of cheaper wine, and a twelve-pack of beer for Sunday to taper off. Who had it better than me? Nobody.

I got a letter in the mail about that time from a New York journal called *Rattapallax*. They wanted to publish one of my short stories. I'd written it just after I'd started drinking again, a response to the Omagh bombing. Rick Pernod had edited the story for me and in the process had taught me a few valuable lessons about the importance of clarity in my work. He'd made only a few suggestions, but those small changes had transformed the story into a fairly tight piece. I'd always been careless in this regard. Every time I'd submitted something before, I'd sent off the rough draft, convinced that whoever was lucky enough to receive my masterpiece would be on the phone in a flash with a book offer and a fat check. Strangely, that had never happened.

I called the editor of the journal and he told me in a voice as mean as a rusty bucket of nails that I should stop by to see him. The editor's name was George Dickerson. Dickerson was not only a poet and editor, but he was also an actor, best known for his role as the detective in the David Lynch movie *Blue Velvet*. I told him I would be there within the hour. I was more than a little keen to hear what he had to say.

The man who opened the door of his fifth-floor walkup an hour later looked like something that had been peeled off the blacktop in the parking lot of a truck stop outside of Nevada. A mottled strip of parchment, infused with the tire tracks of an unforgiving life, pockmarks and windburn, oil stains and all. I could not have dreamed of a more suitable candidate to publish my first short story. I wanted to take him in my arms and hug the life out of the old bastard, but under the circumstances I thought it would be best to resist the temptation.

The apartment might best be described as a den, the den of some curious word-foraging animal. It was a chaotic explosion of paper. There were books and stacks of paper covering every square inch of the place. Sheaves of paper and dusty folders spilled out of every crevice. There wasn't a square inch of the floor still visible. George made no attempt to excuse the carnage or clear a seat for me. He quite simply slumped into it, and with a nod of his head invited me to do the same.

"So you're the new Irish writer, huh?" he said as he leaned over and miraculously located, among the madness, the very file that contained my story. I was tempted to suggest that he spray paint it bright orange so that it would be next to impossible to lose in here, but it seemed George understood this chaos better than I was giving him credit for.

"Yeah, that would be me."

"From the North by the sounds of this story," he said, flipping through the first few pages. The story was called "Bang." It is set in the area where I grew up in County Tyrone and narrated in the voice of an elderly farmer. It had been the easiest short story I had ever written; I had bashed it out in two sittings. The voice of the farmer spoke to me and I just put his words on the page. It was that simple. It was an experience that taught me to get out of my own way and let the writing happen. All my previous efforts and struggles with my egotistical sense of how things should sound had availed me nothing. I wasn't that important, it seemed, in the grand scheme of things.

"I'm from a place called Altamuskin," I told him. "That's where the story is set. All those events were part of my own experience of growing up there."

"Some childhood. You ever think of writing a book about it?"

"I've thought about it."

"By the looks of this story there's probably enough material there for a couple of books."

"I want to make sure I can really write before I tackle that stuff. Writing about home is tricky business."

"You'll get there."

Then he started in about his own stuff. He was working on a book of poetry. He was reaching for another folder to show me something he was working on. That's where he lost me. We're a selfish breed of creature, writers are. I could have yapped away all day when it was my own writing we were talking about, but the minute he mentioned his stuff I was out the door. I thanked him for the honor of being published in his journal and I was gone.

About a month later, I walked into a magazine store between Seventy-first and Seventy-second on Broadway, and there on the shelf next to *Poetry* and the *Paris Review* was the third edition of *Rattapallax*. I was tempted to announce my good fortune to the other folks in the store browsing through the magazines, but I restrained myself. A gentleman in a tweed jacket and the tussled hair of an English professor lifted a copy and thumbed through it right next to me. Then he returned it to the shelf and bought the *Antioch Review* instead. There were three copies left on the stand. I bought all three. I would send a copy to my parents and give the others to friends.

There may be other stories and journals in my future, but none will ever equal the rush of seeing that first one in print, in a store, for sale, in New York City. I felt like my entire existence had been validated in that one simple moment. I was now a published writer.

Inspired by my newfound success, I started on a new novel. It was time to take this thing seriously. Maybe if I put as much effort into my writing as I did into my drinking, I might actually get somewhere. But it was impossible. I was too tired from working during the day to put the required energy into it. Even when I pushed myself to stay with it, there was always the drink to slow me up. Or Oksana. I discovered quickly that dating an eighteen-year-old could be a real drain on the creative process. Teenagers are a particularly selfish breed of creature; they are like writers in that regard. I'd work on the novel religiously for four days in a row, get drunk for three days, die with a hangover for two days, and then by the time I was feeling like writing again I was ready for another drink. After six months I had amassed a sketchy seventy pages. The more I looked at it, the uglier it got. The uglier it got, the more I drank. I needed some fresh experience, some inspiration.

Every summer, Oksana took a trip to Russia to visit her grandparents. This year I was invited to tag along to meet the rest of the family. I leapt at the chance.

Since we had started seeing each other, Oksana had been bringing me all her own favorites to read: Turgenev, Dostoyevsky, and Chekhov. I was drunk with the tragedy of it all: unrequited love, duels to the death—they really knew how to wipe the smile off your face in a hurry, these Ruskies. We spent months reading entire books aloud to one another: Lermontov's *A Hero of Our Time,* Bulgakov's *The Master and Margarita;* her favorite, Pushkin's *Eugene Onegin,* we read twice.

Oksana went a couple of weeks ahead of me to spend the whole summer in Russia, as she always did. I had time for only three weeks.

I traveled with her mother. We had a pleasant, civilized

flight, drinking tea and chatting, reading the *New Yorker*. The thought crossed my mind more than once that this might have been a more enjoyable trip with someone of my own age, someone with as much class as her mother, like my ex-wife.

Divorce can be beautiful to observe from a distance but painful and bloody to execute, like ripping a rosebush out of a thick hedge with your bare hands. This is the real reason people stay in miserable marriages for the rest of their lives. Better to endure the dull ache for a lifetime than suffer the ferocious evisceration for even a flash.

I was more than a little anxious about meeting Oksana's childhood friends and spending what was likely to be an entire three weeks drinking vodka with them. I had begun to distrust my drinking self again. I was not wholly predictable once that first mouthful crossed my lips. Bad things had started to happen when I drank—not all the time, mind you, but enough. Oksana and I fought almost constantly now when we were drinking. I would have to be careful in Russia. I'd heard stories. This was not a country to stagger around with your eyes half closed. Not if you valued your life. I would just have to be extra vigilant while I was there, stay away from the vodka, try to stick with beer. That was the answer. The possibility of not drinking at all was out of the question. My fellow countrymen would never forgive me.

Had I been spending the three weeks visiting Russia with her mother, none of these anxieties would have been an issue. Oksana's parents had always been very civilized with me. I could never quite understand why. I suppose they were just very civilized people. They were much closer in age to me than I was to their daughter. I could just imagine the carnage if my seventeen-year-old daughter, my only child, my little princess, arrived home with a twice divorced, drunken Irish writer/construction worker, fourteen years her senior. I would have to be dug out of him. I'd have his guts for garters. I'd do time for the bastard. But they accepted me warmly into their lives. It might have been better for me if they hadn't.

Oksana's uncle picked us up at the airport. Even though it was summer, I was shocked by how bright and warm it was as we made our way out of the airport terminal. I suppose I had half expected Doctor Zhivago to bundle us onto the back of a snow sled. Oksana, of course, who was supposed to be with him, was nowhere to be seen. This did not shock me in the least. In New York she could disappear for a week without so much as a phone call, then show up casually like she'd just stepped out of the room to use the bathroom, saying she'd met an old high school friend and decided to stay over. Her uncle informed me that he hadn't heard from her in two days.

On the ride from the airport I struggled not to picture her ferociously copulating with one of her former young lovers. This was beginning to feel like one of those Russian tragedies I'd been reading so much about. I pictured a duel on the foggy banks of the Volga at dawn before I left town.

On our drive back from the airport, Oksana's uncle told me a little story by way of warning. A man had been stabbed the previous night just outside the building where I would be staying with Oksana's grandmother. He was a local man. He had lived in one of the flats in the neighborhood his whole life. He had grown up there. He was in his early thirties. Oksana's grandmother had discovered the body that morning as she left for work. She had called the cops to report it. The body was still there when she was on her way home at four o'clock that afternoon. Some kids were poking at it with a stick, so she had to call the authorities again. "But there is no need to worry. The ambulance has taken him away now," he assured me with a bright smile before going on to explain to me how someone had gutted the guy, stolen his clothes and his sneakers, and that it was probably someone from the neighborhood. Possibly someone he knew. These kinds of things happened here, I was informed. I should be careful. People were poor around here, and some were desperate. I should be careful about being overheard speaking English or wearing clothes that made me stand out. I should never go out alone after dark. Ever. Welcome to Russia. Enjoy your stay. Next.

When we pulled up at her grandmother's flat, I was greeted by the sight of a group of young children prancing around playfully in the courtyard. One of them held a short, thin stick with a bloody plastic glove on the end. He was scaring the other kids with it, threatening to poke them with it and then chasing them off, squealing, in the direction of the swings. A scrawny-looking street dog stole quickly across the yard and sniffed the blood-stained tarmac next to where we had parked. He gingerly lifted the other bloody glove in his teeth and scarpered off. This was not *Doctor Zhivago*, I thought to myself, although it did appear as if an operation had taken place here.

Oksana was still nowhere to be seen. I was having tea with her grandmother when she showed up unapologetically an hour later with some story about how she hadn't realized the time. Oksana insisted that we ditch the family as quickly as possible so that we could go meet her best friend, Marina, and start drinking right away.

About an hour later, the three of us, Oksana, Marina, and I, were in a bar on the main drag near her grandmother's flat. Well, I don't know if you would classify it as a bar. It was an unadorned room with some cheap white plastic chairs and tables where you could buy either a small or a large glass of straight vodka. My large glass was served by a surly-looking lady who possessed all the warmth and grace of a hedgehog while retaining the distinct appearance of a small tugboat. She didn't seem at all pleased with taking our money and having to perform the laborious task of refilling our tumblers, even though we were the only customers she had in the whole time we were there. The girls talked in Russian and I spent most of the time trying to figure out what the hell they were talking about. Oksana made it abundantly clear that she was not going to spend her vacation translating for me. Thank God for vodka.

Within a very short time we were sloshed. Unfortunately, it was only six thirty or so in the evening and the girls informed me that we had only just begun drinking for the night. I tried to say something about jet lag and needing to get to sleep at some point, but the girls had staggered off down the street with their arms around each other, singing something loud and bawdy in Russian. It was a bright sunny evening in the former city of Gorky and I decided I'd better go with the flow. We were off to find Marina's husband, Loesha; apparently we were going out for the night to celebrate my arrival. Just then, a stray dog darted out from behind a parked car and dashed into the street, right next to me. The first car to hit it knocked it sprawling into the oncoming traffic in the next lane, where it was dragged for about twenty yards in the opposite direction before spinning off onto the sidewalk. It somehow managed to rise to its feet, and it took off yelping and hobbling past me down the block. Neither car paused; not a single person on the street stopped to see what had happened. It staggered on, whimpering, past the two girls, who were still singing, then veered off into a small park up ahead to the left.

"Didn't you see what just happened?" I said when I caught up to the two girls.

"What?" Oksana said. Marina looked confused.

"That poor dog just got nailed by two cars crossing the street."

"Oh, don't worry about it." Oksana smiled. "It's Russia, Colin; that sort of thing happens all the time." Then, with a roll of her eyes, she translated the conversation for Marina, who said something in a comforting tone to me that I didn't understand. Oksana didn't bother to translate it to me. I could see this was going to be a problem.

When I found the dog, he was lying in the uncut grass behind a park bench. He was whimpering and his body was shaking from the shock. His front leg was broken and he'd been scuffed up pretty bad; he was bleeding in a few places, but not severely. I sat in the grass and tried to comfort him for a while, petting him and telling him it was going to be OK. Two young boys not more than ten years old sat nearby on the swings, huffing glue out of a potato chip bag. They were too far gone to notice either me or the dog, or maybe they just didn't give a shit. I must have been sitting there for a while, because when Oksana and Marina arrived they had Loesha with them. They had brought along an armful of large bottles of beer. I was glad to see them and, more importantly, the beer.

Loesha was a big lad, tall and handsome with a strong jaw and a kind face. I liked him right away. I felt a sense of relief as I shook his hand. I felt suddenly that I wasn't going to be alone here. He spoke sincerely with me, having Oksana translate as he did so. He said it was admirable to take care of the dog the way I did, but there was really nothing to be done about it. He inspected the dog himself and surmised that it would be fine. The leg was definitely broken, but it would manage to live with it. He'd seen much worse. The dog had stopped shaking and had managed to sit up a little. Loesha gave it half of the sandwich he was carrying and it managed to wolf that down.

The girls opened a few beers and Loesha handed me one.

"Welcome in Russia," he announced proudly in an attempt at English as he gave me a broad smile and raised his bottle to mine.

A couple of cops passed by not ten feet away, chatting and

casually observing the setting: two drunk teenage girls guzzling large bottles of beer; a pair of kids on the swings, one so far gone he couldn't keep his eyes open, the other with his head shoved in a bag of glue, still huffing; Loesha and I with our beers hunkered next to a bleeding, whimpering dog. They continued on without so much as a pause in their conversation. Welcome in Russia, indeed, I thought to myself.

The following day, with my throbbing head as tender as a bruised tomato, we made our way to a small office somewhere in town to exchange some dollars for rubles. I had been warned by Marina and Loesha, who had come along to help with the transaction, that I should stay quiet once we were in the office. They were afraid that by speaking in English I would jeopardize the transaction. I didn't quite understand their apprehension. It's not like we were meeting an arms dealer in an abandoned warehouse. After all, this was a legitimate transaction in a legitimate currency exchange office.

The office we went to resembled the bar we had been drinking in the day before. It was a no-frills establishment. A woman sat behind a desk and glowered at us over her glasses. Apart from the pen she was twisting in her fingers and the big black phone perched ominously to the left of her elbow, there was nothing else of interest in the room to playfully ponder as I pretended to be Russian.

Marina placed herself in the chair opposite the lady to conduct the transaction while we stood behind her in silence, fidgeting with our hands. I felt like an idiot for not having exchanged the dollars in my bank back in New York. I hadn't realized that to possess American dollars would be regarded as an offense against mother Russia. Marina handed the woman the hundred-dollar bill I had given her. We had decided to start small in case there was trouble. The woman fingered the bill precariously, staring at it and then at Marina, and then from

Marina to us as if she was waiting for one of us to crack. She turned and held it up to the light of the window behind her, adjusting her glasses while still keeping the corner of her beady eyes on us lest we had any ideas about rushing the desk and overpowering her. The office door opened behind us and an elderly lady walked in with a small dog on a leash. The little dog leapt on my leg and started jumping up and down with excitement. I was relieved for this momentary break in the interrogation. Involuntarily I leaned to pet the dog and without thinking said, "What a cute little puppy."

That did it. I had blown our cover. The office lady spun around in her chair and glared at me. I might as well have torn up a portrait of the tsar and tossed it onto her desk. She erupted in a barrage of Russian invective directed at Marina. Marina shook her head and tried to plead with her, but it was too late. The lady was reaching for the phone. Marina spun around and, with a pleading, desperate expression, said, "Run." Run? I thought perhaps I'd misheard her, or it had to be a Russian word I didn't understand. Marina couldn't speak English.

"Run," Oksana barked at me. Loesha grabbed me by the arm and we legged it out of there and up the street, leaving Marina there for what I could only assume was torture and quite possibly the gallows.

Loesha ushered us into a bar about a half mile away, checking to make sure we hadn't been followed, and over a few glasses of vodka it was explained to me how a lot of these small exchange places were working in cahoots with the local police, setting up foreign tourists on counterfeiting charges. We stayed and drank, not daring to return home lest they lay in wait.

Later, when we did finally return to Oksana's grandmother's apartment, we found out that Marina had been released after about eight hours of questioning. The cops had then driven her home and confiscated her passport, but not before turning her apartment upside down searching for "the rest" of the "counterfeit" American currency. They demanded to know who had supplied it, but she stuck to her guns and told them it had been sent to her as a gift by a friend from America. They kept the hundred dollars that they already had for evidence. Loesha told me how things were so corrupt that the police and the exchange officers pulled this stunt on a regular basis. They'd take the money from the tourists, claim it was forged, and split it up between themselves and the exchange lady. Not a bad payday when you considered Loesha earned roughly thirty dollars a month as a car mechanic.

As a token of my appreciation and because I now realized I needed a full-time bodyguard to look out for my drunk Irish ass, I offered to pay for Loesha and Marina to come along with us on a boat trip up the Volga to Saint Petersburg. Neither of them had ever made the trip. They were ecstatic about the idea. We went down to the pier the next day and booked two cabins on a boat called the *Turgenev.* I tried to appear enthusiastic, but the truth was, I was vodka sick. I had developed some kind of chest infection and I was having difficulty breathing. I was hacking up a disturbing green bile that might have scared a lesser man into an emergency room. I should probably have eased off on the two packs of smokes a day, but I was on vacation, goddamn it. Oksana's mother tried to convince me to stay on at the house with them and rest for a few days. But I hadn't come this far to miss Saint Petersburg. I hid my cough as best I could and soldiered on as if nothing was wrong.

The morning before we were to leave on our trip, Oksana's grandmother took us on a little trip to the graveyard. She brought along some garden tools and fresh flowers and went about tidying the family plot, weeding and pruning the small bushes, planting fresh flowers, and tilling the clay with a small rake. I took the time to browse the enormous graveyard, reading the dates of demise on the headstones and studying the faces in the small photographs on each, looking for some clue as to the great mystery of the unknown. The faces stared back, saying, "Hey, I don't know shit, buster."

I did begin to see a pattern develop. An unsettling number of the graves were those of young men, between the ages of roughly twenty-seven and forty-two. As I found more and more of these headstones, I began to wonder if I hadn't missed some great Russian war. These were deaths that had occurred within the previous ten years; there were scores of them, sometimes two or three in a row. What could possibly have killed so many young Russian men? I wanted to ask Oksana or her grandmother, but I was afraid of revealing my ignorance of world affairs. Perhaps it was a great epidemic of some sort, but why, then, only the men? By the time I had returned to Oksana and her grandmother, I could contain myself no longer. I simply had to know. I had Oksana translate the question to her grandmother. She straightened herself and shook her head solemnly and then raised her hand to her mouth as if she were drinking out of a bottle.

"Vodka," she said.

Vodka? I was astounded. She continued in Russian and Oksana translated, saying that since perestroika, the young men had had trouble finding work to support their families, so they drank instead. I was floored. It was like witnessing the aftermath of a mass suicide of a generation of men. How was it possible that I'd never read a single thing about this, never once heard it mentioned? It explained the emptiness I had felt since I had arrived. This was not the Russia I had envisioned. This was the afterbirth of some savage delivery. Blood had been spilled in the theater. The great country was anew at the cost of thousands, hundreds of thousands perhaps. I comforted myself with the thought that this was the way all things were born on God's green earth and vowed to lay off the cheap vodka and to go see a doctor about my chest infection the moment I touched down again in New York.

EIGHT DAYS ON THE VOLGA
A DIARY

DAY ONE.

We are on an old boat called the *Turgenev*. We said good-bye to Nizhny Novgorod yesterday morning. I drank a bottle of samagon with Loesha before lunchtime, blacked out, and woke up cold, huddled on a bench on the top deck at six thirty this morning. Less than twenty-four hours into the trip and Oksana has stopped speaking to me already. My chest is worse than ever. I might not survive this voyage.

DAY TWO.

We made a brief stop in Yaroslavl today to visit an old gramophone museum. The rest of the day, the four of us drank sweet red wine in our cabin. Oksana will neither speak to me nor translate what the others are saying. Thank God for the wine. Later the girls went to a disco up on deck and Loesha produced a large glass jar of weed. There's enough here to have us chained together in a cold cell in Siberia for the rest of our lives if we are caught. Thank God for the wine and the weed.

DAY THREE.

Another day of drinking red wine and waiting for Oksana to lift the verbal embargo. I spent the day listening to the radio, staring out the window, scribbling in my notebook.

There are four wooden houses in a clearing near the river's edge. A ribbon of smoke files past them almost horizontally over the rooftops. The sky is blue, and white shirts are being pegged to a clothesline by a woman in a red apron. A bare-chested man is cutting logs with a saw that looks like a huge violin bow. The land is flat here, so there is nothing to bracket any of this. There is a green tent on a beach and a dog barking, a broken wooden pier and a dirty yellow boat upturned in the grass next to it. And here is a church and another church and another. I have been told that at one time there were sixty thousand churches along the Volga. They are empty now and crumbling, their minarets silhouetted in the afternoon sun like the helmets of some ancient tribe. We are drifting along on the Volga not more than twenty-five feet from shore. I could jump overboard here and walk off into the woods. No one would ever hear from me again.

DAY FOUR.

We stopped in Rybinsk today. The four of us took a walk and bought jars of pickled mushrooms, dried fish, and various knickknacks. I bought a small aluminum statue of a drunk with a bottle raised to his head. Then I got into a screaming match with Oksana in the pouring rain. She was wearing a tight white T-shirt and hadn't bothered to wear a bra. I had to endure wolf whistles from the boat crew as she stormed ahead of me onto the boat on the way

back. One of them said something loud enough for
Oksana to hear, and I heard her answer, *"Spacibo"*:
Thank you.

DAY FIVE.

Oksana made me a sardine sandwich today. It is a
peace offering. The first gesture of affection she
has shown me in days. The boat will not stop today,
she tells me. We are between Goritsy and Valaam and
crossing Lake Ladoga, the largest lake in Europe.
Land is no longer visible, and I feel particularly
vulnerable. I'm drinking heavily today to quell my
fears, even though my body is screaming at me to
stop.

DAY SIX.

Today we reached Valaam Island at around ten in the
morning, and she was in love with me again. We
walked with Marina and Loesha five miles through
the woods to the Valaam monastery, high on a hill.
There was a definite ache in my liver this morning.
I prayed it was a walking cramp and made a silent
vow to stop drinking the cheap vodka we had been
purchasing.

Inside the monastery two young monks were on
their hands and knees scrubbing the immaculate
stone floor. Others went about reverentially
polishing gold and brass chalices, rails, and
crosses. Every square inch of the walls, the
ceiling, and the dome far above us was covered
with rich colorful frescoes so awe-inspiring that
it caught my heart by surprise. Art for God's sake.
And in that instant, I could believe too. I wanted to

lie down and hold my cheek against the cold stone floor, because I felt that somewhere here in this great silence was the real prayer.

DAY SEVEN.

Today we visited one of the summer homes of Catherine the Great. While we were walking around, a young boy came up to show me a cricket he had cupped in his hands. Oksana leaned over to look and smiled at the boy. The boy's mother grabbed his arm and yanked him to her side. The cricket fell from his hands and made a hop for freedom, but as the boy stumbled to his mother's side, he accidentally stepped on it.

"Why are people so cruel?" Oksana said, and she began to cry. "I want to take the little boy home with us. Did you see his face?"

"It was an accident," I said.

"No it wasn't. People are mean and cruel. They all are, even you and me. We're all mean. People are horrible. Only animals and little children are good. I can't stand it anymore." She turned away from me and started off toward the bus that had taken us there from the boat. I tried to follow but she turned on me. "Leave me alone. I want to be alone. I want to be little again."

DAY EIGHT.

We were in Saint Petersburg today. Oksana and I went to see Pushkin's home.

"I'm not in love with you anymore," she said as I watched a cat that had snuck in and nestled itself

in Pushkin's old writing chair. An old woman in a
blue head scarf noticed the cat and stepped over
the red rope, scolding and slapping her leg with her
hand. The cat bolted off the chair and managed to
scale four shelves of books before she caught him.
"You're breaking up with me in the middle of our
vacation?" "It's over." I was tempted to step over
the rope and take a seat at Pushkin's desk for a
moment. Russian writers suddenly made more sense.
Maybe he kept an old musket in that desk drawer. I
could end it all here, put a stop to all this drama;
one more gunshot as a punctuation mark on the
historical literary landscape. It is late as I write
this. I am alone again in our small cabin, drinking
cheap vodka straight from a plastic tumbler. She is
gone with Marina to the disco. Loesha has slipped
down to the other cabin to fetch the jar of weed.
Maybe that will help take the edge off a little. It is
going to be a long ride back.

I had another week of Russia to endure now that I was single. I
tried to stay focused on getting my ass back to New York in one
piece. Things had started to get a little crazy before we made it
back to Nizhny. People from other boats, complete strangers,
would approach me in the small villages where we stopped for
supplies and ask me to go drinking with them or if they could
possibly have a picture taken with me. Loesha explained that
word of my drinking exploits had spread. People wanted to see
the crazy Irishman. The orangutan was loose. I had become the
town entertainment. At first I thought it was just a little paranoia from all the weed we'd been smoking, but apparently people were really staring at me. Loesha had to remind me that I

was the only non-Russian that he had seen on the whole river trip. A waitress on the *Turgenev* had told us that in the five years she had worked on the boat I was the first non-Russian she had served. It didn't help that I had been spotted sleeping on the deck on numerous occasions or trying to throw my screaming girlfriend overboard into Lake Ladoga in broad daylight. This did not bode well. This was not a country where you wanted to stand out as a crazy drinker. Not in a country where the life expectancy of the average drinking male is about thirty-five years old. It was too late to stop drinking now anyway. I couldn't afford to go into withdrawals in the middle of my trip. I would need at least four days alone in my apartment to detox from this one. I would just have to monitor my alcohol intake for the rest of the trip, keep a bottle near the bed for when I woke up, maintain a steady buzz, keep my chin up. The liver had only just begun to hurt; there was plenty of fight left in the bastard yet.

Before we left Russia, Oksana's uncle and her mother took us on a little road trip to the country to see Oksana's great-uncle. On the way there we passed through Dzerzhinsk, a town the *New York Times* has called the most tainted city in the world. Oksana's uncle advised us to keep the windows up while we passed through so that we wouldn't breathe in the radiation. I couldn't tell if he was serious or not, but I was willing to listen.

Thankfully, Uncle Kosha lived beyond the city line in a wooden cabin way out in the country. He came rushing out of an old tin shed to greet us with outstretched arms when we pulled up in front. Here was Pablo Picasso's long-lost twin brother; I was sure of it. The resemblance was uncanny. His wife, who had been down in the garden weeding the vegetables, hurried up, wiping her hands on her apron, and embraced each of us in a warm hug before ushering the party indoors to find their beautiful daughter, Anna, who had dashed off to put on a clean dress and fix her hair when she had seen the car approaching up the field.

This was the Russia I had read about. There was no phone here to warn them of our arrival. No e-mail in advance. This was how it had been everywhere once upon a time: big pleasant surprises in the simplest of things.

The women shoved us into the comfortable old worn chairs around the living room and went about fussing over us, handing us drinks and grabbing laundry off the clothesline above the stove, kicking boots underneath the chairs, sweeping the dust out the door, while Kosha ran off to alert the neighbors to prepare for a party. It reminded me of my grandparents' house when I was a kid: the smell of a wood fire, furniture that had been sat in for generations, a floor that had been worn into soft grooves around the kitchen table. I had almost forgotten what it was like to be in a house like this.

For the next four hours or so they prepared dish after dish: cucumber, beet, and potato salads all fresh from the garden; there was a chicken plucked and herring boned; mushroom caps were stuffed and served dripping in butter; wine was sloshed into our goblets and we drank and ate and the neighbors arrived with dessert and we sang songs. Picasso took Oksana and danced with her in the garden as the little black-and-white collie spun himself in giddy circles, yapping.

Then came the late afternoon and the vodka; that was when the real drinking began, a shot for every toast. We raised a drink to Oksana and one to her mother and one for her father, who could not be there. At this point the ladies held their hands over their glasses when Picasso came around to fill them again. They would sip their vodka from here on in. Oksana's uncle was excused because he had to drive us back to the city. Oksana gave me a kick in the shin under the table and a raised eyebrow above it to signify that I had to keep going. Pablo was just warming up, it seemed: one for the food, and the ladies who prepared it; another for the Irish and another for the neighbors who had arrived from across the fields with the dessert. I was relieved to see the bottle of vodka run dry after about five shots. I was having trouble getting them to my mouth without spilling them at this point, but Picasso was nowhere near done yet. He had Anna fetch another bottle from the room and bring it to the table. But wait, hold up a minute, what was this? This wasn't vodka. It looked like some kind of hospital bottle. It didn't have a label, but it was definitely hospital brown. Like a large medicine bottle.

"What the hell is that?" I whispered to Oksana. I got another kick underneath the table. "Is that some kind of hospital cleaning fluid?"

"Shhh."

"Is that from a hospital?"

"Anna is a nurse."

"I can't . . ."

"Don't embarrass me or them. Just drink it."

"It could kill me."

"Just drink it and stop being a big baby."

Baby? Did she just call me a baby? I'm no damned baby. Don't you dare call me a baby. I will drink every drop of alcohol east of the Volga. I will drink turpentine, gasoline if I have to. Fill my glass up there, Pablo, you old crotch-muncher. Let's party.

I still don't know what was in that bottle, but it burned like hell. My tongue shriveled and my throat squeaked and tears rolled down my face. Pablo poured us another one. The second one wasn't so bad now that my taste buds had been seared off. The third was like water.

• • •

A couple of nights before we were to leave Russia, Oksana found a kitten outside her bedroom window, crying in the rain. She spent the last couple of days of the vacation getting paperwork for it to take it back to the States. I kept a drink in my hand and tried to maintain an even buzz until we had to leave for the airport. I was glad to be leaving. I wanted to go back and think about things. Everything was happening too fast: the divorce; losing the house; the business; and now I was losing Oksana. Where had it all gone wrong? Maybe this was God telling me that I had screwed up. Maybe I should have stayed with my wife, raised that little girl. So what if I had been miserable with my life for a little while—wasn't everybody?

When we tried to leave for the airport, the car wouldn't start. Oksana's uncle spent an hour under the hood unscrewing pipes and cleaning plugs. Her grandmother suggested that we call the airline and reschedule the flight. She had a bad feeling about this. I insisted we keep trying. I needed to be on that plane. I needed to get out of Russia. Finally, at the last minute, when we had almost lost hope, he got it going.

It was a mad dash for the airport, weaving in and out of traffic, whizzing through red lights. We passed by a woman lying in the street. It looked like she'd been hit by a bus. There was a pool of blood about her head. A small crowd of spectators was gathered. We had no time to stop.

By the time they had checked our luggage and argued for forty minutes over whether or not they should allow us to take the cat out of the country, we were over an hour late for our flight. Ours was the only airplane out of Nizhny that afternoon. If we missed this one, there wasn't another flight for four days.

Oksana took the cat out of its carrying case and held it in

her lap. We barely had time to snap the buckles on our seat belts when the plane roared off, shuddering down the runway, and with a great surge, we were in the air. I glanced out the window and I could see Nizhny drifting away beneath us. My stomach sank down and nestled into the pit of my pelvis from the upward thrust as we rose higher and higher . . . and then there was an enormous bang somewhere beneath our feet and the plane seemed to stop its great ascent and pause for a moment.

"What the fuck was that?" Oksana said, turning to me.

"I don't know."

"Colin. What the fuck was that?"

"I really don't know." I noticed other passengers shifting uneasily, turning in their seats, whispering to one another. I felt my stomach slowly begin to lift up into my diaphragm. I glanced out of the window again at the landscape. We were falling. The captain came on the intercom and began in English.

"Ladies and gentlemen, it appears we have lost our gears. Try to remain calm and we will try to get going again as soon as possible." And that was that.

"What did he say?" Oksana said. I reached for her hand and she let me take it. She leaned toward me and gripped my arm. A woman two seats ahead of us burst into tears. "Oh my God," Oksana continued. "Are we going to die?"

"No," I said, but I did not believe it. "We're going to be fine. Everything's going to be alright."

"I don't want to die, Colin."

The general feeling of panic and commotion had spread throughout the whole cabin.

I racked my brain trying to make sense of the captain's announcement. "We lost our gears"? What the hell did that mean? Did they fall out somewhere? Have you misplaced them? Do you have a spare set somewhere? "We will try to get going again as soon as possible"? That would imply that currently we are not going anywhere. Yet here we are, about five thousand feet in the air. What did he mean, we'll try to get going again soon? It's not like we pulled over to the side of the road here to change a flat tire.

"Colin, I'm scared," Oksana said, and when I looked at her I could see that she was crying. Oksana never cried. Now I was really scared. Other women were crying now. Someone was shouting up ahead of us. Others sat in petrified silence. We were going down. The plane was falling silently. Maybe we should have heeded the signs, listened to the omens; maybe we were really meant to miss this flight. Why the hell had I insisted on getting here? Why couldn't I have . . .

"I love you, Colin," Oksana blurted. "I'm scared. I don't want to die."

"It's OK. I love you too. Everything's going to be OK, I promise. We'll be fine. Relax." I put my arm around her and pulled her close to me and held her tightly. Couples were holding on to each other all around us. Even the little kitten began to cry. God, if you're up there, wake the fuck up, dude. Don't let this fucking plane fall. Please. I will do anything. I will change my life. I will take care of this girl and this cat and I will never drink again as long as I live. I swear it. There was another jolt beneath our feet and the engines roared into action. We were moving again. He had heard my prayer. We had stopped falling. We were starting to climb.

That fall my youngest brother, Gerry, arrived in New York. Gerry had been eight years old when I left home for London. We had never really gotten to know each other. We had never had a drink together. We had some catching up to do.

Most weekends he wound up sleeping on our couch. The

three of us would sit up till dawn watching movies, drinking, me and Gerry sharing stories of our childhoods spent ten years apart in Ireland. Oksana was happier when Gerry was around. They were closer in age and shared similar interests in music and comedians. He brought her all the latest European CDs and she gave him books of poetry. She liked me better now that she knew that he was my brother. He made me bearable. We fought less when he stayed over. We became inseparable. We were like the three drunken musketeers.

In January, Oksana decided the three of us should go ice-skating to celebrate my thirty-third birthday. Apart from the trip to Russia, it was the first time in a year and a half that she'd suggested that we leave the apartment to do anything together. I stopped by the liquor store on the way home from work that evening and bought a bottle of whiskey to toast the occasion properly. I filled a thermos with hot water, whiskey, sugar, and cloves, and we were off to the rink.

I'm not much of an ice-skater, but the whiskey made it bearable. An hour or two later I was doing pirouettes. I'd never seen Oksana so happy. The three of us would hold hands and race around as fast as we could until we wound up crumpled in a pile on the ice and she would drag us to our feet and we'd be off again spinning around like ten-year-olds until we were completely out of control again. But I couldn't shake the feeling that there was something too perfect, too giddy about the whole thing, as if we were just replicating a scene we might have witnessed in some cornball Hollywood romantic comedy.

Pretty soon the flask was empty and I discovered that they had nothing but cold beer for sale at the rink. I was done with skating. I was beginning to feel more like Jack Nicholson in *The Shining*. It was time for a trip to the nearest bar.

The ice rink was in Westchester, not far from where I was working at the time. I had noticed a bar near the job and had never had a chance to check it out. We drove over there and I managed to convince the bartender that Oksana was twenty-one, and about an hour later I was smashed out of my mind. The whiskey was finally kicking in. Things got a little fuzzy. There were a few rounds of shots with a bunch of Irish American guys. I may or may not have played some pool. I got into a fight with Oksana, our first big public scene this side of the Atlantic. I was leaving the bar without her. I was leaving without my brother. We were in the parking lot. There was a scuffle between Gerry and me over the car keys. There was ice everywhere. I couldn't stand up for more than two seconds. I fell about five times, finally smashing the back of my head. I somehow woke up in the car alone and cold. The keys were in the ignition. I started the car and roared out of the parking lot, skidding all over the joint in the darkness and the harsh ice. It had started to snow. I was great at driving in the snow. I'd spent years driving in this kind of weather back home. I could handle it.

I was on a country road on my way toward the parkway. I was nearing a sharp bend doing over eighty. The little Honda was just drifting on the ice. Trees lined either side of the road everywhere you looked. Where was Oksana? Where was Gerry? Jesus, I'd forgotten them. I must have left them at the bar. I'd better go back. I pulled the hand brake and let the car spin a few times down the center of the road before I could point myself back in the direction of the bar. I had managed that little maneuver with ease. Just like the old days. I could sure as hell drive. I was good, there was no doubt about it. I was having fun. The Honda was slipping out of control. I pulled the hand brake again and drifted sideways down the center of the road for about a hundred yards. I was pointing away from the town again, back toward the parkway. I floored it, pushing the little Honda up through the gears: seventy, eighty; there was that bend again. I pulled the hand brake again. I'd left it too late; I knew it the moment I started sideways. I was out of control.

There's a moment of calm that always sets in with me when I'm in a car crash. I've been in many. Everything slows down. Everything is accounted for. It's as if it is all happening outside of myself, like a dream in slow motion. Details are observed that seem ridiculous when you consider the speed involved. The naked tree branches are glittering with ice as I sail past sideways down the road; the shadows of the tree trunks zip from right to left; the front wheels have caught the grass shoulder. The tires are plowing along sideways, threatening to flip the car onto its roof. I can feel small rocks tapping the floor under my feet. There's nothing to do but wait. The line has been crossed. This situation is beyond all control. It will end how it ends. All four wheels are on the grass now. The car seems to gain speed when I leave the road completely. I am spinning through the trees. Tree trunk, tree trunk, tree trunk, no thud yet. How long can I go without . . . the sound of bushes thrashing around the sides of the car, over the windows. Darkness.

When I came to, the first thing I was aware of was the thudding in my head. I checked the other seats and realized that I was alone. Where the hell was everybody? Where was I? How did I wind up here? I was cold. I opened the door and shoved my way out. The moon was high and bright. I was surrounded by brambles. I made my way around the car. I didn't seem to have done any major damage. It looked drivable. The brambles had piled up in front of the car. That's what must have stopped me. Behind me was a path where I'd mowed them down. I got back into the car and started the engine. I tried to back it out the same way I'd come in. The tires spun in the soft clay and snow. I was not going anywhere. I needed help. I needed to get this thing out of here before the cops arrived. This didn't look good. I took off walking back toward town. I remembered that there was a night watchman stationed in the building where I'd been working. Maybe I could convince him to come out there and help me shove the car a little. I reached the building and walked inside the foyer to find him. He was half asleep behind a desk with his feet up, listening to a small radio. He didn't notice me until I was standing in front of his desk.

"Hey, what's up, pal?" I said.

"Jesus Christ," he yelped as he almost fell onto the floor. He jumped up and away from me. For a second I thought he was going to reach for his gun.

"I've had an accident," I said, trying to calm him down a little.

"Jesus, are you alright?" he said, but he was still keeping his distance.

"Yeah, I'm fine. I just lodged my car in the snow up the road here and I need a hand shoving it out onto the road again."

"Man, you need more than that. I'm going to call an ambulance." He moved toward the phone.

"No, I'm fine. I just need some help."

"You're not fine. Have you seen yourself?"

"What?"

"You're covered in blood."

"What?" I put my hand up to wipe my face, and sure enough I was covered in blood. I stepped over to a mirror on the lobby wall. I looked like I'd been attacked with an axe. There was blood everywhere. I checked my face and head. I found a small lump on the back of my skull. As I touched it I remembered the fall in the parking lot earlier. I must have cracked my head open. The blood was caked in my hair, but it seemed to have stopped bleeding. "You're right," I said. "I do look pretty bad, but it's nothing. I have a nick on the back of my head. I must have been passed out on the steering wheel for a while. I just need to rinse this shit off."

"Are you drunk?" he asked.

"Yeah, I've had a few," I said. "That's why we're not calling the ambulance or the cops. I work here in this building during the day. I'm a carpenter. I need you to help me."

He considered me for a moment, shaking his head in disbelief. "Come on," he said. "Let's get you washed off." He led me into the makeshift bathroom and found me a roll of tissue paper while I washed off. I'd lost quite a lot of blood but had stopped bleeding. I was OK. I would survive without stitches.

"What's your name?" I asked as I finished toweling off.

"Pat."

"You Irish American, Pat?"

"Yeah, my old man's from Cork and my mother's from Galway."

"Well, Pat, here's the story. I need you to do a fellow countryman a big favor. My car's lodged in a snowbank about five hundred yards up the road here. I need to get it out of there before the cops see it or I'm fucked. I just need you to rock it a little for me and it should come right out."

"Man, you should just go home and come back in the morning."

"I need this favor, Pat."

He considered me for a second and then reluctantly grabbed his scarf and gloves. "Alright, then, let's do it."

It was a waste of time. The more he rocked, the deeper the wheels got lodged. After a few minutes he convinced me that it was too far off the road for anybody to see. So we walked back together and he called me a cab.

When I got back to Riverdale it was almost five in the morning. There was no sign of Oksana or Gerry. I hadn't tried to call them. I would face that nightmare later. In the meantime I had to leave for work in about an hour. I had no choice. I would have to go, because I needed to get the guys at work to help me dig out the Honda. Ice-skating? What a dumb, stupid idea that had been. What the hell was I doing at an ice-skating rink? Happy fucking birthday, numb-nuts.

After we'd finished the breakfast sandwiches at ten o'clock tea break, I told the lads an edited version of the story, leaving out the ice-skating, the whiskey flask, the head injury, and the excruciating pain in my chest now from where I had whacked into the steering wheel on impact. I told them my car was still lodged in the bushes and I needed at least five of them to get it out. Nobody seemed to believe me at first. There was no shortage of wild stories told on an Irish construction site and most of them were lies. Nobody wanted to be the first to get up. They were warmer where they were sitting. My workmate, a guy called Dermot Kenny from County Meath, stood up. Dermot was a hurler for the county team. When he spoke, you listened.

"Come on, ya lazy shower of bastards," he roared. "Let's go get the man's car out of the hedge. You," he said, pointing at the youngest one of the bunch, a lad called Larry. "Go get a couple of shovels off the laborers. The rest of ye get on your feet. Come on. Up." And they did. All eight of them. Dermot gave me a wink as they rose begrudgingly to their feet, tossing their paper coffee cups and sandwich wrappers into the Dumpster. I breathed a sigh of relief. I had a man in my corner. There were enough Irishmen on the move here to eat the Honda out of the brambles if need be.

It took five minutes with that bunch to get the Honda back onto solid tar. A snowball fight broke out and Dermot Kenny threw a shovelful of snow through the open car window onto my lap. It was a raucous event, boys shoving each other and dropping snowballs down each other's shirts. They inspected the path the Honda had taken through the trees, marveling at how close I had been to a few of the big ones. There were stories shared of other similar car crashes and before we were back at work forty minutes later, we knew each other a little better. Sometimes, I decided, you just needed to almost kill yourself in a horrible drunken car accident to bring people a little closer together. I would never have felt such camaraderie with these lads had I been sober. It's the damndest thing—the worse I screwed up, the more they seemed to like me.

"Broderick, you're buying the first beer this evening," Dermot announced as we stood around the gang box a few minutes later, strapping on our tool belts to return to work.

"I dunno; I might have to go do some patching up at home this evening."

"Jaysus, won't she be there when you get home?" He laughed.

"Yeah, but it's only Wednesday."

"Don't worry about that; the bars stay open every night of the week."

"I suppose you're right. A few quiet ones never killed anybody. The first beer's on me."

"Uh-oh," one of the lads said. "Somebody better get those car keys off of him." That got a good laugh.

"It's alright," Dermot said. "We'll just take a few of the shovels along with us when we go."

I hadn't heard them laugh so much in all the time I'd known them. A couple of months ago I couldn't get myself invited to a funeral in the Irish construction scene, and now here I was, the life and soul of the party. It was good to be back. Dermot was right; Oksana could wait. What the hell was I thinking, going home to explain myself to a teenager? I really needed my head examined.

When I got home that night around ten, Oksana was waiting for me. I came stumbling through the door with a couple of bottles of red wine I'd picked up for a nightcap. I had a nice buzz on already. I'd had a good time with the lads. I'd spent way too long being sore on myself. I deserved to blow off some steam and I wasn't about to let her ruin that for me.

"Have you been drinking again?"

"Hey, don't start. If I want to go for a few drinks with the lads after work, I don't need your permission."

"I can't believe you."

"Believe it."

"Do you remember anything about what happened last night?"

"Of course I do," I lied.

"Do you remember what you said to me, to your brother Gerry?"

"I was a little drunk, that's all," I said, hoping she'd give me some information. I had no idea of what I'd said to either of them. "What, you've never been a little drunk?"

"You were plastered. Gone. I've never seen anything like it. You were like a madman. You should call your brother and apologize."

"For what?"

"For calling him an asshole. For telling him to go fuck himself. He was only trying to get the keys off you so that you wouldn't drive. You couldn't even stand up. He was only trying to help you."

"Yeah, OK, maybe I will give him a call."

"I can't believe you did that."

"Hey, it's not like you two were sober."

"No, we weren't, but we weren't going to start a fight in the bar with a bunch of strangers and then try to drive home. I can't believe you left us there."

"I almost froze to death in the car."

"You wouldn't get out. We left you for a few minutes to see if you'd sober up. We came out in ten minutes and you were gone. You left me with no money, in a bar I'd never been to."

"How'd you get home?"

"Gerry paid for a cab for me. He took me home."

"Oh, yeah, and how was that?"

"Poor Gerry, you really gave it to him last night."

"OK, maybe I'll give him a call."

"Maybe you should consider not drinking," she said.

"You're right," I said, pouring myself a glass of wine. "I will consider it."

"But you're still going to drink?"

"It was the whiskey. I should never drink whiskey. It makes me crazy. I really just need to take it easy, and I will. I promise. You have nothing to worry about. You just haven't gone out with an Irish guy. We're a little crazy sometimes, that's all. It's all part and parcel of the package. It doesn't make me a bad guy, does it?"

"No but—"

"That's right. It doesn't. It's just so American to get all excited about every little thing."

"But I'm Russian."

"Yeah, but you know what I'm saying. You just got to have a sense of humor about these things. You'll look back at this one day and laugh."

"You're crazy."

"Yes. That is correct. And you're crazier, because you're still here."

"I must be."

"Have a glass of wine and lighten up a little."

"I might as well," she said, but she wasn't smiling. She put the glass to her head and drank it down like a girl who needed to forget. I did the same.

• • •

For the next few weeks I kept a low profile. I made sure I was at work a little early every morning. I tried to stay dry on weeknights. I bought some paint and we spent our afternoons fixing up the apartment, listening to music, and reading each other to sleep at night. At the weekends I stocked up with lots of movies and booze and we would hibernate for three nights and two whole days, never once venturing out the door.

A few months later, by mid-March, I was back in everybody's good books. My brother Gerry had forgiven me and he had begun to stop by again once in a while at the weekends. I suggested we take another stab at going out together for the night. Just the three of us. Tony had given me a few free tickets to go see a reading of a play at his downtown rock bar, Arlene's Grocery. They were a little reluctant at first, but eventually they agreed to go. This time we decided to leave the whiskey flask at home.

What I remember of the play night is this: I am at the bar ordering beers for the three of us, sneaking shots of vodka because the beer is not working fast enough. I have not the slightest memory of what the play was about. Of whether I liked it or hated it. I really didn't care. What I cared about was getting smashed. As soon as the show was over, I suggested we take a stroll around the corner to a place called Max Fish on Ludlow. It was on the way back to where I had the car parked, so they were easy to convince. Once there, I assured them that they should just go ahead and get toasted and let me worry about getting us home safely. Which they did.

What I remember next is that they were both loaded. Oksana was swaying on her stool and Gerry had his arm around her trying to keep her upright. Neither of them was in any shape to finish the six whiskey sours they had backed up on the bar in front of them. I can't remember whose bright idea it was to buy so many of them in the first place, but I do remember quite clearly thinking that I should drink them. I was feeling a little woozy and for some reason I assumed the jolt of whiskey to my system would wake me up for the drive home.

What I remember next is walking toward my little Honda. I remember seeing the car as we approached it, and then in the next instant I recall the big yellow sand bins that you see on the highway rushing toward me at about eighty miles per hour. I remember having the thought that I should hit the brakes. Stop. But of course it was too late. The next thing I remember is coming to with a policeman tapping my left shoulder through the open window, and I reflexively reached for the key in the ignition to start the car so that I could escape. I remember him leaning in to take a close look at my face and saying, "What are you trying to do? The engine's on your feet."

I remember then seeing Oksana unconscious in the passenger seat and my brother groaning, leaning over her, shaking her and begging her to wake up. Then I was in handcuffs and I was leaning against the squad car, watching as they were both removed from the vehicle and taken away on stretchers and loaded into the backs of ambulances. There were flashing lights everywhere, many police, commotion. There was a brief flash and I was in the police precinct. I was trying to walk a straight line that they had marked on the floor, but I could not stand up straight. I hung on to one of the officers and I told him that I was going to be sick. He rushed me the bathroom and I blacked out again.

When I opened my eyes, I saw two dark faces staring back at me. I closed my eyes again. My brain tried to put this image to sleep, tie it into a dream I was having, but my head hurt. I opened my eyes again. There were two men sitting not four feet away. One Latino and one black guy. They were staring at me. They didn't look happy. What the hell was I doing in a jail cell?

Why was I not at home in my bed? This is how it comes to you, the horror. Little glimpses. Flashing lights. Snapshots. Ambulances and handcuffs. This was not a dream. I sat up slowly. My entire body ached. I looked at the index finger on my right hand and touched it. It was broken. The two men continued to stare at me. The Latino man spoke.

"You have yourself a nice sleep, motherfucker?"

I decided not to reply. It sounded rhetorical. My brain struggled to piece together the fragments of what I could remember about last night into some cohesive story line, as if the key to my freedom from this nightmare resided in the solution of this riddle. The black guy spoke.

"Yeah, you been on that cot snoring all night. We got to sit here on this cold muthafuckin' flo' watchin' yo white ass."

I nodded and stood up to stretch myself. This was not going well. My brain kept hitting rewind back to that moment when I reached for the first of the whiskey sours. Which one was it? I could remember feeling OK before we entered the bar. What did it matter? Where the hell were Oksana and Gerry? Jesus, I hoped they were alright. Then I remembered that she had not been conscious the last time I saw her. I remembered Gerry groaning. I sat down again suddenly and gripped my head. This could be bad. This could be really, really bad. Please, God, no . . . Please, God, let them be OK. I will do anything. I swear it. I know I've said that before but I really mean it this time. Please, God. Let them be alive and OK. I will never touch another drink as long as I live. I swear it. Please. I bit back my tears. I was in jail. I had hospitalized two people I loved dearly. How was this possible? Our Father, who art in heaven, hallowed be Thy name, Thy kingdom come, Thy will be done on earth as it is in heaven . . . Please, God, get me out of this one. I beg you, let them be alive and well. I will never touch another drink. Give us this day our daily bread . . .

"OK, rise and shine, you lazy good-for-nothing sacks of shit," roared a big clean-cut Irish American–looking police officer rattling his nightstick down along the cage bars. "Come on, up, on your feet, you miserable lowlife, maggot-infested scumbags."

The doors opened and we filed out into the hallway.

"Come on, straighten up . . ." our commander bellowed as the other two cops started down the line, handcuffing the men to one another. "Whaddya think this is, a goddamned holiday camp?"

There was a pay phone on the wall next to me. I should call somebody. I was owed a phone call. I checked my pockets quickly. No change. I noticed a quarter lying on the floor underneath the pay phone. Jackpot. I leaned to pick it up. It seemed to be stuck. I tried to wrench it free as quickly as possible. I heard all three cops begin to laugh at the same time. I had fallen for one of their little gags. I stood up and tried to resign myself to the fact that I was screwed. The black guy in front of me was shaking his head as if to say, "Yup, this sure is one dumb cracker we got ourselves right here." I was going to have to tighten up a little bit if I was to survive this one. This was going to be a long weekend.

We were handcuffed together, all twenty of us, and marched out onto 123rd Street and up the sidewalk about a half a block in the bright sunshine to a waiting police bus. I kept my head low and tilted away from the street in case someone passing by might recognize me. I'd driven by this very spot a thousand times on my way to work from Woodlawn. That was all I needed right now, to hear someone with an Irish accent call my name out of a passing van. I would never live it down. Me, the only white guy, shackled to a row of criminals being marched through Harlem at about eight in the morning. Here I was, faced with the fact that my actions might have caused someone's death, and I was momentarily more concerned with how I might look. I was one self-centered little cookie, that's for sure.

Our bus driver took the scenic route to the courthouse that morning, as if he wanted to impress upon us the true nature of freedom. This was the last glimpse of a sunny Manhattan morning many on this bus would have for a long time. If Oksana or Gerry were badly injured, I would be among them.

We were driven down Broadway past Columbia University with the first bleary-eyed students trudging along to the diner with newspapers tucked under their arms, on their way to mugs of hot coffee and eggs, on past Symphony Space, and Zabar's and the Dublin House with its huge green neon harp, dull in the morning light. One of the inmates roared for some heat and the driver laughed and opened his window instead, treating us to a flood of arctic air. A chorus of shouts erupted in protest as we passed Lincoln Center. "Shut the damned window, nigga." And on around Columbus Circle, where a horse and trap slowed us momentarily. I tried to relax my hands to keep the cuffs from cutting into my wrists as we rolled down Seventh Avenue, and I gazed at Times Square through the rusty cage–covered window of the bus. This was what happened to orangutans. This was how wild animals were transported through an urban environment.

I spent the rest of the day trying to stay out of trouble. Out of the thirty or so crammed into our holding cell down at the Centre Street courthouse, I was the only white guy. Most of us in there were hungover and irritable, jonesing for a drink or a drug or a cigarette, anything to help ease the despair. Many of these men were repeat offenders caught buying or selling drugs. A few of them had been involved in gun battles; some were still bleeding. Others, like myself, were waiting to find out if we had killed somebody in our reckless pursuit of oblivion. Most of these men were going back to jail for a long time. They paced and traded stories, kicked the bars, yelled at the guards, and nursed their heads. Here was a church with real prayer. Here were God's own lumbering wounded animals, unfit for society. A room full of anguish and menace, men with little, if anything at all, left to lose. This is what the end of the line looks like, or at least one of its many tributaries.

I needed to use the phone. I needed to find out if Oksana and Gerry had made it home. After some negotiation I managed to buy a quarter for two dollars off a huge black guy called Charles, who sat quietly tapping his feet as if he were just sitting by the side of the road somewhere waiting for the bus to come along.

Oksana picked up on the first ring.

"Where are you?"

"Jail."

"Colly—"

"Yeah, I know. Are you two alright?"

"We're fine. A little bruised, but we'll survive. Are you alright?"

"I am now that I hear your voice. Where's Gerry?"

"He's right here on the couch eating pizza."

"I'm sorry."

"I know."

"I'm really sorry."

"I know. When will they let you out?"

"I don't know. If not tonight then Monday morning."

"How is it in there?"

"I love it. Making lots of new friends."

"That's nice."

"I'm out of quarters, so I guess I'll just call you when I get out of here."

"OK. I love you."

"You do?"

"Yip."

"You're crazy."

"I must be."

"I love you too."

I hung up and thanked God. I really didn't care now what else happened. I could handle losing my own life but not causing someone else's death. There are worse things than my own death.

At eleven o'clock that Saturday night, the guard strolled past the row of cages, yelling.

"OK, you guys, the judge is going home for the weekend in twenty minutes, so that's it for the night. So make yourselves comfortable, because you're here until Monday morning. Lights out in five minutes."

In a moment the lights in the cage were out, and in the dim glow from the corridor I watched the bodies shuffling around on the floor and on the benches, trying to find a comfortable resting place. Then, by some miracle, there was the sound of footsteps down the hall again and the lights flickered back on as the guard reappeared holding a clipboard.

"OK, listen up, rejects. The judge has time to hear five more cases tonight. When you hear your name, stand at the door of your cell."

No one in my cell so much as twitched a muscle. Not an ear in this whole room was attuned to hearing good news.

"Tray Clarke, Hector Rodriguez, Tyler Jackson, Jeremy Johnson, Colin Broderick."

And there it was. Just like winning the lottery. I gathered myself and stepped carefully over bodies huddled like shrimp on the cold floor and stood at the door of the cell. I did not glance back at my compatriots to gloat. This was not a victory. There was no triumph in this freedom. Some walked, some stayed.

Each of us would pay the last drop owed; that's just the way the thing is in the end.

Within twenty minutes, the judge had scheduled my hearing and I was skipping down the front steps of the courthouse and out across Centre Street into the cool March night. I stopped in a deli and bought myself a cup of hot tea and a pack of smokes and sat down on the pavement to savor them. I stared back at the courthouse and made a vow never to jeopardize my freedom ever again. I had to stop drinking.

The joke was now officially over. I was done messing around with this thing. I just couldn't drink, period. It was that simple. When I drank, bad things happened. I had almost killed two people. It was a miracle that they were not hurt, that I was not hurt; well, I had broken my finger, but that was nothing. It was a gentle reminder of the severity of the situation. I would just take it easy for a while. Stick to the beer and wine. No more hard liquor, ever. I was going to buckle down and get my life right again. Thank you, God, for this little warning. I hear you loud and clear, pal. You don't need to tell me twice.

Oksana was cold toward me for a long while after that little incident despite her manner when I spoke to her from jail. I had shaken her up pretty badly. I felt she was really beginning to view me with contempt. Sometimes little things she did would betray the fact that she hadn't fully forgiven me for the accident, like throwing a ceramic vase at my head or almost taking my eyeballs out with her fingernails, or smashing my favorite antique mirror with a crystal ashtray, or it might even be something as simple as threatening to cut my heart out with the bread knife. They were little signs that things had not fully healed. But I was getting used to all of that. When we woke in the morning to a trashed apartment, broken glass, and spilled blood, the violence that had taken place was merely a testament to the passion we felt for one another. This was no ordinary affair of the heart. This was legendary.

Finally she made it clear that she needed to take a break. She needed to get away from us, from me, for a while to figure things out. I agreed that she should. I assured her that I would help finance the trip if necessary. She was too young for this shit. I didn't want to be the one she could look back at in years to come as the one who had robbed her of all her youthful opportunities. I was no dummy. I understood that life would do a pretty good job of that all by itself. She decided to take a boat cruise to Europe, visit Portugal, Spain, and France before her annual trip to Russia. A friend of her mother's had an apartment she could use in Paris for a few weeks. I could join her there for a week or so if I liked.

By the time she was ready to go we were in love again. I had taken a break from the drink for a few weeks and she was down to about a case of wine a week. She had really buckled down for a few months to save money for the trip. She had begun working in a flower store and now she was taking side jobs organizing the flowers for weddings and parties. I was so impressed with her business savvy that we discussed opening her own flower store in the fall. In two months she managed to come up with almost half the money for her European trip by herself. She was finally in good spirits, and I was happy for her.

Gerry and I stood on the pier and watched her disappear on the enormous cruise ship as it backed out into the Hudson. It was as big and bright as an office block in the dark night. We stood there, waving, until the boat had managed its slow, deliberate arc into the current and drifted off downstream toward the harbor and the Atlantic beyond, filling the night with its great bellowing foghorn. I had not had a drink in about two months. I was thirsty, and she was gone.

We left the pier and marched straight across the West Side Highway and on to Tenth Avenue and Fifty-first Street and into Bull McCabe's, the first open bar we could find. I was not heartbroken at her departure. I was not concerned about who she might meet and fall in love with on her trip. I was filled with the great hunger for booze that only a real drunk can comprehend. There is no beer in the world that tastes better than that first one after a long break. I lifted the cold bottle in my hand and guzzled the crisp sparkling nectar with all the enthusiastic abandon of a hungry child suckling on his mother's breast. I am not absolutely certain, but I may have had a tear in my eye, as if this were my true lover and we were rushing toward each other again after a long and desperate separation. It's OK, I assured it, you are safe now. I will never leave you again.

Then I was in Riverdale, running, on the access road for the Henry Hudson Parkway, being chased by a cabdriver wielding a tire iron. There was some dispute about the payment of the fare. Gerry was there somewhere. Laughing or shouting. And then it was morning. I was on my couch, face down, still fully dressed, and the phone was ringing. That was how some nights happened. They started out with such promise, then they left three or four distinct snapshots before vanishing into the darkness, like a flat stone being skipped on the surface of a clear lake.

Something was happening to me. I could see it now. This was a definite pattern. At some point I had crossed the line. I was now a problem drinker. If I was not careful, I might have to stop drinking completely. I could not afford to get busted again for some stupid drinking offense. I could go to jail. Well, maybe not on the next offense, but I was getting closer. I had one strike against me now. The stakes had been raised. I had another court date scheduled for my last little mishap. My lawyer had warned me to stay clean for the next few months. The prosecutor for the

DA's office wanted to put me away because I had hospitalized two people in the accident. This was no longer a joke. I could not afford to be wrestling with cabdrivers on the parkway. I would have to be extra vigilant.

I answered the phone. It was Dermot Kenny, the big hurling player from Meath who had helped me get my car out of the woods.

"Broderick, you wanker. What are you up to?"

"Saturday mornings I like to shine all the silverware in the house."

"You're probably still lying in bed polishing the brass rail, am I right?"

"Is there some reason you're calling me at this ungodly hour other than to bust my balls?"

"What do you mean, ungodly hour? It's nearly noon, ya waster. The best part of the day's gone and you've missed it."

"Shouldn't you be out practicing your hurling shots or whatever it is you do?"

"I'm at Katie's Cottage."

"Are you patching her thatch?"

"Katie's Cottage, ya wanker. The bar by McLean Avenue."

"That's nice. Are you having the breakfast?"

"They don't serve food. They have a pool table. Are you comin' up for a drink?"

"I shouldn't."

"Don't tell me that little Russian has you by the short and curlies again."

"She's out of town."

"Well then, what are you waiting for? Get up here. I have a job for you."

"A job?"

"You start Monday morning. What are you drinking? I'll have it on the bar for you here when you get here."

"A bottle of Magners and a glass of ice might be a good way to start the day."

"Right, get out of bed, you lazy bastard. I'll see you here in ten minutes."

"Right."

"And do me a favor!"

"What?"

"Take a cab."

"Wanker."

Dermot had a job for me. He wanted me to help him build a bar called the Joshua Tree on West Forty-sixth Street. I told him I didn't think I was ready for it. I had only been working as a finish carpenter for a short while and I lacked the confidence. Over a few beers he assured me that we would be working together as a team and that he would cover me until I got the hang of it. I would be making the same money that he made, which was a real step up from the cowboy wages I was used to. This is how the construction scene worked for me. It was a vicious cycle. The more I drank, the more money I made. The more money I made, the more I drank. The irony of the situation did not escape me. Had I been sober I would never have been offered the job. To be a good carpenter and a good drinker was invaluable in the Irish construction business. Dermot Kenny was one of the best carpenters I'd ever seen at work, and like most of the best Irish carpenters I met in New York, he liked to drink and he liked that I liked to drink. To have a tradesman like Dermot vouch for me was not only an honor, it meant that I had graduated. I was in. There were Irish carpenters in New York who would stab their grandmothers for a job like this.

For the next six weeks, while Oksana crossed the Atlantic and toured Portugal and Spain, Dermot and I tore it up. Most mornings we would meet at the deli on the corner of Forty-sixth and Ninth. We bought our bottles of beer and poured them into large paper coffee cups so that we could take them with us back to the job and drink away our hangovers right under everybody's noses and nobody was ever any the wiser.

By the time I was ready to go to Paris we had finished the bar and I'd saved enough cash to take off for a few weeks.

I had earned my trip to Paris. I was going to enjoy having a glass of red wine the moment I arrived. Drink is the drunk's great reward for every accomplishment. The golden carrot we will follow till the grave. As I sat on the flight sipping a glass of red wine and reading the *New Yorker* under a single bar of light, high above the Atlantic with the other passengers quietly slumbering all around, it was hard to imagine a single reason for not allowing myself this luxury. Here was proof that I could, if I really wanted to, control my drinking. I was not going to get hammered on this flight, because I did not want to get hammered. This was not the occasion for getting hammered. I would have two or three little bottles of red wine and I would sleep so that I would be fresh for Paris. Was I powerless over alcohol? Apparently not. I felt inspired. I took out my notebook and began to write.

Of course, I had always wanted to go to Paris. What young writer reading Hemingway or Fitzgerald has not dreamed of traversing the same Parisian parlors that our great literary grandfathers had so majestically mythologized? But I could hardly consider myself a youthful, doe-eyed freshman; those days were gone. I was really just another literary tourist in search of some clue, some inkling of the inspiration that fueled so much great writing. I was going to drink where Hemingway drank. Piss in the bathroom where he had examined Fitzger-ald's dick and assured his good friend that it was a fine and normal size. I finished my third bottle of wine, put away my journal, and placed a little pillow behind my neck and tried to sleep. If Paris was indeed a muse, I wanted to look my best.

What actually happened in Paris? We drank, we fought, and we drank again; we had the requisite lovers' embrace in an afternoon rain shower as we ran from one bar to another. We fought, heroically and homicidally; we met Rick Pernod, who was passing through after a trip to Prague; we broke up, ate Croque Monsieurs for breakfast, and got back together again; we ate lunch at Montmartre; we climbed the Eiffel Tower and I had an anxiety attack; we drank in jazzy cellars and on red velvet couches and we fought; we broke up and I stormed off by myself to fulfill my obligatory Hemingway tour; I located both Les Deux Magots and Le Dôme, got exceedingly drunk and apparently obnoxious, and succeeded in being physically ejected from both places in the same night. I woke up the next morning, buckled and bent, and crawled to the bowl and cradled it in my arms and felt I understood then what Hemingway had meant when he talked of Paris being a moveable feast.

I was then back in New York again and determined to stay clean. My drunken Parisian debacle had left me frazzled and raw. My relationship with Oksana was hanging by a thread. I decided to give it a rest. I was sick of myself. I was pissing my life away. I was living my life like a dog on a leash. The bottle had me by the collar. I wanted to race ahead with my life. But the fear of dashing straight into traffic kept me somewhat at bay, and then of course I got thirsty and I lapped once more at that precious golden nectar, dove headfirst for that frosty glass of beer . . .

I got a job working for some Irish American guy fitting panels in an office building in midtown. It was one of those union jobs, so I had to try and dodge the shop steward all day long, and when he did catch me, I had to lie about what my name was and tell him that I'd left my union card at home, again. The union carpenters of New York City have zero tolerance for scab workers, so the situation was almost unbearable. All day long other union carpenters on the job would prod me with little questions to see if they could catch me out. "Hey, pal, where were you working last? Didn't I see you on that job over on First? Who was the shop steward on that job, do you remember his name . . . ?" I was dodging and weaving all day long. They knew I was lying and they wanted me off the job as quickly as possible. These guys had their own friends sitting around down at the union hall with families to feed and no jobs to go to, and the thought of some Paddy working for cash while they paid their dues in their own country just infuriated them. I didn't blame them. If the situation were reversed, I would have felt exactly the same way. Only in Ireland we'd have screwed the guy's toolbox to the floor or locked him into a Porta Potti overnight to let him know he wasn't wanted around.

I was relieved when, one bright sunny morning after about a week of this, I was told that I had to take my tool bag and head on over to an office building on Forty-sixth and Sixth to repair some door handles. I was glad for the break.

I sauntered over to Sixth Avenue and found a spot to sit and relax on a low marble bench where I could drink a cup of coffee and smoke a cigarette and read the morning headlines off the news ticker that wrapped around the corner of the block. NEW YORK PRIMARIES TODAY, it read. NEW YORKERS ARE ON THEIR WAY TO THE POLLS . . . I moved my attention to the early-morning pedestrians hurrying along on their way to work. There is no city in the world better suited to the anonymous spectator sport of people watching. Here was the great herd of humanity going about their daily chores, and all were free to grab a front row seat and observe. The ferocious-looking ladies with their sharp little heels and tight knee-length skirts and de la Renta reading glasses went past without so much as a sideways glance, their steely gazes fixed off somewhere beyond, in the great tops of the buildings farther downtown. "This is where I live," was the message those spiked little heels gave as they rattled and clipped briskly by. "I know nothing but concrete and smooth shiny surfaces," they seemed to announce as they knocked sternly along. Then there were the New Jersey and Long Island girls lugging their oversized knockoff Gucci handbags, wearing sneakers over their nylon stockings, a fashion faux pas necessitated by the long, weary commute across rivers and bridges and up long flights of subway stairs. Their faces were still flushed from that early morning sprint to catch the eight o'clock train out of Weehawken or Fort Lee or whatever other foreign land they had migrated from on this fine sunny morning to this great concrete island of dreams, the comfy walking attire they wore a small betrayal of the hip Manhattan chic they tried so diligently to convey. "I cannot afford to live here," their sneakers seemed to whisper as they stepped softly along. There were others, of course: the young Asians with the *Wall Street Journal* folded and tucked under their arms like military batons, hair greased and clamped tight against the scalp like a helmet; the seasoned old office managers with the graying temples and the fat paunch spilling over a tight belt, men who walked with a waddle, carrying faded old worn briefcases with broken latches that would see them through to retirement now. There was a skinny young Latino kid wearing an oversized suit with broad lapels over a bright orange shirt and a broad red tie, looking uncomfortable as he stepped along in a glossy pair of black loafers. "We don't even know this guy," they seemed to scowl. These were some of the faces of that sunny midtown morning that I watched with great enthusiasm for a half an hour or so, enjoying my coffee and cigarettes, the whole damn lot of them scuttling heartbreakingly along. What a bunch. What a vigorous early morning parade of ambition, the industrious, unstoppable march of commerce.

I finished my cigarette and my coffee, slung my tool bag over my shoulder, and took the elevator up to the eighth floor. When I got out of the elevator I was in a marble hallway surrounded by glass doors. I tried a couple of them. They were locked. I knocked a couple of times before I noticed the little buzzer. I gave that a shove. The shrill voice of the receptionist informed me that someone was coming to let me in. I waited for just a moment before some suit rushed up and swung open the glass door from inside.

"Hi, I'm Colin. I'm the carpenter—"

"I'm Tom," he said, taking my hand. "An airplane just hit one of the Twin Towers."

"Really. How the hell did that happen?"

"I don't know—it just happened. Some idiot lost control, I suppose."

"Is it bad?"

"They don't know much yet. It just happened. I think it was one of those small planes. So you're Joe's guy."

"Yeah, that's me. He says you have some locks to repair."

"Yeah, there are a couple that don't work properly. We have some extra ones that they left here in a closet. I'll show you where they are. Just follow me." I followed him around the large office, observing the early morning bustle of the suits as Tom jabbered on about how they had paid a lot of money for this renovation and about how all these new locks were so expensive and they really should all be working and blah blah blah . . . I was busy checking out the new surroundings. The workings of an office held no mystique for me since my days of working in the bank. I understood now that 90 percent of what happened here was clock punching, cooler gossip, and deforestation. Still, there were one or two cute girls who smiled as I trailed along behind Tom. Manhattan office girls seemed to always get a big kick out of having a construction worker in their midst. It added a little spice to the office for the day—and wait 'til they heard my accent . . . This was going to be a nice gig for a few days. Tom led me to the broom closet, where he located a cardboard box full of metal plates and loose screws, the leftover guts of new door hardware.

"Whatever you need should be in here," he said.

"Great, Tom," I said, dropping my tool bag and staring into the mess of mismatched metal plates and screws.

"Let me show you a couple of the locks you'll be working on."

"Cool." I followed Tom again and he showed me the lock to the office supply closet.

"Maybe you could start here," he said, flipping the handle and swinging the door on its hinges. "We need to get this thing locking today before all this paper and whiteout just walks out the door."

"I understand." Tom got down on one knee and produced a small Swiss Army knife out of his pocket and pulled out a little Phillips-head screwdriver to try it in the door plate. I folded my arms and watched with amusement as he fiddled with the chrome-plated screws on the catch plate. An attractive Asian girl in a short black skirt and a crisp white blouse came up, clutching a folder against her chest.

"Whenever you have a few minutes, could you stop by my office? We really should go over these figures before I put the final proposal together."

"Sure, Sue. I'll be right with you," he said, squinting his eyes to studiously examine the tip of the small screwdriver he held and then trying it back in the screw head. "I think if we could just take this screw out and adjust the plate a sixteenth of an inch to the left here, this locking mechanism should catch."

Sue looked at me with an expression that I read as, "Oh, God, does he really think he's a carpenter now?" I raised my eyebrows in mock horror and clamped my hands against the sides of my face. Sue smiled.

"I think we're going to need a larger screwdriver for that, Tom," I said.

"Yeah, you might be right, Colin. If I'm not mistaken we're going to need a number three Phillips head here for this baby." Then, as if he was just now realizing that Sue had been standing there all along, "Oh, Sue, this is Colin, the carpenter. I'm just showing him around. He's going to be with us for the next couple of days, taking care of some bits and pieces."

"Hi, Sue," I said, taking her hand. "It's nice to meet you."

"Hi, Colin. Nice to meet you. Is that an accent I hear?"

"It's possible."

"Are all you Irish guys carpenters?"

"It's the Lord's own trade." I smiled. "Tom's a burgeoning carpenter himself, you know; he's just giving me a few pointers here to get me going." Sue was now grinning like a giddy schoolgirl. Tom stood up. He'd heard enough chitchat for one morning.

"Thanks, Sue," Tom said as he marched off. "I'll be with you as soon as I'm finished showing Colin around. Let's go, Colin."

"Nice to meet you, Sue," I said, following him.

"You too."

We were passing an office just up the hall when some guy in a suit popped his head out the door. "Tom, you have to see this."

"What?"

"There's been another one."

"Another what?"

"Another plane hit the other tower." He popped back into his office again and we followed him in and there on his computer monitor were the Twin Towers, with smoke belching across the blue morning sky.

"Holy fuck, we're being attacked," I said. They both glanced at me and the three of us just stood there, silently staring at the screen. Another suit popped his head in the office door.

"Guys, you have to come see this," he said, and ran off down the hall. We walked out of the office and followed him around to the big corner office, where a small crowd had gathered. When we walked in they were all standing there in complete silence, staring out of the window. We went on in and stood among them. And there it was, as clear as day. Right in front of our very eyes, a sight so astonishing that there was absolutely nothing to be said. I stared into the gaping hole in the wall of the tower that faced me, trying to piece it together. Where was the plane? Where the hell was the plane? Oh, yeah, there it is. That's the tail end of the plane sticking out. Jesus, that's a big hole. Look at those fucking flames. I was trying to count how many floors deep the hole was that the plane had created: one, two, three . . . My eyes were following the flames roaring up the outside of the building. I stared back into the hole. You could almost see all the way through to the other side. That was no small plane. Then I followed the flames again, out and up the sides of the building, and then I could see it: The plane had torn almost clean through the building. I looked up again at the floors above, and it hit me like a punch to the chest: There are people above that hole. There are people above those flames. There were people in that airplane. It was as if we had all arrived at the same conclusion at the exact same moment. There was a collective gasp for air, as if we had all been holding our breath. Maybe we had.

"The Pentagon's been hit," somebody said, and the coin finally dropped. We were being attacked. I had to find my brothers. I had to call Oksana. I looked around the office. Both phones were occupied. I ran to another office. Occupied . . . Another . . . I had to get to a phone. I ran to the elevator. I took it down to the street and ran to the pay phone on the corner of the block and called my brother Gerry on his cell phone.

"Have you seen the news?"

"No, but one of the lads just said a plane hit the towers."

"Two planes."

"Fuck."

"Where are you?"

"In the seventies on the East Side."

"Run."

"What?"

"Get out of the building and get off the island. Have you talked to Brendan yet?"

"No."

"Call Brendan. Tell him to get off the island. I'll call you later. Get back to the Bronx."

I called Oksana at the flower store where she was working, up on Columbus and Seventy-third. She answered on the second ring. "Hey, where are you?"

"I'm on Forty-sixth and Sixth."

"Are you OK?"

"Yeah. You have to get off the island."

"I'm not going without you or my parents."

I stood on Sixth Avenue for a moment and watched the pandemonium unfold. I had to get uptown to Oksana, but traffic was ground to a halt. People were running in every direction, horns were blowing, women were crying, a fine dusting of ash was already beginning to fall on Forty-sixth Street like a light snow. I looked up at the crystal blue sky above and felt the ash settle on my face. A handful of businessmen standing nearby were trying to outbid each other for the services of a limo driver to get them off the island. I looked off downtown and for a moment considered going down there. There would be casualties. They would need help. I should go. But Oksana. I ran to the corner and down into the subway. A crowd had gathered around the ticket booth and they were screaming and pounding their fists on the Plexiglas window as a terrified transit worker backed herself up against the wall inside and tried to shout back that it wasn't her fault that the trains weren't running. I came back up onto the street. The towers were gone. A woman grabbed my arm and asked, "Are we being attacked?" That's when I ran. I ran toward Seventh Avenue as the roar of F-16s thundered overhead. I did not stop running until I reached the flower shop on Seventy-third and Columbus. Oksana was still there waiting for me when I came through the door.

"Where are your parents?" I said.

"I don't know," she cried. "I can't reach them . . . Oh my God, they're here," she said, and when I turned around her mother was already stepping out of the car and running into the store. Oksana ran to her.

"Quickly, grab your things. We have to go," her mother said.

We took the West Side Highway home, getting on at the Seventy-ninth Street Boat Basin. I had expected pandemonium on the highway, traffic jams for miles, but there was nothing. There was not another car in sight, going either in or out of Manhattan. Not one single car. Oksana and I sat in the back, turned around in our seats, staring out through the rear window at the great trail of smoke drifting off the end of Manhattan, and I tried to grasp this surreal image, this perfectly blue sky, this empty highway, this silence, the end of the world as we had grown to know it, drifting off out into the Atlantic just now like the tail end of a white cloak leaving town.

In the months that followed there was a mass exodus. People were leaving the island. Many Irish simply packed their bags and headed back home. What I did was drink. I staggered through the next year, working when I could, waking in the mornings bleary-eyed and beaten. What did it matter anymore? We were all going to die anyway. The hangovers were becoming insufferable. It wasn't the physical pain that bothered me; it was the all-consuming mental anguish. Oksana and I fought almost constantly. She was becoming more volatile, more violent; her hatred of me was unfathomable. I thought of what I was like at her age and I understood that we didn't stand a chance. One night we went out drinking in some beat-up old bar up on Riverdale Avenue. My brother Gerry was with us. We played pool and drank a round of shots for every beer. She got drunk and belligerent, flirting with Gerry to get my goat. I was too exhausted and drunk to deal with it anymore, so I went home and fell asleep. When I woke the next morning she was lying next to me, fast asleep on top of the covers, still fully dressed. Gerry was in the living room, passed out on the couch with lipstick on his face. I went to the refrigerator and poured myself a glass of vodka. Oksana and I were finally over.

After she moved out, I had reached a point where I said fuck it all to hell. I drank like I have never drank before. But wasn't I always saying that? But it was true: Each time I threw in the towel it got worse. Each new alcoholic onslaught brought with it a new level of debauchery. Some subconscious part of me had come to terms with what I could handle and it took more of an effort to push myself into uncharted territory. Every new drinking binge needed to outdo the last. If it wasn't worse, then it wasn't worth it.

My day would start at around nine a.m. in my new favorite bar in Woodlawn, the Catalpa bar up on 233rd Street. A few glasses of vodka and orange juice for breakfast and a hit of coke in the bathroom and I was raring to go. By about lunchtime I'd have settled into a nice beer-drinking pace and by the time the bar really started to fill up, around four o'clock, when the lads would be coming in from their jobs, I'd be back on the vodka again and a few more blasts of coke to help the conversation along. By nine o'clock somebody would have rolled a joint. Someone else might have slipped an ecstasy pill or four into my hand at the bar and I would roll on into the night like that, playing pool, shooting darts, waking to find myself alone, babbling in my sleep on my couch back in Riverdale. I'd reach for the bottle to get it kick-started all over again, call my dealer for more blow at eight in the morning, and he'd come by to pick me up at my apartment and drop me off wherever I needed to go. I'd run for a week like this without food before the terror would finally strike. Then I'd call Dermot to get my job back so I could get back into a pattern of work and food and life. Try to keep the devil at bay. Now that I was a fully qualified alcoholic carpenter I could always get my job back. But Dermot had just about had it with the Oksana drama.

"If I catch you so much as looking at your phone thinking about her I'll smash it to pieces."

She did call and said she'd like to see me. I went, of course. I put on a clean shirt and took her to a nice Italian place up on Johnston Avenue. She came in a tight new dress with her long hair loose and shiny. She'd even worn makeup for the occasion. She looked like she did when I first met her. She was relaxed. Happy even. She was single. I ordered an expensive bottle of wine and another; we talked about how much we'd hurt each other. She asked me where I could see myself in the future and I told her, living in the country, away from it all, writing. She saw herself with an apartment on the Upper West Side, maybe running her own flower store. We were headed in different directions. We kissed over the crème brûlée and she decided to come back and stay the night.

When I came home from work, there was a note for me on the end of the sofa saying she was gone for good this time and that she didn't want me to contact her again. It was over. I was gutted. I curled up on the couch and lay awake most of the night, listening to the traffic down on the parkway.

The following morning Dermot picked me up for work at my apartment in Riverdale at about seven thirty. I climbed into the truck and turned to speak to him. I was going to explain to him what had happened, but the words wouldn't come out and against all the strength I had, I began to cry. He gave me a look of deep concern but said nothing as he began to drive. I looked away and tried to bite my lip, but nothing was going to stop this. I could not stop. It just came and I couldn't stop. I broke down and wept uncontrollably. We went on up the Parkway, through Yonkers, Westchester, and on to Connecticut and still, I could not stop. I tried to apologize but I couldn't stop long enough to get the words out.

"Don't worry, man, just let it out. Keep going," Dermot said. "It'll be good for you." The tears came in floods. My whole body convulsed and I could not for the life of me contain it for a single second. I was humiliated and scared, but I could do nothing to stop it. The dam had burst, and it was going to come out whether I liked it or not. When we reached Bedford, Dermot pulled the truck over on a quiet country road and called our boss to tell him that we'd hit bad traffic and we were going to be a little late. And still it would not stop. There were tears from my childhood, from my school years, tears from the first divorce and the second, the car accidents, Omagh, 9/11, Oksana, myself, there were buckets of tears, oceans of tears, and they would not stop. When I could finally speak, I told Dermot that he would have to drive me to a train station. I would have to go home. I could not show up for work in this state. It suddenly dawned on me that he must be thinking that I'd lost my mind; it dawned on me that he was right, that I had lost my mind, that I was suffering some kind of breakdown, and suddenly I became paranoid that he was going to turn me over to the authorities. I was terrified. And still I could not stop. This is how people wound up being institutionalized. I made him promise me that he would not call the authorities on me. He promised, then he made me promise that I wouldn't kill myself if he dropped me off at a train station, and we shook on it.

After about two more hours of stops and starts I was finally able to have him drop me off at the train station in the village of Bedford.

"I'll tell him you got sick on the way here and I had to take you home again. Don't worry about it. I have you covered."

"Thanks, Dermot."

"Now go home and get some sleep."

After he drove away I sat on a bench in the sleepy little station and I cried for another forty-five minutes. I couldn't stop long enough to pull myself together to speak to the lady at the ticket booth. Commuters passed me by with curious sideways glances. Nobody approached me or said a word. There was nothing I could do but wait out the flood and pray that nobody got frightened and called the cops. Eventually it eased off enough for me to catch the train to Woodlawn and take a cab home from there to Riverdale. I curled up on the couch and

didn't move again until the next morning, when Dermot arrived
to pick me up for work.

"How're ye this mornin'?"

"I'm good. Much better."

"Are ye sure?"

"It's done."

"You're sure."

"Absolutely sure, yes."

"Good."

"Thanks for not turning me in somewhere."

"Why the hell would I do that?"

"I don't know. People are funny."

"Well, I'm not people."

"That's good to know."

"You sure you're alright?"

"I'm great. I just needed to get that out of my system."

"You're done with the Russian now, right?"

"Done. Over and out."

"About time."

"I have a proposal for you."

"Uh-oh . . ."

"I'm going to put on a play."

"You're what?"

"I'm going to put on a play."

"What sort of a play?"

"It's sort of a tragic comedy; I'll give you a copy of it later
to read."

"You do a bit of theatre, then."

"A bit."

"Who wrote the play?"

"I did."

"You wrote a play?"

"Yup, and I want you to produce it."

"What the hell would I know about producing a play?"

"Believe me, Dermot, you'll be great producer. I'll tell you how to go about it."

"You're mad."

"Completely. But we're doing this play."

"And you'll tell me what to do?"

"I'll give you a few pointers. You'll do the rest."

"Fuck it. Why not. It'll be a bit of *craic*, right."

"It will. It'll be a lot of *craic*."

"You're on. Ya mad bastard."

"You're a good man, Dermot. You won't regret this."

"And no more crying."

"No more crying."

"Good, because if I see any more of that shite I'll put you in the damned straightjacket meself."

HERE COMES HOLLYWOOD

IT was March 2003 and I was going to have my first play produced by a carpenter who'd never worked a day in the theatre before in his life. Yet Dermot Kenny was a natural choice for the job. He had all the requirements of a good producer: He was great at telling people what to do, he had a knack for getting things done, he had a good eye for detail, and he was as sweet as marmalade as long as you didn't cross him. In three weeks he had singlehandedly produced more results than a team of professional producers could have managed in twice the time.

The first thing he did was to secure a venue for the play up on Martha Avenue, in the heart of the Irish community in Woodlawn. It was a church function room with a stage and a seating capacity of about 120. He had also secured a separate function room for rehearsals above a bar called Cassie's on 233rd. Then he rallied together a bunch of Irish lads he knew and they started work on building the set. These were professional carpenters and painters. Under Dermot's supervision, they built the walls, installed windows, doors, and a kitchenette. By the time he brought me around to see it he had organized the furniture, hung the window shades, and rolled out a great big rug to soften the acoustics onstage. Dermot had insisted that everything be just right. I had told him about my days in the Irish Bronx Theatre Company and the late Chris O Neill's insistence that every detail of the set be authentic. It had to look like a real apartment. If it looked like a real apartment, the audience was halfway there. They tacked on baseboard and picture rail, hung a mirror by the door, hooked up a microwave oven and a stove and a refrigerator, put a fresh green plant in the corner, and placed a few old magazines on the coffee table. He even dispatched a team of girls to hound the local bar owners to buy advertising in the playbill; anyone who didn't want to pay got a personal visit from Dermot himself. All we needed was a full cast and we were all set to start rehearsals.

By Saint Patrick's Day, I had three of the actors in place. My brother Brendan would play Martin, and my old pal Tony would play the priest. I had worked with both of them in the theatre before and had the two of them in mind specifically when I had written the play. An actress called Tara Foley had signed on to play Brendan's Irish American wife, but I could not find my Rosie. Rosie was the single girl who lived next door. The success of the play depended on Rosie. She had to be Irish, brassy, sexy, but vulnerable enough so that the audience would fall for her in the end. I'd written the role of Rosie with a vision of who she was, and I could not find her, no matter where I looked. As the first day of rehearsals approached, the other actors voiced their concern. Dermot informed me that I had one weekend left or he was going to pick somebody himself right off the street. I was at my wits' end. If I cast the wrong girl, the play would fail. If I didn't choose somebody, the play would not happen at all.

On the last Saturday morning before our first rehearsal, I dragged my ass out of bed with a ferocious hangover and drove to Yonkers to the state-mandated drunk driving class I was attending at that time so that I could get my driver's license back. I had been driving illegally since the accident in Manhattan. I sat through a thirty-year-old video of doctors slicing into jaundiced livers and guys knocking over traffic cones, and when it was done I walked two blocks to the nearest Irish joint for a drink. I pulled open the door to the bar-restaurant, and there before me was my Rosie.

"Good morning. Would you care for a table for one?" she said, beaming a bright all-American smile, her lush red hair falling in curly waves down around her shoulders. It was her, exactly as I had imagined her.

"Naw, I'm good," I croaked. "I need a drink."

"Well, go right ahead, the bar's right over there, and have a nice day."

This was the girl I was looking for, in the flesh. She had the vibrant Celtic appeal of a girl you might see on an Irish tourism poster and the dramatic body and poise of a dancer.

I went on to the bar and ordered a beer and then another. I snuck a glance over my shoulder now and again in disbelief. I had found her three days before our first rehearsal.

The chef came out of the kitchen and sat next to me, trying to spark up some conversation about the Yankees or the Mets. I can't remember which. The common assumption is that if you are in a bar in New York and you have a beer in your hand, you are a sports fanatic. I didn't know enough about the game to bluff my way through a conversation, so I nodded a lot and tried to look concerned as he rattled on about innings and plates and pitches. I let him go on for about five minutes before I asked him about the redhead at the door.

"Oh, she has a boyfriend," he said, eyeing me a little suspiciously.

"No, I didn't mean it like that," I said. "She looks like an actress."

"Ah, yeah, I think she said she does do something along those lines alright."

"Really?"

"I think so."

"Do you know her at all?"

"A little. She's very friendly. A lovely girl."

"Maybe you could bring her over here for a minute."

"For what?"

"I'd like to talk to her."

"You want to talk to her?"

"Yeah, just for a second or two."

He went off reluctantly and brought her over to where I was seated and introduced us.

"Fiona, this is Colin. Colin, Fiona."

I took her hand and she smiled that red-carpet smile of hers again. "It's nice to meet you," I said.

"It's nice to meet you, too."

"Liam here tells me you might be an actress."

"I'm a dancer, actually, but I've done a little bit of acting."

"You're American."

"From New Jersey."

"I thought you were Irish, with the red hair . . ."

"I got the hair from my mother's side . . ."

"I see," I said. There are times in your life when you meet someone and you know automatically that you connect, and it was like that with Fiona. I knew right away we would get along.

"How do you think you would be with an Irish accent?"

"Oh, she's great with an Irish accent," Liam chimed in. He'd been observing the proceedings with some amusement. "She's been imitating us around here every day. Go on, do a bit for him. Go on."

"Aren't you supposed to be in the kitchen . . . ," she said, cocking an eyebrow in Liam's direction, ". . . frying something?" Liam grinned.

"Could you do it in a play?" I asked her. "If you had to?"

"I suppose so," she said, breaking into a Dublin dialect on the spot. "If you really wanted me to play a wee girl from Dublin I suppose I could give it a try. Sure, why not."

Liam applauded a little too enthusiastically. I ignored him as I took a look into Fiona's big, bright Irish eyes. I was done for, again. She had me.

"Great," I said. "I have a part here that's perfect for you."

"You want me to audition for a play . . ."

"No, you've got the part."

Three weeks later Fiona broke up with her boyfriend of two years and moved into my apartment in Riverdale. We were both on the tail end of unhappy relationships, it seemed, and we were just happy to be happy for a change. I explained to her straight up that I was an alcoholic and that I would be drinking extensively and that if we were going to be together she was going to have to understand that simple fact from the outset. She was not to try and stop me under any circumstances. If I wanted to kill myself drinking it was my choice. I was an adult and I could do as I pleased.

Fiona assured me that she would try not to stand in my way. She was going to be too busy studying for her college finals and going out enjoying herself in her free time to be bothered about saving my skinny Irish ass. It seemed I had found just the very girl to drink myself to death with. Her only reservation was that she didn't want to watch me do it in the Bronx. "If you're going to drink yourself to death, why not do it in style? Why not Manhattan?" I liked her way of thinking.

Fiona was a city girl. Manhattan was her playground, and she was chomping at the bit to get back there again. She had a group of friends she'd gone to ballet school with and on any given night, one or two of them were knocking around town somewhere in search of a party here, a club there. These were girls who knew exactly where to go and, more importantly, it seemed, where not to go.

The Manhattan nightlife and club scene were foreign to me. The only time I had ever spent hanging out in the city was during the years I had spent sober, and even then I had only managed to explore some of the coffee shops and restaurants. I had never been in a position before to really explore the other Manhattan, the one that began at midnight and went on until dawn.

One of the first clubs Fiona took me out to was a place called the Frying Pan, a notorious dance club on an old boat anchored off one of the piers in Chelsea. This was not somewhere that she and her friends normally came to party. The Frying Pan, I was to learn, was for the bridge-and-tunnel crowd, the Goomba Johnnys in for the night, sporting their dazzlingly white wife beaters, bottled tan, and fat gold chains. On this particular night there was a private party for some of Fiona's friends on the boat, and she wanted to take me along to introduce me to them.

I wanted to make a good impression, so I made my own way into the city that evening and started drinking at around five somewhere on the Upper West Side. By the time she called me at about ten thirty, I was in a transvestite bar on Twenty-second Street with a Tina Turner impersonator in my lap, entertaining a table full of her friends. Transvestites are the most fun to party with. Nothing shocks them. I have always felt completely at home in their company. Maybe they were just trying to seduce me. Whatever the case, I was enjoying myself immensely, and when Fiona got there she loved the scene too. The queens ushered her into the pack, fussing over her new outfit and her spiked heels and making sure our drinks never ran dry.

When it was time for us to go, one of the queens called a

friend of hers to come pick us up. Within a few minutes her friend Dave arrived in a Range Rover to drive us over to the pier. Dave, she informed me, could get me anything I needed to keep me wide-awake and happy for the rest of the night.

The drug scene in the city was a tidier affair than I was used to in the Bronx. Dave cruised around Manhattan in his hunter green Range Rover, listening to Roxy Music, in an eternal loop of bars and clubs. He assured me that with just twenty minutes' notice he could meet me anywhere below Fourteenth Street seven nights a week. Dave was a guy who took pride in his product. He charged twice as much as everybody else, but his cocaine was cleaner than the first snow. I assured him that as long as it kept me awake to drink I was all for it.

By the time we arrived at the Frying Pan we were in a festive mood. I went off to the bar to get us a couple of vodkas while Fiona tried to locate her friends. On my way back to find her, I fell and landed flat on my face on a metal step. Somehow I managed to save the drinks. I gathered myself and went off to find Fiona. When I found her she was with her friends, who gasped in horror as they saw me for the first time, with blood streaming down my face, holding Fiona's drink out to her as if nothing had happened. I proceeded to shake a little bump of cocaine out of a little baggie onto the back of my hand as they watched in bewildered horror. One of the club's bouncers came running up and handed me a white hand towel.

"Maybe we should get you to a hospital," he said. "Looks like you're going to need a few stitches."

"It's nothing," I said, wiping my face with a handful of napkins I grabbed from the bar. "My face is numb. I can't feel a thing."

The bouncer seemed to be happy enough that I wasn't planning on getting the cops and a lawyer in there to sue the place, so we were given special treatment and free drinks for the rest of the night.

When we showed up for rehearsal the next day, Dermot and Brendan demanded to know who had beaten me so badly. Fiona had tried to patch me up a little with some surgical tape, but my eye was black and blue and the gash on my eyebrow had developed an ugly dark scab during the night. I tried to convince them that I'd fallen at a club, but they weren't having it. I lay down on the couch we were using in rehearsals and fell asleep as they continued to run their scenes without me.

After suffering my initial introduction to her friends and my 1980s Irish Catholic altar boy look, complete with gold buckled loafers and oversized shirt collars, Fiona insisted she take me out shopping in the West Village. She needed to buy me some new clothes for my fresh start in the world. Fiona was a twenty-two-year-old drama queen who never left the house without her four-inch stilettos; her image was everything. She could put up with me drinking myself to death, but my wardrobe needed a serious makeover if she was going to be seen in public with me while I did it.

She took me to SoHo and dragged me around the boutique stores on West Broadway and bought me skin-tight T-shirts and black pants, a two-hundred-dollar pair of oversize sunglasses, and a new pair of Doc Martens. Apparently, I was ready to party.

With Fiona by my side and Dave's number in my speed dial, I set off on a mad dash about the island of Manhattan like a wolf that had been starved and let loose in a hen run. We swilled twelve-dollar martinis at Vintage up on Ninth Avenue. Sipped wine at the Mercer Hotel, slugged screwdrivers all over the East Village and whiskey neat at underground dance clubs in Chinatown. Everywhere we went, we met actors and writers, producers and directors, hopeful Midwestern transplants, recent college grads, and trust-fund posers who invited us to their tables to help drink daddy's generous allowance. I began to feel more at home; I began to get a sense of myself. I was the Irish writer guy, the drunk; I was a playwright and a novelist, a poet and a storyteller. I was no longer the crouching wallflower; I was the life and soul of the party, the roaring maniacal scream machine; you couldn't shut me up. I had spent a decade of my life with the cotton wool in my mouth, a decade of my life listening, and now that I was free I talked, I talked till my throat hurt, I talked till the lights came up and the last drinks were drained, I talked till the bouncers ushered me out onto empty sidewalks at dawn, I talked until the sun came, until my body ached with talk and my head spun like a lighthouse lens in a deep wretched storm.

DJs, bartenders, and bouncers all over town began to remember our names. My veins throbbed with the glamour of it all; Manhattan buzzed and pulsated in tune with my own highly medicated heart. Fiona led me around like a bright star. When Fiona walked into a bar, she lit up the place like a sparkler. She had an air of celebrity about her, and people noticed. She took me to the little boutique dance clubs around West Broadway and the Meatpacking District that only a true city dancer would know, and I would watch as they would clear the floor for her while she danced. When Fiona danced, everybody watched. I stood at the bar and sipped my screwdrivers and felt the great pull of the earth beneath my feet. I understood now the place where I was standing. This was the New York I had heard about. This was the city that never sleeps. This was what people stayed and died for.

• • •

On opening night of my play, *Father Who*, 120 people showed up. Fiona's performance as Rosie stirred the crowd into such a frenzy that some sexually repressed young Irish gentleman actually yelled, "Slut" from the audience. Fiona came backstage after the scene and burst into tears.

"I can't go back out there again," she cried. "They hate me."

"Of course they hate you. They're supposed to hate you at this point in the play. Go back out there and piss them off," I said, massaging her shoulders.

"I can't," she sobbed. "They hate me."

I had to think fast. "Remember Glenn Close in *Fatal Attraction*?"

"Yes."

"Did the audience hate her?"

"Yes."

"And whose performance do you remember most from the movie?"

She wiped her tears away and braced herself for the next scene.

The play was a huge success. We sold out all ten shows, over one hundred people a night. My parents flew in from Ireland and attended all ten shows in a row, reveling in my success and the attention they warranted as parents of the playwright/director. I had finally shown them something, at last, that proved that I was not completely delusional in my aspirations to be a writer.

Pauline Turley, the artistic director for the Irish Arts Center in Manhattan, came up to see the show. I had talked with her about how the show was being received in the Bronx and she'd expressed interest in seeing it with the possibility of bringing it into Manhattan for a run. I sent for a car to pick up her and her date. I reserved the best seats in the house for them and made sure they were served refreshments before the show began. The immediate future of the play and of my theatrical career hinged on this one performance. If this went well, I was off to Manhattan with my first show. If not, then it was back to the drawing board for at least another year or two.

As the play began, I stood in the back of the theater and prayed for luck. The house was packed, the lights came up, and the cast were off and running. The audience shuffled in their seats with their heads strained to make sure they didn't miss a beat. I glanced over at Pauline Turley and noticed the way she studied not only the stage but the audience's reaction to the material. I could barely stand to watch. There is a scene at the beginning of the play where a phone rings onstage to announce the arrival of the priest. It is a pivotal scene and it had gone off without a hitch for the first eight shows, but on this night the phone would not ring. I gripped my arms across my chest and prayed. This could not be happening. The phone would not ring. The seconds that passed seemed like an eternity. My brother, as Martin, covered as best he could to buy time onstage, but in the awkward moments that followed, the audience was lost. They had felt the break in the performance. By the time the phone did ring, it was much, much too late. The show that night was a disaster. I walked backstage and lay down flat on my back and held my head in my hands as the crowd's uneasy shuffling and coughs filled the air. The play would not be going to Manhattan. "It seems to work well for a local production," Pauline said with her hand on my shoulder before we parted that night. I was gutted. I needed a very strong drink.

• • •

What is there to say about what happened next? It bores me now to recount it. By the time the play ended I was on a full-fledged drinking binge from morning to night, working a day or two here and there to make enough money to continue the session. I was resolved to drink myself to death. Fiona tried to convince me that I should take it easy. I got worse. Fiona got a job as the "whore on the door" at Bouley restaurant down on West Broadway and moved back to Manhattan, where she belonged. She got an apartment with her friend Suzanne above a bar called Jake's Dilemma on Amsterdam Avenue.

Two months later, I was forced out of my own apartment in Riverdale. I could no longer pay the rent. I packed my books into about forty boxes and moved into an attic room in my brother Brendan's house in Yonkers.

It's easy to explain to a drinker how you could wind up on a six-month bender, but for the nondrinker it's a little ridiculous to comprehend. I took to selling some of my most prized books so that I would have drinking money. A signed first edition of *The Gonzo Papers* by Hunter S. Thompson for $150; *The Grapes of Wrath*, signed by Steinbeck, for $200; a Bukowski hardback limited edition, hand bound in boards by Earl Gray, No. 22, signed by Bukowski with a doodle of a dog next to his name, for $200. Once the Bukowski was gone it got easier. These were books that I would never see again, books that had been given to me as gifts, treasures discovered at street fairs and old bookstores around town over a period of twelve or thirteen years, and I was practically giving them away for drinking money. I unloaded bags of books, signed first editions, rare hardbacks, and treasured paperbacks no longer in print. It was a bibliophilic slaughter. But when I decided to drink, that was what I did. The hangovers were worse now. I now had the added horror of waking up to the realization that I was selling off my most prized possessions. Books I had kept with me for years were now being pissed away in an afternoon at the Catalpa.

I was losing my mind and it was beginning to scare me. The Iraq War had started and I became consumed with what was happening to the world, what had happened to my beautiful America. I sat in bars reading every newspaper article related to the war, watching the continuous news coverage, chewing the ear off anyone who would listen: cabdrivers, strangers next to me on the 4 train, barflies like myself. One afternoon, in a suicidal depression and very drunk, I called the CIA and told the guy who answered the phone that I wanted to go to Baghdad. "What exactly is it that you do, Mr. Broderick?" he asked with great professional courtesy.

"I'm a writer," I said.

"And what makes you think you would be of any service to the CIA in Baghdad?"

"I don't know," I told him. "I just figured you guys could get me into the middle of the war if I wanted to go."

I woke up hours later in my dark attic with the phone still in my hand, and my mind tried to block out the first thing that it remembered. I called Tony.

We hadn't talked since the last night of the play. I had been avoiding him. Tony was still drinking, but his drinking was somewhat civilized in comparison to the game I was playing.

"Tony, I did something very bad."

"I'm sure it's not that bad."

"It's bad."

"Mmmm. Did you kill somebody?"

"No."

"Well, then, it's not that bad."

"It's bad."

"What did you do?"

"I think I called the CIA."

"You what!"

"I called the CIA."

"No. What do you mean, you called the CIA?"

"I was drunk and I called them."

"This is bad. How do you call the CIA? How did you get their number?"

"I called Information. They gave it to me."

"Tell me you didn't call the CIA."

"I called them. It's bad, right?"

"When did you do it?"

"A few hours ago."

"Jesus."

"What should I do?"

"I . . . I really don't know what you should do. I can tell you this much: This is not something you're going to undo very easily."

"Should I call them and tell them I was drunk?"

"I don't know, Colin. This could be bad. People are disappearing."

"I know, I know. What do you think I should do?"

"I don't know. I'll be honest with you—I don't even like being on the phone with you right now. You're putting other people at risk here. They're probably monitoring your phone calls right this very minute . . . Jesus."

"I'm sorry, Tony."

"I don't know what you should do with this one. I really don't."

"Tony—"

"Sorry, Colin, but you're in a dangerous place with this one. You should really think about getting some help."

"I know."

I called Fiona and told her the same story. She started sobbing.

"Jesus, Colin, can't you see what you're doing?"

"I know. I'm a fuckup. I've lost it."

"Look what you're doing to everybody around you."

"I know. I don't know what's wrong with me."

"You need help."

"I know. I know."

"Stop drinking. You're going to die. If you could only see yourself. Do you know what you look like when you drink? It's disgusting."

"I know. I'm sorry. Can I see you?"

"No." She continued to cry.

"I'm a little scared."

"I'm scared for you."

"Meet me tomorrow for coffee just for a few minutes, please. I just need to see somebody. Please. One coffee."

"Colin—"

"Please, Fiona."

"OK. Call me tomorrow around lunchtime."

"Thank you."

I lay in the bed in the dark, staring up at the ceiling. I had nothing to drink left in the room. My brain felt like somebody had taken an eggbeater to it. I was empty and sick and hungry for a drink, but too sick to go get it. I twisted and turned, wrestling with the blankets. What had I done? How could I have gone this long, months now, without sobering up for a single day? My body was beginning to convulse; my chest ached until it felt like my heart was going to pop. I was gripped by a horrible, nightmarish fear that there was something in the room with me, and simultaneously that there was not, that I had in fact just lost my mind. I reached out cautiously and switched on the lamp by the bed. I was face-to-face with the devil. I closed my eyes and reopened them. The devil's face was next to mine, nose to nose like a semitransparent ghost head, his eyes staring directly into mine, and without speaking he seemed to say, "Got ya." I closed my eyes again, buried my face in the pillow, and I prayed to God and to the saints and to the souls of everyone I had ever known who had passed. I kept my eyes closed and I prayed. I prayed for an eternity, until I sensed the sun come up and I fell asleep, my body creased and twisted in knots, and when I opened my eyes he was gone.

I got up and showered, put on some clean clothes, and went to meet Fiona for coffee. Every person I saw on the street was a CIA agent. I was being followed down the block, onto the train, all the way into Manhattan; they were everywhere.

We met in a diner on Seventy-ninth and Broadway, where I sat with my back in a corner so that I could try to pinpoint the undercover agents who were following me.

Fiona sat down across from me and began to cry again.

"I'm really sorry I've put you through all this," I said, hoping she didn't notice the way my hand shook trying to put a spoonful of sugar into my coffee. "I know this is disgusting to you, but I'm done now. It's over."

"I don't think I can see you again for a while."

"I know. But thanks for coming today. It means a lot to me. I needed to see someone."

"I talked to Tony today. You've really scared him with this one."

"I know."

"You're scaring everybody."

"I know. It's over. Maybe I should go to Baghdad for a while."

"Jesus, Colin, do you hear yourself?"

"I'm a writer. This is the war of our times. I'm just saying maybe I should be there to witness it."

"Can you see yourself? You can't even hold your coffee without spilling it. You're going to kill yourself like this." She started sobbing again and I caught a man nearby glance in our direction and then go back to reading his *Daily News*. Was he the guy who had followed me off the train? What if they've poisoned my coffee and he's just waiting to see me keel over here on the table? I pushed my cup aside and played with the spoon.

"I have to go," Fiona said, sliding out of the booth.

"Thanks for coming out," I said. "I really appreciate it."

"Do me a favor and don't call me for little while."

"OK."

She leaned over and kissed my cheek and gave my shoulder a tight squeeze before disappearing out of the diner. I paid my bill and walked around the corner to the Dublin House bar on Seventy-ninth and Broadway and ordered a glass of whiskey. My body was telling me that I had reached the last stop on this particular ride, that it was time to stop drinking and pay the piper. I had to dry out. I took the 4 train back to the Bronx and went up to my little attic room with a bottle of water and lay down on the bed and settled in for the long ride back to sanity.

The scary thing about drinking alcoholically for years is that you become aware of how your body will react to detoxification. You recognize the symptoms as they're happening and they are as familiar to you as a cold. I was nineteen years old and living in London the first time I went through the delirium tremens. When I started to hallucinate that a little girl was standing at the bottom of my bed, staring at me, I didn't know what was happening and it scared me half to death. But as the years go on you become accustomed to this kind of horror. You understand that for every day spent on a run, the price will be a little higher, the nightmare of detoxification will have intensified just a little more. It is simple mathematical logic: What goes up must come down, and the higher you go, the longer and more terrifying the fall. It is the gripping fear of this inevitable nightmare that keeps the alcoholic drinking after a while. Jumping through the porthole back to sobriety means a temporary loss of sanity, and no matter how many times you've gone down that path, it never gets any easier. After a while the alcoholic drinks to maintain sanity. There is no enjoyment in the booze at the end of a run. Each drink is a battle, a temporary relief from madness. The alcoholic knows that when he can find the strength or motivation to put the last one down, he is in for hell. There is no escape. I envied the Americans I met who were always off to rehab for the comfy comedown. For most drunks, rehab is a luxury we will never know. Three thousand or thirty thousand dollars or whatever a week or two in a clinic costs these days can buy an awful lot of booze or pay off an awful lot of debt. Most of the drunks I have met don't stop the run until every last penny is consumed, every bridge burned. We lay in our attic rooms and slip the devil's noose around our necks and we fall back into the nightmare of reality.

That is how it feels coming off a drunk. I heard a heroin addict one time talk about how just the feel of a light breeze on his exposed ankles was almost unbearable. It is the same for the real alcoholic; the return to normalcy is unbearable. In those days of transition, the weight of the world, of what we refer to as normal everyday living, is unthinkable. The thought of going back to a job, repaying debt, getting a haircut, buying a pair of jeans, the sound of the clock ticking from across the room, saying I'm sorry, calling your mother, everything, is unbearable. The heart bends and creases, the muscles in your back spasm, the liver feels like it's been whacked with a baseball bat, you sweat poison for days, your mind runs into the darkest recesses it can find:

You have AIDS, cancer, liver disease, heart disease, spots on your skin, your hair is falling out, the devil has his tongue in your mouth and he's suffocating you with it. The room does not spin above your bed like some psychedelic collegiate dreamscape; it whirls and twists into dark unknowable horrors; real people plunge gleaming knives into your chest; vicious black dogs rise from underneath the bed and sink their teeth into your face; filthy giant roaches fly above the bed, waiting for their chance to latch on to your chest and sink their teeth into your skin; the CIA bursts into your room and shoots you for trying to roll out of the bed onto the floor. Your greatest fears will manifest themselves; a vision of hell tailored specifically to your every need will envelop you. There is no escape from any of this; it comes and goes, and after a couple of days you can rise again, if your heart has survived, and splash water on your face and step into the shower and rinse the putrid stench of death from your skin and hair and then start the slow return to the world, with trembling hands and a fragile heart and a swear to God that you will never, ever let it get this bad again.

Now that I had stopped drinking again I had to find a job. I needed to get back into the workforce. If I could get just one week of carpentry work, I'd be as good as gold again. But most of the guys I knew in construction liked to drink. If I was in a bar around Woodlawn and I happened to meet a guy who was running his own job, I could have a few beers with him and before you know it we would be best friends and I'd be starting first thing in the morning. But once I had stopped drinking, I was less convincing. Maybe it was easier for me to play the role of the construction guy after I'd had a few. Maybe when I was sober they sensed that I had no real passion for carpentry. Maybe they sensed that if I wasn't desperate for money, we wouldn't be having this conversation at all. Maybe I was just a delusional, paranoid, out-of-control, fucked-up alcoholic and they all knew it. My brother Brendan finally pulled a few strings with one of his buddies and got me a job.

I was drinking again within a week. Another month or so passed and I was talking to Tony again and staying over at Fiona's place a few nights a week. I was sipping my wine, smoking the occasional joint. The devil had taken off on a little winter hiatus down to Saint Bart's and I was feeling human again.

I finally had the realization that if I were to continue going out with Fiona, I needed to earn some real money. Fiona was an ambitious, energetic, high-maintenance girl who didn't need to be wasting her time on some juice-head construction worker living in his brother's attic apartment in Yonkers. It was time to get busy.

I convinced Tony to let me use his new country house upstate to get away for a few weeks so that I could be alone to write. I'd had an idea for a screenplay floating around in my head for a few years now. All I needed was some quiet time to put it on paper.

Tony and Fiona drove me the three hours north to Tony's new farmhouse. I had two cases of red wine and a case of beer along to keep me from getting lonely, and a large bag of weed to help me sleep at night.

When we reached the village of Sidney, it was twenty below and the snow was just beginning to fall. At the house we lit a fire in the potbellied stove and drove the five miles to town to pick up enough food supplies to keep me alive for a couple of weeks. By the time we got back to the house an hour later, there was a severe storm watch alert for all of Delaware County coming over the car radio. Tony turned up the volume and shook his head as the alert continued. They were predicting a foot of snow within the next twenty-four hours. He was going to have to head back to the city right away. Fiona had to be back in the city for work on Sunday night. Tony had an important meeting downtown on Monday morning. If they didn't get out now they could be snowed in here for a week.

"You can come back with us if you like," Tony said as we pulled in back of the house to unload the groceries.

"Maybe you should come back with us," Fiona said. "You'll be snowed in here. What if something happens to you and there's nobody around to get help?"

When Fiona came back for me two weeks later, I emerged from the farmhouse to greet her with my first screenplay in hand. I was in the movie business. Hollywood, here I come.

As soon as I got back to the city I called my old friend Jerome O'Connor over at St. Dymphna's on St. Mark's Place. Jerome had some experience with this kind of thing. He had produced one movie already, called *An Everlasting Piece,* about two guys selling toupees in Northern Ireland. Jerome had managed to procure a $15 million budget for the film from Steven Spielberg's DreamWorks, with Barry Levinson signed on to direct. The movie ran briefly in a handful of theaters and then all but disappeared from sight. According to Jerome's version of the story, Spielberg pulled his support of the project to court favor with the British government, which had just given him an honorary knighthood. Jerome sued Spielberg for $10 million.

Under the circumstances, Jerome was a dubious first choice for a connection to pick in the movie business, but I was a newcomer to this vicious arena of entertainment and I didn't know where else to begin. I was under the naïve impression that I would sell this screenplay in a heartbeat and have enough money in my pocket to take a year off to write a book.

Jerome read the screenplay, and when he called me three days later, he offered me five thousand dollars to option the rights to it. I was ecstatic. I wasn't back from the country for a week and I had sold my first screenplay. Jerome was going to have his lawyer draw up the contracts, and whenever we had them signed, I would have my money. In the meantime he had a little job he needed doing. There was this guy named Craig who wrote for *The Muppet Show*, and Jerome had told him he would do a little renovation for him at his Upper East Side apartment.

"It's about two weeks' work, maximum," he said.

"I was really hoping to just stay out of the construction business for a while now," I told him. "I have a book I've been trying to get to."

"Believe me, I feel exactly the same way, but it's only two weeks' work and it's money. All you have to do is supervise. Show up and read the newspaper if you want to. I'll pay you well. In the meantime I'll have my guy draw up your contracts and we'll get this screenplay moving."

"I don't know . . ."

Two weeks later I was in the Muppet guy's apartment, knee deep in rubble and trying to placate his sobbing wife, who had been under the impression she would be living in a dust-free environment while we demolished their apartment. I was exhausted and covered in dust from head to toe.

Apparently Jerome's lawyer was out of town, so it was going to be a little while before I would see any of the option money. On top of that, Jerome informed me that he was almost broke and that he had to invest the little he had left in buying materials for finishing the Muppet job before he could pay me. I couldn't believe it. I had been suckered back into the construction business and now I was really broke. I needed the money. I would have to stay and work my way out of it again. The construction business is worse than the Mafia; there is just no way out.

Fiona's roommate, Suzanne, had moved out and I took her place. I was now sharing her rent and officially living in Manhattan for the first time. The apartment was above a bar and the noise never stopped. At four in the morning, seven days a week, the floor was vibrating with the raucous screaming of drunk frat boys yelling Bon Jovi lyrics at the top of their lungs. The only way to get to sleep before dawn without committing mass murder was to consume approximately three to four bottles of red wine with a constant relay of joints all night long, which I did. I didn't really consider this drinking. Not only did I need to drown out the incessant din from downstairs in the bar, but I needed to numb myself to the fact that here I was, back working construction again full-time. When I worked construction, I justified my drinking by the fact that I was so miserable and exhausted that I could not do the writing I was born to do. The truth was, I always had an excuse.

I was getting pretty sick of this whole writing thing. Why did I bother with it at all? I'd been doing it now, on and off, for about fifteen years and I hadn't made a single penny. Was writing really making me happy? Had it ever really given me anything to equal the work I put into it? I was tired of being the outsider. I felt alienated from my fellow countrymen. I'd had to deal with snide underhanded remarks from other Irish guys about my sexuality for years on the job. To most of the guys, announcing "I'm a poet" was equivalent to saying "You're hot and I want to have gay sex with you right now while you're wearing your tool belt." After the success of the play, the return to the construction scene was worse. The general consensus in the construction business is that if you're standing there with a hammer in your hand, you can't have been much of a writer to begin with.

• • •

Two months later I was still working for Jerome O'Connor. His lawyer had returned to town but Jerome was broke now and still couldn't give me the money he owed me for the screenplay. He had one more little job for me to do and then he would be able to pay me in full. He hadn't mentioned my screenplay in weeks.

Jerome hired a guy from Dublin called Frank Murray to drive the van. Frank was to handle the garbage removal and material deliveries. When I got talking to Frank, it turned out that Jerome had managed to coerce him onto the job in much the same way he had with me. Frank had been the manager of the infamous Irish band the Pogues at one time, but he was currently out of a job, out of money, and out of a place to stay. Jerome had offered him a couch to sleep on and told him he could work off the favor by driving the van for him.

I liked Frank. He regaled me with his stories of working with Shane MacGowan and of partying backstage with the Rolling Stones, Elton John, and Eric Clapton. We were working in the apartment on Ninety-first one afternoon and I mentioned the screenplay I had given to Jerome.

"You should give it to me to read," he said. "I know some people."

"Jerome sort of thinks he owns it right now."

"Have you signed a contract?"

"No."

"So you own it."

"I suppose so."

"Maybe you should bring me a copy of it tomorrow," he said. "My girlfriend's father is a movie director. Maybe I'll take it down to Virginia with me this weekend and have him take a look at it . . ."

I was willing to try anything. We were in the middle of a

heat wave in New York that August afternoon as Frank left the apartment up on Central Park West where we were working, and some of the boys informed me that they couldn't see the work with the sweat in their eyes. I complained to the electricians that none of the air-conditioning units were working. They looked perplexed, saying there didn't seem to be any power reaching the apartment. I looked out the window at the honking cars on the street below. The streetlights on the corner were out. We were in the midst of a blackout.

In five minutes the entire work crew was on the street and scattering in all directions. I called Fiona. She was down at the Jersey Shore at her parents' beach house. No answer. I lit a cigarette and pondered my options. If this was another terrorist attack, I was going to be safer off the island now. I had to get back to Woodlawn. This would be an evening to spend at the Catalpa.

I was right. By the time I showed up, most of the lads were there already. The door was propped open and my new drinking pal, Henry Smith, or Hank as we called him, sat outside on a bar stool with a beer in one hand and a joint in the other.

"How was school today, Colly?" he asked, handing me the joint.

"The teacher sent us home early."

"Well, you have your homework cut out for you here," he said, leaning his face back so that he was able to catch the full glare of the warm sun. "We have to get all this beer drank before we run out of ice."

"I'd better get started, then," I said, and handed him back the spliff and went on into the dark bar, blinking at the sound of familiar voices calling my name.

The night of the big blackout we stayed in the Catalpa until dawn, drinking by candlelight. All night long, stragglers kept showing up with stories of being trapped in subway cars for hours, of being caught in crowded elevators. One lad had walked all the way back to the Catalpa from his job in Brooklyn just to be around the people he knew. At around midnight, Kenny Manion and a guy we called the Big Bamboo went off up the street and came back carrying their guitars and a bodhran and we had a sing-along until the sun came up the next morning.

When we emerged squinting from the bar after daybreak, New York was still standing. She had not been pillaged in that dark night. The wounds of September 11 were still too fresh then for everyone, except maybe the coldest-hearted hoodlums. The peace of that night, of the big blackout, was a testament to the goodness still left in people. It was evident, if only for a brief moment, that a small glimmer of decency still resided in the hearts of the masses. We had huddled together in little groups all across the great city and protected and comforted one another. It was a tiny glimpse of how things could be, of how they should be; a small window we peered into for a single night that showed how things should operate in a more civilized society. And then in a flash it was over.

Within a week of the blackout, Frank had returned from Virginia with word that the director had taken a look at my script and wanted me to give him a call as soon as possible. I was ecstatic. Within another week, I was done working for Jerome and made the call.

"This is Colin Broderick, a friend of Frank Murray's. He gave me your number a few days ago. He said that he talked to you about my script over the weekend . . ."

"Ah, Colin, how are you. Yes, yes, I've only had a chance to glance at it, but it looks great and Frank tells me he really enjoyed reading it. He also tells me you're a master carpenter. A man of many talents, I believe." He had a deep, powerful pull in his voice, like the undertow of a rogue wave. There was a sturdy, resonant, masculine quality to it. A voice to be believed, the voice of a commander, a man you might put at the helm of an $80 million movie project. I found myself a little intimidated by the voice on the other end of the line, a feeling I was not accustomed to under any circumstance. Perhaps I was just desperate for this guy to like me.

"It sounds like I owe Frank a few drinks," I said.

"Maybe you should come down to Virginia and I'll buy you a drink."

"That sounds like it might be fun."

"I don't know if Frank mentioned it to you, but I have this house down here that I've been fixing up. The contractors are just putting the final touches on it now, but if you'd like to come down to Virginia for a couple of weeks, I'm sure we could use another finish carpenter on the job. In fact, why don't you take a friend with you."

"I'm sure I could. I'd have to ask around, of course, but I think I have just the man for the job."

"Well, why don't you go and give him a call and let me know as soon as possible. I have a house here where you men could stay. You'd have your own bedrooms, of course, and my butler, Mark, would be there to cook you breakfast and dinner and take general care of things while you're here."

"That sounds great," I said, trying to sound like this was the kind of setup I was used to on any construction job. "I'll give him a call and I'll get back to you later."

"Wonderful. I look forward to hearing from you, Colin, and I'm looking forward to meeting the great Irish writer in person."

A week later, I had negotiated wages and two weeks' work for three of us carpenters. My buddy Hank and my brother

Brendan were coming to Virginia with me. The following Friday, we packed up Brendan's jeep, kissed our girls good-bye, and took off for the Blue Ridge Mountains.

Within the first two weeks in Virginia, I had managed to challenge an entire polo team to a tequila-drinking contest. I had passed out on the director's shoulder after about ten shots and had to be carried out of the bar unconscious. The following day I was offered the job of finishing the renovation of the mansion on the hill. I accepted the offer and stayed in Virginia with Hank and Brendan for almost a year, drinking barrels of the local wine and smoking weed with my new friend Mark, the director's personal chef.

Wayne, the director's son, arrived from New York about this time and moved into a cabin on the property on top of the mountain, just above the main house. Wayne, who was just a few years younger than I, was an accomplished chess champion and a writer also. He'd written a novel, a love story based on a relationship with a girl he'd met in New York. He had given me the manuscript to read and I was impressed. Wayne could write.

One night during dinner, the director announced what a great writer he thought I was. He raved about my screenplay for about ten minutes before Wayne stood up and abruptly left the house without a word. Apparently Wayne had given his father his manuscript about six months earlier and had yet to hear a word about it. He was understandably upset.

A few days later, without a word to anyone, I took the opportunity to escape the family tension and slipped off back to New York to try to salvage my own relationship with Fiona once more. All the drama in Virginia was taking its toll on her patience. She was just about ready to move on. Hank and Bren-

dan had long since returned to work in New York and she was
annoyed that I had refused to do the same. I did what I normally did on my return to New York: I drank for three days
straight. Then I got on a train and went back to Virginia with
my relationship in worse shape than when I had arrived.

When I returned to Virginia the following night and went
back to the main house where I was now staying alone, putting
the final finishing touches to the job, I was shocked to discover
bullet holes and spent casings everywhere. The place looked like
a war zone. There were bullets lodged in the mirrored panel
doors, in the new cherry wood floors. Windows had been shot
out; there were holes in the drywall; broken glass and bullet casings were strewn all over the new lacquered floor in the big front
room. As I stood there alone in the mansion on the top of the
hill, my blood running a little cold, the house phone rang, giving me a start. I reached for it.

"Yes," I said.

"Colin. Did you just get back?" It was the voice of Calvert
Marks, the new general contractor.

"Yeah, what the hell happened up here?"

"Wayne shot up the house. He was upset that his father read
your movie script and not his."

"What?"

"He's lost it."

"Is he in jail?"

"No, he's around somewhere. The cops arrived yesterday
morning and had to surround the cabin and talk him out with a
bullhorn. You should get out of there in case he comes back . . ."

"He's still got the gun?"

"Yeah."

"How the fuck does he still have the gun?"

"His father didn't want to press charges, so they had to let
him keep it."

"Great. Was he after me? I didn't tell anybody I was leaving for New York. I could have been here . . ."

"I don't know. The police put him on the line with his father while I was standing there and Wayne said it was because his father read your script and didn't read his."

"Jesus. You couldn't have called me in New York and warned me before I came back?"

"We're supposed to keep this whole thing quiet."

"Even if it means me getting shot? Oh, shit—"

"What is it?"

"He's here."

"Wayne?"

"Yup. He just pulled up outside the window."

"Fuck. What's he doing?"

"He's just sitting in his jeep outside. Is he going to shoot me?"

"He's not well right now and he still has the gun. Be very careful."

I hung up the phone and ventured out into the dark night. I was on the top of a mountain, a mile up a rough lane, me and some guy with a gun who may or may not want to shoot me. Is this how these things happened? House lights flickered as far as fifty miles away in the distance, and beyond that the black silhouettes of the Blue Ridge Mountains sat against the night sky for as far as the eye could see. Wayne sat unflinchingly, staring straight ahead as I approached the jeep. I took a deep breath and opened the passenger door and jumped in, trying to appear nonchalant. I landed on something hard and metallic. I reached under my ass and pulled out from underneath me a heavy semiautomatic Glock handgun. I closed the passenger door and held the gun for a moment in silence before speaking.

"Nice gun."

"Yeah."

"Is it loaded?"

"Yeah," he said, but he didn't look at me.

"Is this what you shot up the house with?"

"Yeah."

"If I hand you the gun, will you do me a huge favor and unload it, please?"

"Yeah."

"Are you sure I can trust you?" I said, moving the gun toward him across the center console, being careful to point it at neither him nor me.

"Yeah."

I let him take the gun and watched him remove the clip. "There. You feel better?"

"A little. What the hell happened in there?"

"I don't really know."

"Was it something to do with your father not reading your script?"

He took a deep breath and let it out slowly. I continued. "Would you have shot me if I had been here?"

He turned to look at me again.

"I'm glad you weren't here," he said. "I was drunk. I can't remember the whole thing. I was pissed off."

"Are you still pissed off?"

"Naw, I think I'm over it."

"Maybe you should think about getting off this mountain, dude. It's got to be a little lonely up here all by yourself in that cabin."

"Yeah."

"Whaddyasay you and me head down to the pub and grab ourselves a cold beer?"

"I don't think that's such a good idea right now. I think most people around here heard about my little run-in with the law here yesterday. They might not feel too safe having me in there with a beer in my hand."

The director tried to salvage the situation by offering both Wayne and me writing gigs on some Civil War television series he was supposedly producing. He assured me that Fiona would have a role in his next big movie. But nothing was really happening. His career was in a nosedive and I was his carpenter-slash-gofer-slash-analyst; I was going nowhere once again and now I was having trouble sleeping at night, imagining Wayne on the prowl outside my darkened window, armed with a piece from his ever-expanding gun collection. Every time I found myself in a lighted room at night, I expected the shattering of glass and the thud of a slug in my chest.

Things had gotten about as strange as I could handle. I was drinking heavily and I didn't care who knew it. The director had tried to talk to me about my drinking. He tried to explain the thing to me in his own logical terms. "You only have one set of plumbing," he explained. "When you wear out the filters and the pipes and the pumps, it's over. You should really stop drinking, or at least stop drinking the way you do. It won't last. It can't last. It's just a mathematical certainty." He was right, of course. I had another drink.

I was alone with the director in the big stone cottage one rainy Saturday afternoon. He was fielding phone calls from debt collectors while I finished reading Joe Eszterhas's *Hollywood Animal*. The work on the house was basically finished. I was spending weeks now fine-tuning the place, hanging pictures, adjusting hinges and door catches, passing the time waiting for the next big thing to happen in my life. As I finished the last page in the book, I turned in the swivel chair I was in and proclaimed loudly, "I've got it."

Ever the gracious listener, he set down his pen and leaned back, knitting his fingers behind his head to listen.

"It sounds big," he said with a grin. "What is it that you have?"

"I've finally figured out the movie business."

"I'm listening."

"You are never going to help me make my movie. Jerome O'Connor was never going to make my movie. The only way I will ever get a movie made is if I go out and make my own movie."

He tipped his head back and laughed in perfect English, "Ha, ha, ha," applauding as he began to speak.

"You've got it. That's the movie business in a nutshell."

"And you're still doing it. All this time I've been here, you've just been keeping the ship afloat looking for the right money to make the next movie . . ."

"Welcome to Hollywood."

". . . I've just been part of the machine you keep in place to keep you going until you get the next big check."

"And you've been paid for your time, have you not?"

"I certainly have," I said as I put down my book and stood. "I'll be leaving this weekend. I'm going back to New York and hiring a cameraman and I'm going to start shooting my own movie this weekend."

"I'll be sorry to see you go. But I wish you all the best. It's been great having you here and you managed to get my house finished. I don't know if I could have gotten it done without you. What's this movie you're going to shoot?"

"I'm not sure just yet, but I think I'm going to start with a documentary about the Irish in New York and about how the community has been affected by nine-eleven."

"That sounds like it just might work."

"It's a start. Maybe I'll have to interview you at some point."

"Anytime, my friend. Anything I can do to help."

One week later, I was sitting on my couch in my little apartment above Jake's Dilemma on Amsterdam Avenue with a camera guy I had hired. He was filming me as I verbalized my first thoughts about what the movie was that I intended to shoot. This was the beginning of my documentary. It was official. I was making my own movie. "I'm making a documentary and I should have this wrapped up in a couple of months," I told the camera.

That one line became the mantra that I lived by for the next three years. "I'm making a documentary . . ."

The reality was that I was back in New York working construction and drinking heavily. Whenever I could afford it, I called my cameraman and told him that we needed to shoot something. Ironically my cameraman, Brandon Herman, is the cleanest-living American ever to don a pair of chinos. He is a reliable, honest, nonsmoking, vegetarian teetotaler who was operating his fledgling production company from an office in the basement of his parents' house in Staten Island. Brandon became caught up in the idea I had for the movie. He was convinced that I would actually complete the project or at least die in the process, either of which might make an interesting story.

The inside of my head at this point felt like a child's rattle strapped to the blade of a blender. "It's a documentary about the Irish in New York. No. It's a documentary about terrorism. No.

It's a movie comparing the Omagh bombing to the collapse of the Twin Towers. No. It's a movie about the ever-shifting perception of what the word 'terrorism' really means. No. It is a documentary about what it's like to be an Irish writer living in these perilous times. It's a documentary about the collapse of the American empire. It's a documentary about the difficulty of making a documentary. It's a documentary about an Irish guy who has absolutely no idea how to make a documentary, drinking himself to death while trying to shoot a documentary. Yes, that's it. I think."

If I'd had trouble convincing those around me of my sanity before the camera appeared, then I had completely lost them now. I was interviewing writers, filmmakers, politicians, girls in bars, ex-lovers, and random homeless people I met on the street. I flew to Ireland with Fiona and surprised my parents by showing up at their door unannounced, after not being at home in Ireland for four years, with my cousin Declan behind me filming the whole thing. What did any of this mean? I didn't really know. I just kept drinking and rolling the tape. I showed up at Gaelic football matches in the Bronx and interviewed representatives of the GAA, drunk and stoned off my head. I covered the Saint Patrick's Day parade on Fifth Avenue, loaded. I attended every antiwar rally in New York. I quizzed topless protesters and firemen, and I drank.

Fiona was sick of the whole thing. Sick of me, sick of my drinking. We stayed together anyway and rented a new apartment, a fifth-floor walkup on Ninth Avenue in Hell's Kitchen.

My old pal Hank called me with the offer of a job working on a renovation out in the Hamptons for the summer. Fiona warned me that if I left her alone for another summer, it was over. I'd already wrecked an entire summer for her by staying in Virginia. I took the job in the Hamptons.

The first night, an Irish guy called Cairn Cassidy picked me up at the train station and drove me to a huge house in East Hampton. Cairn was twenty-seven years old. He had a round comical face and the kind of strong thick body that you didn't want to mess with. Cairn was my new boss. As we pulled up outside a mansion by the water on Georgica Pond he announced, "Here it is. Home sweet home. This is the house we're fixing up. The owners are gone to Europe for the summer, so we're just staying here for now until they get back. Unfortunately I don't think there's a bed for you just yet. But if you can get through tonight I'll get you a mattress sorted out tomorrow."

"And where am I supposed to sleep? Is there a couch?"

"No furniture."

"A blanket? Pillows?"

"No and also no."

"But you have a bed for yourself?"

"I have a bed."

"And I don't?"

"You could jump in beside me, I suppose; I just don't know if that would be very comfortable. It's a small bed." Cairn laughed and I had to laugh along with him.

I spent the first night trying to sleep on top of a stack of new doors in the big living room. I was thirty-seven years old, hungover as usual, twisting and turning, sweating profusely, and battling an army of vicious mosquitoes without a pillow or a blanket, cursing my life and everything that had brought me to this point. Somewhere soon, this would have to end. When the sun finally came up over Georgica Pond, I was stiff and angry and covered in mosquito bites. I sat up and watched as a small crew of bleary-headed Irishmen emerged one after the other from the bedrooms down along the dark corridor. These bedraggled-looking strangers were my new workmates and housemates. Cairn emerged from his room showered and fresh and introduced me to the other men.

"This is Budgie, Saucy, Corky, Gary Rocks, Doulta, the Grim Reaper, and . . . where the fuck's Smith . . ."

A door opened down the hall and I was relieved to see a familiar face. Hank emerged, looking scorched and gaunt. I hadn't seen him since he'd finished working in Virginia.

"Whassup, Spiel," he muttered as he ambled past on his way to the refrigerator. "Welcome to hell."

"Who the fuck's Spiel?" the one called Budgie said, grinning.

"That's Spielberg right there," Hank said, pointing at me. "Colly's in the movie business. Isn't that right, Colly?"

And that was that; I was Spielberg for the entire summer in the Hamptons. Spiel for short. I was with the most insane group of individuals ever assembled to build a house. A typical morning might have started with Gary Rocks casually wandering about the outdoor decking buck naked, displaying his humongous appendage while we struggled to avert the ghastly vision as we wrestled with herculean hangovers. Gary was not a drinker and so he thrived on this early morning routine, knowing the discomfort he inflicted on the rest of us.

Our days were spent suffering our hangovers in the unbearable heat. Invariably one or two workers were already on the "missing" list by lunchtime. Corky asleep in the back of a closet, Smith hitching a ride with the delivery guy to the nearest bar in East Hampton.

As soon as the work was done for the day there was a beeline for the Blue Collar Bar on Sunrise Highway outside of Southampton, where the bartenders wore short skirts and shorter tops and Saucy would dash off to the bookies next door to catch the last races of the day at the OTB. We would settle in to get hammered and play pool until the bar was closed for the night. Then I'd stagger out and hitch a ride home with the Grim Reaper on his motorcycle at speeds of over 150 miles an hour with no helmet. And in the morning we'd crawl out of bed and do it all over again.

For a while Cairn tried to play the role of responsible boss. He tried to rein us in, telling us that the drinking was killing productivity on the job. He was concerned that the Reaper and I wouldn't last the summer if we continued the way we were on the bike. But it was futile. He may have been our boss, but at twenty-seven he was younger than nearly every man on the job, and besides that, he was in the bar drinking right along with us every night. Eventually he just threw in the towel and joined the madness.

Pretty soon the casualties started to pile up. There were broken ribs and mild concussions. Cairn broke his wrist in a late-night fence-jumping competition and had to have it set in a cast. Two days later, frustrated that he couldn't hold a block of wood to put a nail in it, he borrowed my utility knife and cut off the cast. He grabbed a two-by-four in his broken hand and asked me to hand him the nail gun. I reluctantly handed it over, and with his broken wrist he fumbled with the block of wood and shot a three-inch roofing nail into the same hand. The nail went straight up into the broken wrist, leaving nothing but the head peeking out of his palm. He looked at me with an expression of absolute horror and surprise and then managed a tight smile as his eyes began to water up. Very calmly he asked me to hand him a pair of pliers, which I did. He got a good grip on the head of the nail, closed his eyes for a second, and then yanked the nail out in one quick snap. All without a whimper. I noticed the blood drain from his face as he turned away and walked off down the lawn. He circled once or twice, swerved dramatically, and dropped onto his ass. Out cold. I called a couple of the lads and we got him gathered up and off to the hospital again over at Southampton for a new plaster. He was one tough cookie alright, Cairn Cassidy.

A week later the Grim Reaper fell asleep behind the wheel of the new Subaru he was driving and slammed into the oncoming traffic on Route 27 out of Southampton, flipping an SUV and totaling both vehicles. Luckily no one was badly injured, but the busy stretch of Route 27 that runs between Bridgehampton and East Hampton had to be closed for about three hours while the wreckage was cleaned up, causing complete havoc with a snarl of busy summer traffic. The local police were not amused. Word was spreading about the lunatic drunken Irish construction crew in town.

The work kept coming. If there's two things the Hamptonites love, they're a remodel job and high drama. They became our enablers, fueling our drinking escapades for the perk of informing their dinner guests that their job was done by the finest authentic Irish craftsmen. For me it was a glimpse into a world of material excess that is hard to fathom. Imagine having your brand-new hundred-thousand-dollar swimming pool ripped out because you felt it might look better fifteen inches to the left, uprooting a row of thirty-foot spruce and having them replanted because they were two inches too close to one another, gutting your Italian marble bathroom because it didn't match the carpet in the new bedroom.

The only celebrity I met while I was there for the summer who seemed to have miraculously survived the slide into dementia was Jon Bon Jovi. One hot afternoon toward the end of the summer, Hank and I were installing a set of steps on the front of a house in East Hampton and he came over with his wife to introduce himself to the workers. He'd been watching us work in the heat and wanted to come by and say hello and tell us what a great job he thought we were doing. The couple stuck around for half an hour or so, posing for pictures and signing autographs, proving that money and fame didn't need to turn everyone so fortunate into an empty self-serving narcissist.

Every couple of weeks, I'd show up in the city to see Fiona and the apartment we'd rented on Ninth Avenue. She didn't want to hear the stories about me getting kidnapped by a group of neo-Nazis or almost drowning in a late-night canoeing accident with Budgie on Georgica Pond. She'd heard a thousand stories like them already. What she wanted instead was for me to get involved in making our new apartment a home. We were in a relationship of convenience, it seemed. It's not easy to get an apartment in Manhattan, and once you have one that you like, neither party wants to be the one to move out. Fiona wanted me to go look at furniture, talk about paint colors. She wanted to fix the apartment and maybe fix me into the bargain. She wanted me to take the weekend off and come down the Jersey Shore to spend the weekend with her family at the beach house. Normal people stuff, the stuff people do without thinking, every single day of their lives. But I wanted nothing to do with it. I wanted to drop my bag in the door and go to the nearest bar and drink, or sit on the couch and roll joint after joint and drink and watch movies. She'd take pictures of me passed out, sprawled on the couch, fully dressed, and hand them to me the next day.

"Take a look at yourself! This is my boyfriend. This is what I'm living with. Do you like how this looks? It's disgusting. Can't you see how disgusting this is? You pass out alone here on the couch at ten o'clock at night, too wasted to get up and take your clothes off and go to bed. You wake up and you have to have a drink, or go to the bar. Don't you care what you're doing to yourself, what you're doing to me? I can't take this any longer.

I'm too young for this shit. My friends call us to go out to dinner or go to a party and you're too wasted to leave the couch. You don't make me feel safe or wanted. Why the hell am I still with you? Why can't you stop?"

"I can."

"I will."

"It's a bad time right now."

"After this job is over in the Hamptons, I'll stop."

"I drink when I can't write."

"Things have been tough for me."

"I can't stand the pain and misery I see all around me."

"I'm sorry. Come on; I'll get cleaned up and we'll go out for a really nice dinner."

I had a million excuses. Every one of them ended with me holding a drink in my hand. I was losing a lot of weight; I could see it myself. I had done nothing with the documentary in months. Nothing but talk, that is. Fiona's friend Suzanne called. She wanted us to come over to the lounge-bar at the Hotel Edison and meet her friend Don. Don was a documentary filmmaker. He'd made two documentaries already. I was reluctant to go. Documentary filmmakers are assholes. But at least we'd be drinking. I went along.

The Edison Hotel piano bar is one of the best-kept secrets in New York. It's one of those old–New York places nestled in the heart of the theatre district that you would never even think of walking into. It's a cozy little wooden nook of a place that never bothered to glam itself up for the onslaught of Midwestern tourists. There's a piano player in the corner who gets more enthusiastic as the night goes on. Some old Broadway actress might get up and sing a few bars of some old show tune, and you never know who might duck in from the cold.

Suzanne introduced us to Don, and the four of us took a round top by the door and ordered drinks. Don and I started to talk movies right away. It's rare to meet a guy who knows and loves movies as well as I do, but Don did. I was glad I'd been dragged out the door. I hated meeting new people. But with Don it was easy conversation. He had produced two documentaries of his own with his partner, a director named Jack Haines. He'd started out as a bar-back in Jake's Dilemma, the bar we'd lived above on Amsterdam Avenue. He'd been behind the bar working, lugging buckets of ice, the night his first documentary premiered on HBO. He had been a wrestler in college. He had been trained by the writer John Irving, my favorite living American novelist. I was blown away. I named him every book John Irving ever wrote. At some point I glanced at Fiona, who was sitting directly across from Don, and I caught her and Don in a simple glance. She had fallen for him, and he was falling for her. I braced myself for being upset, but it didn't happen. Instead I felt a sense of happiness. She looked happy. Fiona was happy. I had not seen her so happy in a long time. In an instant she had been transformed into the same girl I'd met three years earlier. Her face opened like a flower. I was happy for her. I was happy for both of them.

I returned to the Hamptons the following Monday afternoon. By Wednesday Fiona had called to ask me if I thought it would be OK if she went to see a movie with Don. He'd insisted that she ask me so I wouldn't think they were sneaking around behind my back. I told her to go and have fun. Less than three weeks later, we were going out together for a drink, only now Fiona was on Don's arm. It was the most natural transition in the world. We had gone from being lovers to being friends without a single piece of smashed ceramic. I suppose that was what had kept us together in the first place. We had always been good friends. To celebrate their newfound romance, Don whisked her off to New Orleans for a spur-of-the-moment vacation.

It was the morning of August 29, 2005, and hurricane Katrina had just rolled ashore. I took the afternoon off and sat in the Blue Collar Bar and watched the reports come in, praying that they'd make it out alive. Don did get them out of there. They hitched a fifteen-hundred-dollar ride with a couple of Creole guys who drove them to safety on the back roads. It took them three days to make it back to New York, but they were alive and well.

With Fiona gone, I was alone and single for the first time in eleven years. I had an apartment in midtown and a job in the Hamptons. I was making a documentary. I had no one to try and tell me what to do or when to come home. The orangutan was free.

My new friend Don invited me to a party and introduced me to a friend of his called Courtney. She was about my age, an attractive girl with long sandy hair and deep brown eyes. She was smart and cynical and pretty funny to be around, until she'd had about two or three pints of vodka. She lived in the city also. She had her own car and a place up on Central Park West. She was into photography and cooking. She was an independent operator. She didn't need some guy to take care of her. I couldn't even take care of myself. We were perfect for each other.

It became obvious pretty quickly that she was an alcoholic just like me. She informed me nonchalantly that she'd been to rehab twelve times already. We had another drink and rolled another joint and had a good laugh about it all. We were never going to quit drinking again. We were sure of it. We'd just be careful. We were old hands at this game. We could do this thing with our eyes closed. And we did. We sputtered and sparked like two wet mosquitoes on a heat lamp for about a month and

a half before we decided we should really quit drinking for a
while. We made a pact that neither of us would drink again
without the other. I had given my body a terrible beating over
the summer. I was becoming fearful that this was how it would
all end, with me broke and drunk in Hell's Kitchen, drinking
myself to death with the rehab queen. I thought about death
constantly. My liver was swollen and bruised. My brain felt like
a piece of Swiss cheese; my thoughts ran like mice through the
holes. We were going to nurse each other back to sanity. We
would keep each other sober.

And we did, for a couple of months. At the weekends we
went for drives to the country and visited old graveyards and
abandoned mental institutions. She took pictures and I started
talking about writing again. Courtney took me shopping for
fresh vegetables and whole-grain breads I knew nothing about.
She cooked and we ate elaborate meals in the afternoons like
real, normal people. We took walks through Central Park as the
leaves began to turn and the evenings cooled, slipping into
the rusty corrosion of a long, hot New York summer. I was beginning to feel hopeful again. Maybe I could finally turn this
thing around. I came home from work one evening and she was
on my bed swilling cheap vodka out of a half-pint plastic bottle.
She was plastered. I was surprised. The sight of her disgusted
me. Even on my worst binge, I would never buy cheap vodka in
a plastic bottle. The very thought of it repulsed me. She was
barely coherent. Somehow I couldn't help but feel responsible
for this mess, that this was my doing, that I had created this,
that this was her way of saying, "I know you don't really love
me." I was a coward. She was right. I didn't love her.

"I want you to go," I said. "This is over. I want you to leave."
I had never witnessed a real alcoholic on a slip before, someone
I cared about. The scene horrified me. I couldn't identify myself
with it at all. She became belligerent. The person before me

bore no resemblance to the girl I had said good-bye to that very morning. I wanted her out of my sight. She went into a fit of melodrama, insisting that she take anything of hers that she'd brought over to my place: a few books, a pair of pants, some shoes. I got a small cardboard box for her and helped her pack. It took over an hour to get her out of the apartment. I watched her through the window as she hailed a taxi out on Ninth Avenue. Two days later she was back.

Within a week, her mother had come to town to take Courtney off to rehab number thirteen. Between us we helped her down the stairs and into the backseat of her mother's truck outside of my apartment building. We hugged good-bye. It wasn't yet noon and already she was too drunk for tears. I was relieved to see her go. It had been a rough seven days. Her mother put her hand on my shoulder and told me that I should seriously consider getting some help for myself. Then I stood there and watched them drive away, disappearing into the thicket of midtown traffic.

As soon as I was sure they were out of sight, I strolled up Ninth Avenue and went into McCoy's Bar and ordered myself a beer. I was done with women. For good.

The next six or seven months are a blur. By about Christmas of that year I was unemployable. I was drinking massively seven days a week. I had used up all the goodwill my fellow Irishmen in the construction business could muster. If I worked at all I showed up smelling of drink and left for the bar at lunchtime. There was just no place on a construction site they could hide me any longer, although some were still kind enough to try. Not even my own brothers could get me onto a job as a favor. I didn't look like somebody you'd want to be associated with anymore. I quite simply didn't care enough anymore. I didn't want to work construction. I wanted to write. I would pick up a pen and stare at the page. I'd put the point of the pen on the page to begin and start scrawling lines in swirling circles, ripping through the page with the tip in frustration. I couldn't write a single word. I'd rip the page out and have another drink. The inside of my head was a scrawl. My head was too mangled to write. The words were in there, the lines were in there, but it was a bramble patch, a cluster of incomprehensible squiggles, scores, and dots like a bad Jackson Pollock knockoff. The only way to untangle the pain in my head was to drink. But when I drank I couldn't write. Soon the money was going to run out. Soon something would have to happen. A change would come. I figured I had about enough money left to keep me drinking until about sometime in February, if I was careful. Then . . . I'd figure something out. Something would happen. A miracle would come. I would win the lottery. Jerome O'Connor would call and tell me he had a buyer for my screenplay. I would be discovered by some elderly millionaires who were willing to sponsor my every creative whim. Something had to happen. Wasn't that how my story was supposed to end?

I threw a New Year's party to celebrate the arrival of 2006 and my being single on the eve of my thirty-eighth birthday. I was drunk before anyone had even arrived. About thirty people showed up. At midnight, we went out onto the roof to watch the explosion of fireworks over in Times Square just a few blocks away. I decided to slip down the fire escape on the back of the building and enter my apartment through the kitchen window to fetch another bottle of wine. I stumbled on the way down and slipped over the side rail of the ladder, almost falling the five floors into the backyard. Somehow I managed to catch the outside railing with my right hand as I was falling, and for a

moment I hung there, suspended on the outside of the fire escape with nothing beneath my feet but air, only my right hand
holding me there. How simple it would be just to let go. But my
hand would not release. It had a firm grip. I was not going anywhere just yet. I was not supposed to die just yet. Here was my
miracle. Was this what I had been waiting for?

There's a story told often in recovery circles about a guy of
unshakable faith and prayer who finds out that his village is
about to experience a great flood. He gets on his knees and
prays to God, asking to be saved. The police come by and tell
the guy it's time to go. But he stays, saying he has faith that God
will save him. The waters rise and the guy stands in his upstairs
window and prays. "I have faith in Thee, O Lord." Some guys
come by in a dinghy and offer him a ride to safety. He joyfully
tells them that he is safe where he is and that the Lord will keep
him safe. A little while later he is on the roof and the water is
still rising. A helicopter arrives. They toss him a rope, but again
he thanks them and refuses to go. He assures them that he has
prayed and the Lord will protect him. After he drowns he meets
God and asks Him what happened. God berates him, saying, "I
sent you a policeman, a dinghy, and a helicopter, ya dumb
clown." (God's got an Irish accent, by the way.) "What sort of
sign were you waiting for?"

I had spent five years going to meetings once upon a time. I
knew all the stories about the warning signs, but they were all
wrong. I had not died. I was alive. I had been through car accidents, I had been stabbed and hospitalized and almost
drowned, and now I had fallen off a roof and still I was alive. I
had been drinking for seven years now and I was still alive.
Everything I had been told was untrue. God had saved me from
every mishap. God was telling me that I *should* drink. That I
should pull out all the stops and just roll with it. Drink like I

had never drunk before in my life. Forget work, forget health, forget family and friends. Just drink. And I did. I drank.

The last days of the big Manhattan binge go something like this: I wake up on my couch around seven in the morning and look around the room for the nearest beer. If there's not a beer left on the coffee table, I get up and get one from the fridge, pop it open, and light a smoke. I close the bathroom door quietly behind me and try to muffle the noise I make puking so as not to wake Theresa. I'm sick almost every morning by now. I've convinced myself that it's a good way to start the day, expelling the previous night's toxins. Then I sit in my kitchen and watch out my back window. The gray mist slowly clears over the top of the Rockefeller building and Times Square and I drink.

After I consume whatever beer or vodka I have left in the apartment, I make the dreaded inspection of my wallet and pockets to see what I have left from the night before. I find the usual debris: crumpled dollar bills, a broken cigarette, some girl's phone number scrawled on a paper napkin; if I'm really lucky a little cocaine in a baggie, but I'm not lucky very often anymore. It seems I've used whatever luck I had coming and now it's time to face my karmic tsunami.

Before twelve I've finished whatever beer was left over, so I venture out onto Ninth Avenue for some supplies. I call Hasan down at the deli and tell him what numbers I need to play for the midday lotto. I will win today. I am sure of it. Then to postpone paying Hasan for the tickets I go to a different deli and buy more beer, cigarettes, come back home, have a few cold ones, and try to figure out a way out of this mess I'm in. Where am I going to get the money I need to pay my rent, my phone bill, the power, to pay back the thousands of dollars I've managed to borrow from friends and acquaintances, the money I need to finish my documentary? Ah, yes, the elusive documentary started two years ago. It was supposed to take six weeks, as I recall, and here it is, between fifty and sixty hours of footage later, sitting in a cardboard box in my friend Don's closet. I am right on target. It's a piece of cake. Another beer . . . Everything is under control. Another . . . I'm a writer, goddamn it! Another . . . can't you see I'm working?

By two o'clock I have cooled my nerves enough to face a short stroll up the street to McCoy's Bar. I'll feel better if I can manage to get out of the apartment for a while. Then I can always say, if anybody happens to ask, that I was out and about. It just sounds better, as if I'm actually doing something constructive. It seems that all I do anymore besides drink is convince people I'm doing stuff.

"What did you do today?"

"I was busy."

"Oh yeah, doin' what?"

"You know, I was out and about all day."

"Really."

"Yup. Busy day."

With the right baseball cap and a pair of shades I don't look too bad in daylight. Besides, there are always five or six characters in worse-looking shape than I am on Ninth Avenue between my apartment and the bar. The way it looks right now I'm probably about a month or two away from being exactly where they are. When they ask, I give them whatever change I have left in my pockets. I might need that kind of karma working for me pretty soon. I take a last quick glance around to make sure that nobody I know is watching me and I duck into

McCoy's. I mount my stool at the end of the bar, where I can watch the ladies stroll by through the open windows, and I unfurl the newspaper on the bar before me.

"How're you, Colin? The usual?"

"Yeah."

"Rough one last night?"

"They're all rough."

"Here ye go. That'll straighten you out."

"Cheers, Mary."

I sit here for a while and try to pull it all together again. Even after the four or five beers I consumed at home, my brain still feels like someone poured hydrochloric acid on it. I try to concentrate on the newspaper, feign interest in whatever nonsense sports they play on the telly, and send out a general vibe to the other drinkers that I just want to be left alone. I have to get another three or four of these beers into me before I start the daunting task of checking my cell phone messages. I have to check my messages and then I have to make whatever phone calls I need to make to clear up last night's drama. There is always last night's drama. Then I have to make a few more phone calls looking for a job.

When I am working, I am a carpenter. The truth is, I am a pretty good carpenter when I'm not hungover. I have to make these phone calls about work before it's too late in the evening. Pretty soon I'll be too drunk to pretend I'm sober anymore, or to give a shit about finding a job. It's not easy to get a job when you're slurring your speech on the phone.

Right. To get warmed up I'll make a few phone calls to my friends.

"Hank, whassup, buddy?"

"Colly, you old corndogger, what's the good word?"

"Same old ding dong. Did you talk to your boss about that job for me?"

"Yeah. He doesn't need anybody right now. Try Patsy—I think he just started with some guy this morning. I heard he's crying out for finish carpenters."

"Cool. I'll give him a shot. Where'd you see Patsy?"

"Met him briefly last night in the Catalpa."

"Oh, yeah, how was he?"

"He was buckled. He was asked to leave at one point. Then he fell asleep on the bar. He was still there sleepin' when I went home. Where are you at it today?"

"McCoy's for a few cold ones."

"I could use a few of those myself."

"Sick?"

"As a small hospital."

"Yeah, they're going down nicely. I'll have one for you."

"You're a pal."

"Right. I'll give Patsy a call and I'll get back to you later."

"Right, Colly. Later."

Ring, ring.

"Patsy."

"Colly, what's the *craic,* boy?"

"Same old dingaling, Patsy, and yerself?"

"Ah, not so bad. Nursing another major hangover here, ye know yerself."

"I hear ya. You started with some new guy this mornin'?"

"Yeah; who were ya talkin' to, Hank?"

"Yeah."

"How's he today?"

"Sounded alright on the phone."

"Yeah, last I seen of him last night he was plastered over the bar in the Big C, passed out cold."

"He made it to work this mornin'. I just talked to him."

"That's the shot, that's the shot. Com'ere, any luck yerself, Colly?"

"Not yet, still lookin'. I heard your guy might be lookin' for carpenters."

"Yeah, he might be but he's a pure bollox, Colly."

"Oh yeah?"

"A real scumbag. I'll give ye his number if you want it, but I mightn't even last the day with him."

"Naw, I'll hold off. I'm not that desperate. If you hear of anything else let me know, alright, Patsy?"

"No bother, Colly. Will do."

"Later, Patsy."

"Alright, Colly. Take her handy, boy."

I was that desperate, but the truth was, I just couldn't face it anymore; the Irish construction scene was making me ill. Everything about this damned city was making me ill, and a few days' work wasn't going to save me now. It was too late for that. Six thousand dollars in back rent, the phone bill, electric bill, cable bill, the money I needed to finish the documentary, not to mention the hundred or so it takes me just to get through a quiet day. What good was a few days' work? I needed a miracle.

"Will ye have another one, Colin?"

"Does a bear shit in the woods, Mary?"

"I couldn't tell ye. I never seen one."

"When are we gonna run away and get married, Mary?"

"As soon as I can ditch Pat and the kids, we'll be on the first plane to Vegas."

"I'll book the plane tickets this evening."

"And what about all yer other girlfriends?"

"We'll bring them along for the *craic*."

"Maybe I should bring Pat and the kids, too."

"Fuck it, Mary, why not? We'll make a day of it."

• • •

They're amazing, the curative powers of alcohol. It's like a healing lotion, a balm for all aches and pains, an instantaneous solution for boredom, depression, doubt. A fountain of youth, and there's so much of it. How in God's name will I ever drink it all?

Back to the newspaper; I don't want to get too drunk too fast. It's early in the day. Stop flirting with the bartender; she's a married woman, for chrissake. Here's an interesting story: David Blaine will attempt to hold his breath for nine minutes after being submerged in a sphere of water for ten days. That I have to see. I reread the article. I love it. Blaine's a lunatic. He could die. That's the boy. Push it to the limit. Lincoln Center's right up the street and he'll be submerged tonight. I'm going. This I have to see. The modern-day Houdini.

My phone rings; it's my German roommate, Theresa. She's twenty-two years old, six feet tall, blond, gorgeous, and I'm sort of in love with her, or is it just that she won't let me sleep with her? It's something.

"Hey."

"Colin, what are you doing?"

"I'm out for a run in Central Park. I'm just coming around by the reservoir right now. It's such a beautiful day to be alive."

"So you're drunk again."

"Not just yet, but I'm getting there."

"Colin, what are you cooking me for dinner tonight?"

"I was thinking maybe duck, potatoes au gratin, a little spinach—no, sauerkraut—sauerkraut for the sour kraut . . ."

"OK, so you want me to pick up some Chinese on the way home?"

"Naw, I'm OK."

"Colin, you have to eat something. You want, I will cook you something. Bring home a bottle of wine, I will get the food. OK. Maybe we watch a movie together."

"OK, Theresa."

"Six o'clock. Don't be late, Colin. You know you don't want to make me angry."

"I know, Theresa."

"You still in love with me, Colin?"

"Head over heels, Theresa. You're the only one for me."

My ex-girlfriend Oksana introduced me to Theresa at the end of January. Theresa had just arrived in New York to study for the semester at Queens College and she didn't know anybody and through some terrible mix-up it turned out she had nowhere to stay. So, being the perfect gentleman, I offered to rent her my couch. She's very German. I tell her I need to check her chest because I believe she's so cold, she has to be heartless. She tells me if I touch her chest I die. We are like an old married couple: We watch television together, we bitch and complain to each other, we never have sex. It's a perfect relationship for me right now. I can drink all I want. Stay out for days and she can't say anything to me about it. She has been trying to feed me, which is a problem.

I try to eat at least once a day. But it's an effort. Sometimes I'll go three or four days without eating a single thing. I can't quite comprehend how I'm still functioning. I figure there must be a lot of calories in the alcohol I'm consuming. It's the only explanation. Everyone I know has begun to comment on my weight loss. At this point I weigh about 115 pounds. I lie and say I weigh 135. I'm not sure anybody believes me anymore. I sometimes catch a glimpse of myself in the mirror or a shop window and I'm horrified by my appearance. I have at least one person every day tell me that I need to stop drinking, that I will die if I continue this, and yet . . .

"Mary, I'll have a screwdriver with Absolut, easy on the orange juice."

"Is the beer not working?"

"Does it ever?"

A few beers are a nice way to get over the hangover, but that's about it. To catch a decent buzz I need something a little stronger. Beer's for little babies, toddlers. Besides, I look better after a few stiff ones. Two or three screwdrivers and I'm like Errol Flynn in his prime. The likeness is quite unsettling.

"Mary, I'll see you later."

"Bye, Colin. Are ye off?"

"Unfortunately."

"Take care of yourself."

"Right."

"Where's the big party at tonight?"

"Quiet night at home with the missus."

"Right."

Stop at the store. Buy another pack of smokes. Check the midday lottery numbers. I've lost again. Is this some kind of joke, God? Are you fucking serious? You know what? Fuck you. Yeah, you heard me right. Fuck you. We're through. No more mister nice guy. From this moment on you can kiss my ass. You're an asshole. Can you hear me, God? You're an asshole.

I buy more lottery tickets for the evening draw at seven thirty. Please, God, let me win this one. Give me a small miracle. Just a little one. Please. You've punished me enough. I didn't mean what I said earlier. You know I was only joking, right? Of course you do; you're God, for chrissake.

Stop at the liquor store. Pick up a couple of bottles of wine. Stop at the video store. I'll pick out a nice movie to watch with Theresa. Wave to my landlord. Smile. "Hey, Carl." I owe this man a lot of money. Try not to look like I've been out drinking all day. Don't check the mailbox. It's full of bills. I never check my bills anymore. Why bother? When they're really serious about switching something off, they'll actually call me. Then I call them back and tell them I'll pay it next week. Buying time, buying time. Waiting for the miracle.

I'm living in a fifth-floor walkup. I'm panting by the time I get to the third floor. I want to stop and lie down in the hallway. I can't take it anymore. Where am I going? What the hell am I doing with my life?

"Colin, you look like shit."

"Thanks, beautiful."

"You're drunk again."

"Thank God you're not my girlfriend."

"Come on, Colin, you know you love me."

"You're a pain in the ass, Theresa."

"You want I give you a pain in your ass."

"Leave my ass alone or I'll throw you out on the street."

"I throw you out on the street."

"Let's eat and watch a movie. I have to go out."

"Card game tonight?"

"Card game tonight, yes."

Once a week I go to a card game. I almost never win. I say "almost" because I've been told that I did win one night, but I was too drunk to remember it. But on a good night I can get through the card game without losing more than two hundred dollars or so. We have a bottle of Jack Daniel's and a keg in the corner, so I can drink all I want. I can light a cigarette without having to go outside, listen to some music, and shoot the breeze until four in the morning. It's a good pastime for a guy who doesn't have a job or his rent money and who's usually too drunk to notice that the guy he's betting against is sitting with a straight flush on the board. I suppose people who don't have to be drunk all the time find other ways to have a social circle, like knitting groups or bowling leagues or feeding the homeless, but at the moment anything that doesn't involve drinking heavily, gambling, or sex just doesn't seem to work for me.

I play poker with a bunch of American guys: actors, directors, editors, musicians, a select group, some of them quite famous. People you would know. No girls allowed. It's boys' night out. We listen to rock music, get stoned, and drink funnels of beer. I'm their token crazy Irish writer guy, so they let me stick around. They weren't quite sure what to make of me for a while, but I think I'm growing on them. It's hard to tell. I'm always drunk.

The game's starting at eight o'clock. I try to eat as much of the Chinese food as I can so that Theresa's not too disgusted by my drunkenness. I have a few glasses of wine and we watch *Entertainment Tonight* and *Access Hollywood*. Theresa has ruled the remote control ever since she moved in. I kiss Theresa good-bye.

"When are you going to bring me to the game?" she says, curling her bottom lip.

"Never."

"I can beat all of you."

"I don't doubt that you could beat us, but can you play cards?"

She jumps off the couch and grabs me. She throws me onto the bed on my back and jumps on top of me, straddling me. She leans her face down close to mine and says in that deep, husky voice of hers, "You want I should beat you, Colin?"

"Yes. Please."

"Oh, you like me to beat you, hah?" She slaps my face and grabs me loosely by the throat with both hands.

"You want to hurt me, Colin? Hah. You think you can hurt me?"

I grab her firmly by the throat and she writhes on my lap, groaning playfully. She tightens her grip on my throat. She smiles at me, dropping her elbows down onto my chest so that all her weight is on me. My heart is racing. There's a moment where our eyes are locked and neither of us is saying anything. She's inches from my face. It's gone as far as it's going to go without going further. I toss her off onto the bed beside me and get up and head for the door.

"Don't wait up," I say, lighting a smoke.

"You want to go to a club later on?" she calls.

"What? No."

"Please. I want you to come with me."

"I'm going to die if I don't stop partying, Theresa."

"OK. I call you later. We go to a club."

"I'll call you later."

"I wear a very short skirt just for you."

I walk around the corner and slip into the Collins Bar on Eighth Avenue. I order a Jack Daniel's on the rocks and a bottle of Bud. I like it in the Collins Bar. It's one of the last great Manhattan bars. It's dark and old and the people who drink there are drinkers. The old neon sign is still up outside, nestled between two porn stores like a whiskey sandwich. I need to settle my nerves before the card game. Theresa has me all riled up. I have another Jack Daniel's just so the half-finished bottle of Bud doesn't feel lonely. Soon they will be together.

I leave the bar and stop to light a smoke on the corner of the block. A tall, husky transvestite hooker asks me for one. I oblige. She holds it to her lips as I light it for her. She flutters her long lashes and gives me her best come-to-bed eyes. I want to tell her she's too old to still be doing this. But I smile because this is why I love New York. And anyway, what do I know? Maybe I'm just too damned particular.

"You want some company?" she asks, adjusting her gold sequined miniskirt.

"It's tempting," I lie. "But I'm on my way to a card game and I'm already running late. Another time perhaps."

"I'd make it anytime for you, honey." She smiles, running a long fingernail down the side of my face.

"You stay safe out here," I say. "I heard it's a full moon tonight."

"Don't you worry about me, sweetie. I'm a werewolf." She winks at me playfully and disappears into a throng of tourists walking north on Eighth Avenue and I slip into the flow of foot traffic headed south.

I arrive at the game early and pour myself a shot of Jim Beam from the house bottle. I drink it in a swallow and pour myself another. A few of the guys are settling in. Ethan and Allen look like they just woke up or are just going back to bed; I'm not sure which. Tim looks like he just got here from his softball game. Fred's hooking up the keg. Pendy looks like he's drunk already. Doodles glances around the room furtively, anxious for the game to begin. George is sipping his Starbucks silently, studying each and every one of us from behind his wire-rimmed glasses. Doyle and Hyams stroll in just behind me, so engrossed in whatever discussion they're having that it's doubtful they notice that anybody else is in the room. Mick's already here, organizing the chips. "What's up, you crazy Irish fucker?" he shouts at the top of his lungs. "Fuck you," I shout back. "I'm gonna whip your ass tonight, you fuck."

"Oh yeah?"

"Oh yeah. No more mister nice guy. I've just been lulling you guys into a false sense of security."

"It's been working." Mark laughs as he plugs his iPod into the sound system.

"Yeah, we're feeling pretty secure," Steve adds.

I laugh too as I walk around and get all the handshakes and high fives out of the way.

"Whassup, Josh . . ."

"Yo yo yo, Mr. Gladis . . ."

It's the same old story every week. They know I don't take it seriously. I'm here for the beer.

"You sure you don't want a funnel for that drink?" a guy I know only as Fingers asks.

"Maybe later."

He's referring to the fact that I drank eighteen beer funnels last Wednesday night, doubling the previous record of nine. I thought my liver was going to explode for two days after I pulled that little stunt. It didn't, but at thirty-eight years old and in the shape I'm in, it probably wasn't such a hot idea. But hey, I'm Irish, I have my reputation to uphold. To hell with the liver. As the T-shirt says, THE LIVER IS EVIL. IT MUST BE PUNISHED.

My uncle Brendan was the craziest, wildest, most successful drinker I ever knew. He's still a legend. I admired him since I was a little kid. He died in a hospital bed in Belfast when he was forty-two. I remember going to visit him the night he died. I didn't even recognize him. I walked right past his bed twice before he called my name. His liver had packed it in. He was like a big yellow balloon. He put up a good face even then, telling drinking stories to me and a few of my cousins. He was joking with the nurses, making fun of the state he was in. He was dead six hours later. He was forty-two years old. I was seventeen at the time. It seemed like he'd done alright. I was thirty-eight and a half now, 115 pounds, twice divorced, a sore chest, a sore liver and kidneys, and an ever-increasing reputation as a party animal. Eighteen funnels? Forty-two's getting awful close. I can make it.

By midnight I'm very stoned and drunk. I'm being careless and losing more money than I can afford. I decide to stop the hemorrhaging. I take a bathroom break and call Theresa.

"You ready to come get me?"

"You win lots of money?"

"I'm unbeatable. I'm on fire. I need to get out of here."

"I'll be ready in ten minutes."

"Get a cab and pick me up outside the game here."

It's one in the morning when we walk into the club. We're on Little West Twelfth Street. There's some guy next to me who can't believe how hot Theresa is. He wants us to sit with him at his table. He's sitting alone in a big booth overlooking the dance floor. He wants to buy me a drink. He's saying something about the IRA. I know he's more interested in Theresa's legs. Who wouldn't be? He asks me what I want to drink. Vodka. He orders a three-hundred-dollar bottle of Grey Goose and three glasses. Theresa downs a glass of vodka and dances for us. He's slipping me a bag of coke. I'm off to the bathroom. I'm outside in the little courtyard, smoking a joint with a posse of rappers. They mention Belfast. The IRA. Everybody assumes I'm a terrorist. I suppose I look like one. I'm back inside. I can relax now and watch Theresa dance. A lot of people are watching Theresa dance. She dances alone. My new friend is asking me if we're dating. I tell him that she's just been following me around. I can't get rid of her. He's thinking he stands a chance. I drink his vodka and snort his cocaine and let him think whatever he likes. The music's pretty good. The seat is comfortable. I can watch Theresa dancing. When it's time to go she'll take me home. She always takes me home.

Suddenly it's Friday night. I've been drunk all week. David Blaine's been underwater for six days. I've been up to Lincoln Center to see him every day. I'm amazed. I'm not sure why. Maybe it's his endurance. Or the fact that he's doing it under the microscope, in front of a constant crowd of spectators. It's a surreal scene. The human goldfish. I go up to the glass and hold my hand up to him. He presses his hand against mine on the glass and we just stare at each other for a few seconds. For a moment we make eye contact and I'm not sure which of us is closer to drowning. I want to be on the inside of the glass, submerged, people feeding me through a tube, floating. Anything would be easier than this. I'm drowning.

Theresa's friend is visiting from Paris. She arrived Wednesday. She doesn't drink very much and is astounded and disgusted by my complete disregard for my life. I tell her I think she should lighten up a little. On Saturday morning I take them to the street fair at Twenty-sixth and Sixth. It's a bright, sunny morning, so we walk. I drink all the way down there. I have the girls wait while I pop into bars and drink a quick vodka every few blocks. I need it to feel better. It's only eleven in the morning and I've already had five drinks. My head feels particularly bad today. I leave them at the market and go into the nearest bar and order more vodka.

It's the first real hot day of the year. A perfect day to get drunk. The bar I choose is a little too upscale for the condition

I'm in, but I just need to drink. A kid having lunch with his mother is staring at me. I mouth the words "fuck off," but either he can't lip-read or he's just a cocky little bastard. I know I'm losing it, but another bar might be blocks away; I just don't have time to waste. I must get alcohol into my system now, this instant. I call Theresa to let her know where they can find me when they're done shopping. By the time the girls arrive, I'm shit-faced. It's only about one thirty on a beautiful sunny day in the city. I register the disgust on Theresa's friend's face. So I order another one. Then I wake up on a gurney. I'm in a hospital. I'm in the hallway of a hospital. Three nurses stand nearby. I check myself, move my arms, move my legs. Everything seems to be working.

"Excuse me, nurse."

"Yes?" All three look at me. They appear concerned.

"Am I being held here?"

"No. You were brought in on a stretcher about three hours ago; you were unconscious."

"Cool. So I'm free to go, right?"

"We would rather you'd stay where you are for a little while longer."

"Yes, but I can leave if I want, right?"

"Yes, you can leave if you want, but . . ."

"OK. I'm leaving."

"You really should just stay where you are."

"Thank you. That's very kind of you."

"If you insist on leaving like this, you'll have to sign this release form."

"No problem. There you go. Thank you, ladies. Have a nice day."

I walk outside; it's still a beautiful day. I light a cigarette and walk to the corner of the block. I'm back on Ninth Avenue and

Fiftieth Street. Two blocks from my apartment. It's only four thirty. I walk straight up the street to McCoy's. There's a nice crowd for a Saturday.

"How're ye, Colin."

"How are you, Mary."

"Are you OK?"

"Never been better. I'll have a screwdriver, please. Not too much orange juice."

"You got it, handsome."

This is shaping up to be good evening after all.

Six months later I sit out on my fifth-floor fire escape overlooking Ninth Avenue on a sunny Sunday afternoon. There is a street fair in progress down below, and for ten blocks on either side of me the entire avenue is thronged with thousands of people filling the street. The smells of fried chicken and peppers and hot buttered corn waft up along the avenue, rising above the heads of the great mass, above the canopies and salsa music to where I sit with a glass of straight vodka and a can of warm beer, sucking on one cigarette after another as if the very essence of life itself could be inhaled from them. I am sick, empty, broke. My marrow aches. The vodka stopped working days ago. I scroll through the list of names in my cell phone, looking for a name to hook my attention, someone I can call, someone to come to my rescue, someone to entertain me, someone to take me out of the mess my head and body have become. There is no one left. Not a single person that I have not alienated or scared or disgusted in some way. I have become the guy nobody wants to drink with. All my friends have warned me by now. They say things like, "You're going to die." "Have you looked in a mirror lately?" "Have you any idea how disgusting you look?" "I'm afraid your legs will break, they look so thin." "Do you really want to die?" I have laughed at them all, called them pussies, wimps, and losers. I weigh a 118 pounds. I have not eaten solid food in weeks. The very thought of food makes me nauseous. I have been talking to myself. I start my day by vomiting. If I stop drinking for more than four hours, my chest hurts so badly I'm sure that I'm having a heart attack. The crowd in the street below disgusts me. Their smiles make me sick. Their sunny music and rank food make me want to throw furniture into the street. What the hell is everybody smiling about? I want to scream down at them, "We're all going to die, people. Snap out of it. Everybody's going to die." I don't want to die, and then another part of me wants to throw myself at it, run at it, just get it out of the way. It's the waiting that's killing me, all this sitting around, passing the time, pretending like it's not happening. My roommate Theresa left and went back to Europe a few weeks ago, so I don't even have that to come home to anymore. My apartment is a mess of overflowing ashtrays and empty bottles and beer cans, the home of a bum. I have been living like an animal, an ape. I met a girl in a bar in March and I can't get her face out of my mind. She was bartending in one of Tony's places, Scratcher, down on Fifth and the Bowery. She was so exotic and mysterious that my heart had jumped with a sharp, terrifying jolt the moment I saw her. Here was the one God had created in his most inspired moment. I'd turned to Tony and said, "I'm going to marry that girl." But she was with someone else. Someone she'd been with for five years. I am too sick to even go there for a drink. I don't want her to see me like this. I am too sick to see anyone. I haven't so much as kissed a girl in six months. I've met a few but wound up drinking myself into a blackout in their presence. One, an English ballerina named Kelda Dearden, I met over in Scruffy Duffy's on Eighth Avenue and invited her out. I took her to a party, but when I woke up I was on my couch at home, alone. I can't remember what happened or how we were separated. When I went to her hotel to see if I could track down my cell phone, she'd left it with the concierge with a note that said: "I sincerely hope you manage to exorcise your demons. Take care of yourself. Kelda." I had no idea what she meant. I still don't.

I have lost my internal editor. The original editor, the innate editor, the editor of myself, the editor of my sanity. He has taken a vacation or has simply stepped aside as my life has become a stream-of-consciousness mess. My vision of the world and of myself has disintegrated to the degree that what I am telling myself can only be considered the truth for that very second, for the instant in which the words are spoken. But at least I am doing that, right? I am telling the truth for that very second. I am being, in a word, sincere. I treasure sincerity. I treasure it in myself. I treasure it in others. Isn't it enough that I think it is the truth? Isn't it? But then it becomes this race to pin the truth on everything from morning to night, to live in the sincerity of the moment. Because without the truth comes confusion; my waking moments become a series of stabbing, pinpointing, trying to nail the truth of myself. Where am I? What have I become? If I could somehow articulate the truthfulness of this very instant, then I would be alive and truthful in it. I would have pinpointed my own existence. I would have located myself in all of this confusion. And the only way forward is to continue in a long line of these moments, where my only sanity lies in the perfection of the truthful, sincere moment. Anything else is just confusion, headaches, anxiety, and madness. So then it isn't the truth that will set me free; it is the feeling that truth has been achieved, if only for this fleeting second. And even if it isn't really truth, it is still something. Isn't it?

I take a good swig of the vodka and I stand and hold on to the rail of the fire escape. I grip it tightly in my fists and try to will myself to make the leap. One short burst of energy and it will be over. I just have to get my feet off the ground and over the rail and I will be finished with this nonsense, with the pain of this existence. I don't want it anymore. I don't want to drink anymore and I don't want to live without drinking. I have nobody waiting up for me to come home. I search below me for a clean spot of concrete or tar to make sure I hit solid. I don't want to misstep and land on top of one of those canopies. I might be saved, paralyzed, a quadriplegic; I'd be a laughingstock, or worse: pitied. "Look at Broderick in the wheelchair. The poor bastard. You know, he could have been a writer." I lean farther out and start to feel the center of gravity shift in my body. If I lean a little farther my feet will quite simply leave the ground of their own accord . . . I can unstick myself, be free, I am a disgusting mess . . . I want to leave this part of me behind . . . I want to be clean again . . . new again . . . young again. As long as I don't land on a pedestrian, I'll make it . . . Wait—what if I land on someone and kill them and I survive? I have to time this just right. There is a girl outside the front door of my building, on the step below, smoking a cigarette. She is going to get an eyeful . . . Just keep going . . . My head is getting lighter; I am almost all the way up on my toes. But at the last second something stops me; I catch myself; the gravity returns to the soles of my feet. I plant them again. I hurry back inside and shut the window and sit on my couch and cry, but there are no tears in it. It is a dry, painful cry, like something you might hear out of an animal with its leg caught in a trap. There is not a tear of moisture left in my body. I have more disgust than grief. I curl up on the couch and hold my gut. I need to get out of here. I need to get out of this neighborhood, to get off this island. I need to go somewhere away from people and see if there isn't some way to come back. There has to be one last chance to get back.

I call Tony.

"Tony, I need help. Please."

On the sixth of the sixth, 2006, I pack the few things I have into the back of a small U-Haul truck Tony has rented for me. A friend comes up from Brooklyn and spends the day with me, lugging my stuff down five flights of stairs. It has to be the hottest day of the year. With each step I take up and down the five flights, I pray that the pain in my chest will not kill me, not today. I am too close to the end. I just need to make it to the country. By the time we are finished I am ready to collapse. I haven't had a drink since the last can of beer I had for breakfast, around ten in the morning. I have to stay sober to make the three-hour drive alone upstate to Tony's farmhouse. Tony has to drive his own car. I am driving the truck. Carl comes out of the fruit store downstairs and gives me a big hug even though I still owe him some back rent.

"Take care of yourself, kid," he says, clamping my shoulder in his big meaty hand. "Eat something, for chrissake."

"I will, Carl."

"When you come back, come and see me. We'll have a drink."

I make one last stop, around the corner on Forty-sixth Street outside Don's apartment, to see Fiona. We hug good-bye and she begins to cry.

"Are you going to be OK up in that house alone?"

"I'll be fine."

"Are you going to stop drinking?"

"I'm going to try."

"Please stop, and take care of yourself."

"I'll give it a shot."

I get back in the U-Haul and take off toward Tenth Avenue. I glance at the digital reading on the clock radio on the dashboard and the time reads 6:06. I am leaving Hell's Kitchen and driving north to try and piece my life together again.

It starts to rain just then as I drive up Tenth to Amsterdam Avenue and on through Harlem, Washington Heights, and In-wood, and onto the Major Deegan at 231st Street, and up past McLean Avenue.

I have reached the end of another chapter in my life. The city is shrinking in my rearview mirror. By the time I reach the Tappan Zee Bridge the rain has stopped and I roll down the window to breathe in the fresh, clean country air.

As I reach Route 17 West, the sun is ahead of me and sink-ing over the lip of the world, a vast orange orb bathing the after-noon sky with its fiery glow. I turn the radio up a little louder and find myself singing along, tapping my fingers to the beat. I have survived. I am making it out alive.

Three and a half hours later, as I pull into the driveway of Tony's farmhouse, Tony is arriving as well. He felt it might be safer to spend the first few days with me to make sure that I don't die in the initial stages of the drying-out process. The first few days of horror and hallucination will be hell on the heart. I am glad he is going to be there with me in the house.

Over the next four days I writhe and shake and sweat. Tony had planned to stay for two days but winds up staying for five once he realizes how sick I really am. I sweat so much that I wake up soaked, cold, and shivering, and have to move to a drier place in the bed, and then in a little while to another one. I re-peat this process for about three days, trying to drink as much water and tea as I can manage. The nightmares are horrendous. On the third day, I eat a bowl of soup with a trembling hand. I have to struggle to keep it down, but I have to start again some-where. I have weighed myself earlier in the day and was dis-gusted and scared to see that I'd dropped to 115 pounds.

On the fourth morning, I shower and sit down with a pen and a notebook and begin to write this book. Tony leaves me with a bunch of supplies and takes off for the city, telling me I should stay here in the farmhouse for as long as it takes to get well.

The following night, I wake from a nightmare to the phone ringing. It is Budgie. Our good friend Cairn Cassidy is dead. I think I am still dreaming. Gary Rocks has just gone over to the morgue to identify the body. Cairn has been killed driving a motorcycle he just purchased the previous day in the Hamptons. He was twenty-eight years old. It seems ridiculous that he is gone and that I am still here.

It would make sense to say that I'd reached the bottom and that I was done now, that I was appreciative that I had survived and for the chance I'd been given to start my life anew. But it did not end that way. That's the ending Hollywood would have us believe. The truth was a little messier. After I'd sobered up for a couple of months upstate in the farmhouse, I got invited to a barbecue by a local guy called Mike McWeeney, who delivered lumber to the house for a deck I was building for Tony. This was a country barbecue. There was going to be some hard drinking involved. The truth is, I wanted to be able to go to that barbecue and just kick back for the night and have a few cold ones, like a normal guy. The truth is that I sat down on the porch that afternoon and opened a can of beer and sat there, staring at it for ten minutes, deliberating. Could it really be that bad that I would have no control over my life after I picked up that first one? The truth is that the big orange animal in me wanted to just rip the can apart with its teeth to get into it and the human part of me was scared I might not be able to stop the beast if

I let it start. The truth is that after ten horrendous minutes I picked it up and I drank it.

One week later I came out of a blackout behind the wheel of an old car Tony had left in the garage for me to use in case of emergencies. It was nighttime on a country road and there were flashing lights in my rearview mirror. I was busted again. I wound up spending thirty-six days in an upstate jail. Is this what they talked about at the meetings when they said the active alcoholic's life ends in hospitals, jails, and death? There was no romance in any of this. There is nothing romantic about being yelled at to get out of bed at six thirty in the morning to eat a bowl of cereal and drink a mug of rank coffee out of a plastic cup that somebody else has gnawed around the edges. There is nothing romantic about the fact that your breakfast comrades are neo-Nazis, drug dealers, child molesters, redneck crack addicts, and gangbangers. The real truth of the matter is that Hollywood will never quite capture that experience on the big screen, because there are unpleasant smells involved that you don't want to think about while you are trying to digest a good story. I learned how to make jailhouse hooch in a Ziploc baggie. I learned how to light a cigarette using two staples, a wall socket, and a piece of toilet paper. On the night of my release, I had a beer in my hand within twenty minutes of walking out of jail. And then the next day I stopped drinking again and went back to working on this book.

I found out through Tony that the bartender that I'd met six months earlier had finally dumped her boyfriend. I got her phone number and gave her a call. She was a writer also. She had a few good stories of her own. A good story is like wine to a writer. We were drunk on each other. We spent hours on the phone bouncing easily from one topic to another without the slightest hiccup: literature, addiction, philosophy, religion, politics, sex, and love. Finally I'd found a woman who viewed the world with as much skepticism as I did. I was not alone. She offered to come up to the farmhouse to sleep with me, knowing that I had not been with a woman for a long time. The next time Tony came upstate he picked her up in the city and brought her up to visit.

Renata came into my life bearing a box of condoms and three new pairs of boxers for me and I collapsed into her arms and we held each other. It was as if I had been running toward this moment, this girl, my entire life. Her face is like the sun and I stood in her glow and I smiled.

After a few days she went back to the city, and then in December she came up with her dog and her cat and she stayed for a month. I invited my brothers and their girls up to the farmhouse for Christmas. Tony arrived from the city at seven in the morning on Christmas Day, badly hungover. I had stopped and he had gotten worse, it seemed. For the week covering Christmas and New Year's, I drank with him. Then I stopped again. I had only been drinking for a few days, but it had scared me. Other people can drink. They drink and they stop. I have one drink and I'm drinking morning, noon, and night. That is what happens. There was no in-between place anymore.

I was writing again. I'd been working on my book for six months and the old feeling was beginning to come back to me. I was becoming human again. It was becoming more and more apparent that every time I drank, all of that disappeared instantly. But I had a small taste for what my life could be again without alcohol, and I wanted it. I wanted it desperately.

I came back to Manhattan at the end of January and moved in with Renata and her golden retriever, Graham, and her cat, Angelicka, in a small studio apartment on the Upper West Side. We went to meetings together and stayed sober; then one night in March I decided I wanted to try drinking again. I wanted to drink with Renata in the city. I wanted to have that experience with her. It felt unfair that we couldn't go out and tear up the town together at least once. We were both writers, after all. We decided to have a couple of bottles of wine to test the waters. We made rules: (1) No drinking before six p.m.; (2) We could get drunk any two nights of the week that we wanted, but we couldn't drink the rest of the week; (3) If it caused problems we would quit again immediately.

I was drinking again, and within one week all the rules were out the window. Soon I was drinking from the moment I got out of bed in the morning until I fell asleep at night. I stopped writing and took a job as a carpenter, building another bar, the Whiskey Trader, in midtown. I was back where I had started. Within a matter of weeks, the fights started. I was drinking whiskey in my tea before going to work in the morning. I had to try and stay drunk all day long and try to hide it from Renata. We were fighting for the first time since we were together. The walls of the small apartment were starting to close in. I had only been drinking again for a few weeks and already my friends were berating me for my behavior. Don had just been looking at some of the footage for my documentary and he had told me that if he had to take an honest stab at how it was going to end, his guess would be with me being dead. I tried to keep up appearances, but the orange beast was wrestling its way out again. But he was ugly to me now. He was an embarrassment. He didn't care about simple, everyday things like hygiene or taking a stroll by the river with the dog at midnight or eating a nice meal with the in-laws. He didn't care about keeping the peace; he didn't even care if he lived or died. For the first time in my life I saw the beast for what it was. It was me. When I drink I am the beast. I am the orangutan. There was no magic involved, no romantic transformation. Alcohol quite simply robbed me of my humanity.

I woke up one Sunday morning at the end of June and

opened a can of beer and sat in bed, trying to force it into me slowly so as not to puke. Renata returned from a walk with the dog, and seeing me there, she said, "We have to talk about all this. This is pathetic."

She went on outside onto our small patio and I watched her light a cigarette and sit and pet the dog in silence. Here was the girl I loved and wanted to spend the rest of my life with, sitting on our patio with tears in her eyes at noon on a beautiful sunny Sunday afternoon because I would rather continue drinking than give us a proper chance. I got up and walked outside and sat down across from her and said, "I'll stop. Tomorrow. I'll go get myself some help. I don't want to lose you." She sat in my lap and held me to her and kissed the top of my head and said she would quit with me. We decided to drink whatever alcohol we had left in the apartment for the rest of that day, and that would be it.

After all I had been through, after all the near-death experiences, it came down to this: My last night drinking was with the girl I love more than anything in the world, chatting and reading poetry to each other, sipping whiskey and actually enjoying it, reading Yeats and e. e. cummings, and making love until the sun came up. It was a beautiful night. I had finally met somebody I wanted more than I wanted a drink.

In the morning I went on to work, and for the first time that I could remember, I had no hangover. I was not sick or confused. I did not crave another drink. The beast in me was quiet.

I still don't claim to know what the answers are. I don't know how some people stop and some don't. I can only tell you my story, how it went for me and for the people around me. A lot of the lads I drank with are still drinking, some more, some less. It's their choice. In my opinion, that first drink is always a choice. Tony stopped, started, and stopped again and has so far stayed stopped. I see how much more beautiful he is without drinking and it makes it easier for me to accept that I'm a better guy to be around as well. I went back to AA meetings for a while and that helped me to get my head clean, and then I stopped going to the meetings because I felt I didn't need them anymore.

I stopped smoking. I stopped eating red meat. I exercise when I can. I work hard now to maintain the life that I want. I will fight to protect it. My life and my thoughts are my own. I am no closer to knowing if there is a God or not. But I can assure you that if there is, I'm going to have a word with him about his sense of humor. I am still paying the price for ten years of recklessness. The rest of the mess I will get sorted out one piece at a time. At least I have my health still intact; I've known a lot of others who were not so fortunate.

I married Renata and we moved to Prague with Graham and Angelicka, and we write. In March of 2008, two months after my fortieth birthday, we found out that we are going to have a baby. One week later I sold this book. My life has been opening in ways that I never would have expected. In the end I have no regrets. I wouldn't swap the life that I've had with anyone on earth. I'm glad I drank. I'm glad I had the life that I did. At least it was mine.

ACKNOWLEDGMENTS

And now to the most difficult part of the book. Who to thank and who to leave out.

Unfortunately, there is no way of doing this without leaving someone out; so here's what I have for now. For Renata, thank you for showing so much belief in this book and in me that you finally made me see it too, I love you and I'm sorry. My darling daughter Erica who makes me smile every single day, you rock. To my parents, Claire and Michael, who have supported, carried, and loved me through all of the madness, thank God you were my parents, and thank you for dealing. To my brothers and sisters, without whose support I might have cracked: Michael, Brendan, Noleen, Louise, and Gerry, I will repay you, sometime, but don't wait up for it. To Tony, there are no words to thank you; you saved my life again and again, you are my brother and I will love your big, beautiful heart always. To the writers who encouraged and nudged me along the way: Billy Collins, Malachy McCourt, Colum McCann, Jimmy Smallhorne, Stephen Smallhorne, Patkie Jo Gilheany, Sean O' Driscoll, Elizabeth Bassford, and Rick Pernod, thank you. To Dymphna, Caroline, Sylvie, Brian, and Stephen, what on earth were you thinking? To the Rev. Michael Kelly and all the lads at Big Money Wednesdays, suck it. To Kathleen Daly for your generous support while I was in jail, thank you. To Eugene and the entire Catalpa crew, thanks for the memories. To Chris Campion for introducing me to his agent without ever reading a word I'd written, I am forever indebted to you. To my agents, Jane Dystel and Miriam Goderich, thank you for deciding to change my life. To Carrie Thornton, Philip Patrick, Emily Timberlake, Jean Lynch, Rachelle Mandik, Linnea Knollmueller, and Maria Elias for making me look good, thank you. John Hyams for the cover art, thank you. Jon, for saying, "Stop," thank you. Brendan O'Shea—thanks, dude. To all the ladies in my past, lovers and wives, thank you for carrying me along the way. To Paul, Des, and Padge and Mary for your unflagging belief in me, thanks, guys. Dermot Burke for sparking a light that never went out. Ying and Melanie, thank you both. Carl Mazzalla for helping keep a roof over my head, cheers pal. Andrew, Amanda, Megan, and Rachel for your help, thank you. To Anna and Nicky, thank you for your support. Brandon Herman, for putting up with my madness. Marika and Jindra, thank you for everything. For those I have drunk with throughout the years—that includes Barry, Paddy, Budgie, The Vamp, Teaker, Pat, DJ Johnny, Brendan, cousin Frank, Mark, and Dermot—thanks for listening. To my godson Christopher, RIP little man. And to those of you who have been there and I have not mentioned, you know who you are. Thank you.

ABOUT THE AUTHOR

COLIN BRODERICK is a writer/carpenter from Northern Ireland. He lives in Manhattan with his wife, Renata, and their daughter, Erica.